WAR LE

OF

MORTON EUSTIS

TO

HIS MOTHER

FEBRUARY 6 · 1941

TO

AUGUST 10 · 1944

•••

WASHINGTON, D. C., 1945

Printing Statement:

Due to the very old age and scarcity of this book,
many of the pages may be hard to read due to the
blurring of the original text, possible missing pages,
missing text and other issues beyond our control.

Because this is such an important and rare work, we
believe it is best to reproduce this book regardless of
its original condition.

Thank you for your understanding.

FOREWORD

THE LETTERS THAT APPEAR in this book were written by Morton Corcoran Eustis, 1st Lieutenant, Army of the United States, who was killed in action in France on August 13, 1944.

The letters cover the entire period of his Army life, from February 6, 1941, shortly after he left New York for Fort Devens, Massachusetts, to August 10, 1944, three days before his death at Domfront, in Normandy. All the letters were written to his mother, with the exception of a few, as indicated, to other members of his family and to friends. They were written with no thought of publication although, as he said, he expected someday to use them as notes for a play or a book which he hoped to write after the war. They appear in this volume exactly as he wrote them, with no changes other than the deletion of passages of a purely personal nature. His mother has had them printed, so that his family and friends might have Morton's own account of how, in spite of handicaps of age and defective eyesight, he succeeded in achieving his ambition to become part of the combat forces and to fight at a time when his country had need of him.

He was born in New York September 18, 1905, the son of William Corcoran Eustis and Edith Livingston Morton Eustis. His father served as a Captain in the United States Army in the first World War and was attached to the staff of General Pershing at Chaumont. His maternal grandfather was the late Levi P. Morton, former Governor of New York, Minister to France and Vice-President of the United States. On his father's side, he was a great-grandson of William Wilson Corcoran of Washington, banker, philanthropist and founder of the Corcoran Gallery of Art.

Morton's childhood was a very happy one. He lived in the winters at Corcoran House on Lafayette Square in Washington—the red brick house which occupied the site of the present United States Chamber of Commerce. In the summers he was usually with the family in the country at Oatlands House, near Leesburg, Virginia.

At the age of fourteen he was sent to Groton, where he received his

i

education under Dr. Peabody. Even at that early age Morton had the same strongly developed characteristics that determined his course of action in later life. According to Mr. Tuttle, one of his masters, "He had the rare ability, at variance with his manner, of driving himself past endurance at the task he had set. It was for this reason he was such a good football player. No one had to ask him to give all he had. He gave all he had to give without being asked. Nor did any amount of success ever cause him to talk about himself. He always gave the credit to the other fellow."

After finishing at Groton, he went to Harvard, graduating with the class of 1928. Later he joined the staff of the *New York Evening Post,* and subsequently became associate editor of *Theatre Arts* magazine under the inspiring leadership of Mrs. Isaacs. In addition to numerous articles on the theatre and related subjects, he wrote two books, *Broadway, Inc.* and *Players at Work.* He tried his hand at writing plays, but his real talent was as a critic and a writer about the theatre, as he proved in his many articles on that subject. Regarding his ability as a journalist, Miss Rosamond Gilder, Associate Editor of *Theatre Arts,* said: "Morton had a flair for news, the ability to go out and get a story, a gift for swift and accurate reporting. His writing was vigorous. He was a true craftsman with a sense of style and a respect for his medium."

During these years he lived in New York. Although he had a large and varied circle of friends, many of them in the theatrical world, he liked best to gather his little group of intimate friends for an evening of bridge or music in his apartment. And while he was shy with strangers, among friends he was often the gayest member of the party and had a sense of humor and a pointed wit that spared no one.

He was a man of strong convictions, with high standards of loyalty and duty in every relationship of life. The deep and lasting impression which Morton made on his friends is described by Joseph Alsop who said: "In everyone's life, I think, there are a few people who constitute, as it were, fixed points around whom the general pattern develops. Morton had the knack of becoming the fixed point in the lives of almost all who knew him reasonably well."

Morton enjoyed life and lived intensely, wherever he was. He was

ii

always happiest with his family and spent much time with them when his work permitted. He particularly enjoyed the country and was never so happy as when he was at Oatlands. He loved the beautiful old house, with its yellow walls, its high portico supported by white Corinthian columns, and its balustraded terrace with the dark green magnolia tree in the center. The garden, too, gave him infinite pleasure; and he was proud of his mother's achievement in restoring it and creating so much ordered beauty with terraces and walks under towering box-wood. He took the greatest interest in everyone who worked at Oatlands, and all the friends and neighbors were devoted to him. On Sundays in Virginia, he played the organ at the village church. He was a vestryman of the Episcopal church at Oatlands.

Morton liked to ride and play tennis and to engage in seemingly endless games of intricate croquet. He enjoyed bathing in the pool and lying in the sun. Indeed, he craved the sun and never found it too hot, even in Virginia in summer. He loved his horses, and to him Rory, his Irish setter, and in later years, Von, his police dog, were almost like members of the family.

He enjoyed travel, particularly in Europe. Next to his own country, he loved France and felt at home there among a people he both liked and understood. He hated Fascism in all its manifestations, wherever found. And so, when war came and Hitler marched into Poland, Morton never had any doubts that the danger which threatened the civilization he loved in Europe, threatened also our own way of life here in America and, perhaps, eventually our very existence as a nation. At the time France was invaded he wanted to go to her defense; and later, just before France fell, he was on the point of flying there, to serve as a driver in the American Field Ambulance Service, when his orders were cancelled.

By October 1940 he had made up his mind to enter the Army. He enlisted as a Private in Squadron A, New York, which in due course became the 101st Cavalry. In February 1941, he was sent with his outfit to Fort Devens and from this point his military history may be read in his own words.

As his letters indicate, the making of war had no charms for Morton. He was essentially an individualist, with a strong aversion to being regimented under normal conditions. But his never-failing sense of humor, his determination not to lose sight of his objective, enabled him to meet with patience and even gayety long periods of boredom, of frustration and drudgery, such as the interminable K. P. assignments at Fort Devens and the dreary period of waiting before he could enter the Officers' School at Harrisburg. As Peter Nicholas, one of his friends, said: "In the 101st Cavalry he did the most menial work so well and with such a magnificent sense of humor that it was always a joy to be with him."

Later, when the pace of war had accelerated, the imagination which Morton had shown in his writings, turned to inventiveness in finding and adapting new guns for his armored cars. His unselfishness and thoughtfulness of others showed in his consideration for his men. He was constantly trying to get better food for them or to give them pleasure or, when danger threatened, to expose himself in order to save them. Captain Richard Story wrote: "In a hospital in England I had to censor a lot of mail and one day I came across a letter addressed to Morton from one of the men who had been in his platoon, and again a day or two later, another from another man. Of close to a thousand letters that I censored, I think those were the only two cases of enlisted men writing to their officers; and it is the best possible testimony of the affection in which his men held him."

It was a long, hard road from Fort Devens to Domfront. But Morton deliberately chose the hard way, because he was determined to get into a combat unit and he wanted to be prepared for the opportunity when it came. He consistently refused back-of-the-line assignments, even though the work might be interesting and might result in promotions in rank. So, when he found himself, after two years training in the field, sitting at a desk in Egypt, he determined to transfer from the headquarters job and to take his chances in the ground forces, hoping that eventually he would secure a combat assignment for which he believed himself fitted both by training and temperament.

That he succeeded was due entirely to his own persistence. He tells in his letters how, after his transfer to the ground forces and a long plane ride to North Africa, he sat for weeks on a cliff above the

Mediterranean with no prospect, so far as he could see, of ever being assigned to a combat unit. In fact, he described himself as the "forgotten man." But here again his strong will power came into play. Hearing that an armored reconnaissance unit was encamped forty miles away, he walked part of the intervening distance and talked the commanding officer into giving him his chance. Thereafter, as he said, he was "happy as the day is long," in charge, at last, of a scout section, with an armored car of his own and a machine gun at his right hand. "I'm really content now," he wrote, "for the first time since I've been over here. I'm just where I want to be, which is the second most important thing in my life at the moment. The first is that I do a good job when and if the going should get tough."

He did do a good job, both in Sicily and afterwards in France. For his part in the attack on Palermo, he received the Silver Star "for gallantry in action." In the words of the citation "Lieutenant Eustis's coolness and courage under fire, coupled with his aggressiveness and disregard of his own safety in fulfilling the mission given to him, reflect great credit upon himself and the Armed Forces."

Again in Normandy he was decorated, receiving the Bronze Star Medal "for meritorious service in France during the period 29 July 1944 to 30 July 1944, in connection with military operations against the enemy." The citation states that he came "under enemy fire at least ten times and by his quick action in locating and destroying enemy tanks and ground positions made it possible for the company to move forward on its mission."

Finally, he was awarded, posthumously, the Oak Leaf Cluster to the Silver Star "for gallantry in action on 13 August 1944 in France." He had been given the mission, with a platoon of medium tanks and fifteen dismounted men, of crossing the river and attacking Domfront in Normandy. The citation reads: "Lieutenant Eustis, with utter disregard for his own personal safety and under heavy small arms fire, rode on the turret of the leading medium tank in order to best direct the advance. He was always present at the point when contact with the enemy was made. Lieutenant Eustis was killed by an enemy rocket projectile while firing a fifty caliber machine gun, from an exposed position, at a dismounted enemy patrol, which had forced his own dismounted men to take cover. Lieutenant Eustis's courage and habitual contempt for the enemy was largely responsible for the success of his Platoon."

Lieutenant Frank Jordon, who was Morton's best friend in the Battalion and was fighting beside him when Morton was killed, wrote: "I am sure that he died instantly. . . . I know that, if Morton could have had his way, he would have preferred going the way he did. Morton is buried near Percy, which is a town about fifteen miles north of Domfront. He is buried in a well-kept American cemetery. Only a few days before, Morton and I were discussing some friends we had lost and both agreed that we were leaving them in good company."

Lieutenant Jordan, himself, was killed shortly afterward as a result of enemy action. He and other friends of Morton's in the Battalion lie buried in graves that mark the triumphant march of the 2nd Armored Division through France and Germany. And of Morton and his friends, as of other American soldiers who have given their lives in this war, it may be said as truly as was said by Pericles of those who died for Athens centuries before:

"In a moment of time, at the climax of their lives, they were rapt away from a world filled, for their dying eyes, not with terror but with glory. . . . So they gave their bodies for the common weal and received, each for his own memory, praise that grows not old, and with it the grandest of all sepulchres, not that in which their mortal bones are laid, but a home in the minds of men, where their glory remains fresh to stir to speech or action as the occasion comes by. For the whole earth is the sepulchre of illustrious men; and their story is not graven only on stone over their native earth, but lives on far away, without visible symbol, woven into the stuff of other men's lives."

DAVID E. FINLEY

Washington
April 1945

vi

MAY 8 · 1945

The war in Europe is over. And he did not live to see liberated Paris again. But I like to think that, in a small way, small because he was only one among countless thousands, he contributed to that victory which is being celebrated today.

His letters tell the story of his struggles, his aspirations, during four years in the army. But they do not tell what some of his friends felt, that his sacrifice was, in some intangible way, a fulfilment. With much to live for, with talents which had not yet fully reached their prime, there was that in him which, until the war, had never quite found expression. He was searching for something which did not come his way, something which demanded more of him than life had hitherto offered, and strangely enough, the calamity of a world war threw the opportunity he had sought in his path. He never hesitated, and even in England, before D. Day, when he told his cousin: "I do not think I shall come back," he had manifested entire contentment and serenity. And again, I like to think that he was supremely happy, not because he did not enjoy life, but because of that unfulfilled desire to give all of himself to a cause he believed in.

I do not think anyone enjoyed life more than he did,—a sense of fun, of nonsense even, of innate gayety, pervaded his relationship with all his friends. A party was a success if he were there. A drab aftenoon became amusing if he dropped in. I remember one evening at Oatlands, when he made the rafters ring with stories of life at Fort Devens. Cousins and friends were present then. But with the family alone, and what a love of family he had! it seemed as if he were the pivot on which the life of all revolved. His sisters, his aunt, how close they were to him! Family problems, and what family is without them, were brought to him and his good sense and wisdom seemed to solve them easily, so that burdens were lifted and one wondered why one had thought them burdens at all. With all his gifts, and he had many, "A most original and penetrating mind," as a literary friend wrote,—he had a way of deprecating all his successes, refusing praise or laughing it off. It was a curious sense of modesty and sensitivity in him, coupled with a certain shyness and an instinctive desire to give the credit to some one else, which hid from strangers many of his dominant characteristics. I must add, however, that people who worked for him adored him, just as later the men in his platoon considered him a friend.

A very human personality, a rare combination of fun and gravity, of generosity of mind coupled with generosity of deed—such, I think, was the author of the letters that follow.

His brother-in-law has written an able and vivid sketch of his life and has described his many qualities. My only excuse for adding these words is to speak a little more intimately about him than perhaps any other person could. It is all inadequate but it may help towards a better understanding of the underlying motives and directives of Morton's character and life.

E. M. E.

THE LETTERS

AMERICA

···

FEBRUARY 6, 1941 TO OCTOBER 31, 1942

To be prepared is half the victory.
DON QUIXOTE

We did not leave from Grand Central after all, but from the freight yards at 137th St. We had Pullmans, with thirty-nine to a car, two to a lower, one to an upper. Thank God I got an upper!

They woke us about six, for no good reason, and gave us some terrible coffee; then we lay around till Ayer hove in sight around nine o'clock. . . . Another wait of about an hour before unloading,—waits mean nothing in the army. Then the train pulled up near the camp and we decamped.

On the march to our quarters, I was pulled out (as one who looked strong, I fear,) to carry a box of butter, and arrived fairly exhausted in consequence. Fortunately it was a beautiful day, cold but sunny and clear. I hate to think what it would have been like, if it had been raining.

Although one could not exactly call the quarters heaven, they are on the whole better than I expected. We are in two story wooden barracks, about 60' by 25'. Our platoon is on the second floor with half of another platoon, twenty-eight men to a room—about three feet between beds, real cot beds with springs, mattress, sheets, pillow case, comforter and three blankets. Downstairs there is a bathroom with running water, three showers, six toilets, for about fifty people, but the water is hot so the *facilitées de la maison* are unexpectedly good on the whole.

Yesterday everything was disorganized, no lunch till 2:30, dinner at 8, loading and unloading most of the day. Fortunately I escaped any mess duty or other detail, except for unloading the trunks and barrack bags and we got more or less settled by about seven. Each barracks has its own furnace and is nice and hot. The mess barracks is only two houses off and there is a recreation room just next to it.

Physically speaking the surroundings are ugly as all hell; there is not a blade of grass nearby, and the company streets, now nicely frozen, will be a sea of mud come the thaw. However, considering what it might have been, it is luxury.

Although we have not yet settled down thoroughly, the schedule is

3

roughly as follows: Reveille, 6:15; assembly (outdoors in the freezing cold and pitch dark) with exercises, 6:30; clean up barracks, make bed, etc., breakfast, 7; drill call, 8; lunch, noon; drill—;recall, 4:30; supper, 6:00; lights out, 10:30.

This is all if there are no details: as there are more than you can shake a stick at we will probably be on some detail every three or four days. One can't pretend that it is exactly one's idea of bliss, but it certainly could be worse.

There are movies every night, canteens where you can buy beer, cigarettes, etc., and they say you get into a kind of vegetable state where it all seems rather pleasant. I must say I slept like a log last night and am now comfortably lying on my bed writing, as the day is being given over to cleaning house.

FORT DEVENS, FEBRUARY 8, 1941

Well, come the revolution, I ought to have no trouble getting almost any kind of job. They certainly give you a varied experience in non military life in the army. In the four odd days I have been here I have washed windows, cleaned dishes, piled up rocks and loaded them into trucks, stoked four furnaces for a twenty-four-hour guard detail, raked, graded, sewed, polished and God knows what other menial tasks. The Army does this without kicking (well, say without too much kicking) and gets hardly any sleep while the $19.00 a day workers crab if they work more than forty hours a week. Most of us have worked forty hours in two days without any serious injury to our morale or solar plexus; and believe me, the more people that get drafted, the more kick there is going to be against labor refusing to take its share of the burden.

Being orderly, I have had a fairly soft job on this guard as it was a poisonous night, pelting rain and a driving wind and at least I didn't have to march up and down in it for two hours on end but just sally forth every hour or so to my furnaces.

I don't honestly see, if this keeps up, how we'll get any time to learn anything about drill and mechanized equipment, but that is not my

4

lookout. Like the Jesuits we are dedicated to a life of poverty, chastity and obedience. And that seems to be that!

FORT DEVENS, FEBRUARY 15, 1941

It was the greatest break in the world running into Cabot and Emily at Groton.* I breezed up there in a taxi and would have gone barging into the dining room if I hadn't run into George Lodge in the hall who told me he was waiting for his parents. So I waited too, and we went off for a picnic lunch which couldn't have been more fun and then took a walk. After they left, I went to call on a few masters at school, then to Johnny Hallowell's and stayed there until dinner.

Johnny had asked me, Harry Nicholas, Steve Whitman and Herbert Martin, our captain, to come to supper. It was rather frightening for me, a mere buck private, to have to give the message to the captain of our troop that he was expected to dinner, but it all passed off very pleasantly and there was no nonsense about difference in rank once we were assembled at Johnny's!

Our plans, according to Captain Martin, are to stay here for at least twelve more weeks, roughly speaking, up to the first of May. Then, in field maneuvers with the First Army Corps, somewhere down south for some three months. Our base camp will remain Camp Devens.

FORT DEVENS, MARCH 1, 1941

Inspection by the Major is just over and I have hurled all the equipment that was laid out in serried ranks on my bed, into my barracks bag. *Un point, c'est tout.*

As luck would have it, the axe struck just about 20 minutes after I spoke to you last night and I was put on K.P. for the coming week, starting at noon today. While I shall doubtless curse inwardly for the next seven days,—washing, scrubbing greasy pots and pans, washing floors, etc., the relief when it is all over will be such that it will be well worth it.

It sounds like hell on earth when you describe life up here, but it

*Senator and Mrs. H. C. Lodge, Jr.

isn't actually so bad, largely, I think, because there are congenial people to do the dirty jobs with. And although standing on your feet for fifteen hours and a quarter (as I did in officers' mess) isn't exactly a picnic, a sense of humor helps a lot. And you do learn something even from the lowliest and most menial task you are obliged to perform.

K. P. finally ended last night and no one could have been more pleased than I was to get out of that G. D. kitchen! However, that is out of the way for a couple of months, pray God, and that in itself is worth a great deal. By that time a lot may have happened and we may be in the Near East for all I know.

Thank goodness the Senate finally passed the Lend Lease bill.

I have just finished a day loading ashes into a truck and dumping them in the A.M. and tearing down half of a hill of gravel in the afternoon to fill in the land where the officers park their cars.

All very stimulating!!

But good exercise. . . .

Easter, I got a day pass and they let us off in time to go to Groton for the Easter service—ten of us. Dr. Crocker referred to us obliquely in his sermon. It was a lovely service, as it always is, and I enjoyed being there very much.

Cousin Susie,* by the way, couldn't have been nicer, and had, as usual, delicious food. It will be a great haven to be able to go to for a break every now and then.

Steve and I were talking to Sergeants Mortimer and Alfred Clark about the whole prospects for the future. They were both extremely blue about the future of everything and everyone connected with the

*Mrs. William F. Wharton.

6

101st Cavalry. What was depressing was their conclusion, reached, I gather, after several talks with the Captain, as to the chances of becoming officers.

Specifically, in my case, they said that the age question was an extremely serious drawback towards getting a commission. Apparently the Captain, who is the one who has to recommend you, feels, as do many others, that the army does not want people over thirty for jobs as line officers and that consequently he would, I imagine, be indisposed to recommend them. An even more, or just as, serious handicap is my eyesight. I got into this thing only by faking as I was really 20-200 when you were supposed to be 20-70. And they have an even stiffer exam for officers which it would be next to impossible to fake.

Well, in the course of the conversation, I mentioned that I had, on several occasions, thought of getting transferred into some branch of the service in which my special qualifications would be of some value and asked their advice. The unanimous reaction was that I would be a fool if I didn't immediately try to get a commission, even, if necessary, at a desk job. I told them I didn't want a desk job, and I don't; but they still said they thought I should try anything because the chances in this set-up were so slim. I don't know quite what to say. I'd rather stay on here and work my way up, but if it's going to be a dead end, then I think it's foolish. I should obviously have looked into all this before taking the plunge—as God knows you urged me to do. However, I wouldn't have missed this and the situation may, of course, change overnight if we get into war.

FORT DEVENS, JUNE 25, 1941

The observation school has really been a wonderful break for me, whatever comes of it. We have been out every day on maneuvers, working out the problems involved. We have had dive bombers dropping flour bags on us, have been gassed, have gone up in observation planes—have done almost everything, in fact, except drop from a plane in a parachute. And it has all been practical experience, instead of empty lectures.

7

My plan for the week-end of the 4th is to take a plane arriving in Washington somewhere around 9:30 P.M. (Standard) Thursday night. That will give me three consecutive nights in Oatlands which will be wonderful. Neilson will know about what we want in the way of fireworks. What about music? We might get the same fiddlers or perhaps some that were a little better.

I think we ought to ask everyone from the neighborhood.

FORT DEVENS, AUGUST, 1941

I am writing from regimental headquarters where having won the coveted honor of being chosen "Miss Devens" from the guard, I am acting as Colonel's orderly! Miss Devens is the person who is picked by the officer of the day as the best turned out for the guard mount. And he acts as a kind of messenger boy at RHQ instead of walking his post on guard. You're supposed also, to get 24 hours off as a reward once the day is over, but unfortunately that does not hold good on Saturday which is inspection day . . . I'm sure you'll be both amused and incredulous to hear that I was chosen as the best turned out from a group of thirty men! But it was a mass effort on the part of several members of the 3rd platoon, who lent me various bits of their clothes and equipment which produced the winning result.

I went into Boston last night to dine with David.* But as ill luck would have it, the hotel never gave him my message and he dined in solitary splendour in the dining room while I waited upstairs on the roof. However, I saw him for about an hour before I left. He's coming up to spend the evening here tomorrow and then d. v., we both expect to motor to the Walkers the next day.

I hope we can all get together somewhere, somehow, the next week end, if we get off. That is a big if, as we're supposed, I believe, to be on maneuvers.

[Later]

We had a lovely three days—the bulk of the third platoon—because we smashed up three of our four cars in the maneuvers down on the Cape, while indulging in a hair raising cross-country dash after some

*David E. Finley.

8

negroes in a light truck. . . . So when the time came to go out on this week's maneuvers in the pouring rain we all stayed back at the camp and have had a gloriously lazy time, going out every night and doing little in the daytime except bunk fatigue, plus a little cleaning here and there. And since we're all a very congenial group, it couldn't have been more fun.

AUGUST, 41

Well here I am homeward bound as it were, after a delightfully restful and pleasant three days at Anne and Grenny's.* Aunt Helen† spent one day with us, but most of the time we were just lazy except for a trip over to Darien to pay my respects to Mrs. Isaacs, and I enjoyed it all thoroughly.

AUGUST 18TH, 1941

Tomorrow we go on more maneuvers, in New Hampshire this time. By the way, the sleeping bag made the greatest difference. I have had the first comfortable night I have ever had in the field.

SEPTEMBER 12, 1941 (TO R.G.) ‡

We are engaged in mad maneuvers all through New Hampshire, so tired and hungry most of the time that you are hardly aware of the fact that you are supposedly fighting a war! You manage to have a certain amount of fun notwithstanding, but when you stagger back to camp at the end of four days you just crawl into bed and sleep for fourteen hours and still are tired the next day. Then the day following you set out again. Worse than the lack of sleep (we never pitch camp, if we pitch it at all, till about one A.M. and then set out again at about 3 A.M.) is the fact that the mess truck can never find us, and so, on the last walk, we went twenty-nine hours one time without food and twenty-four hours a half day later. Actually the life is

*Mr. and Mrs. Grenville T. Emmett, Jr.
†Mrs. H. Morton.
‡Miss Rosamond Gilder.

damn good fun in one way when on maneuvers, but monotonous and deleterious as far as your sanity and stomach are concerned.

Heigh Ho! Have another beer. Incidentally, I have uncovered blushingly a new talent, as song writer, and have now composed, with the assistance of a vague collaborator, ten songs, two of them with original music, one of which will undoubtedly become the "Mademoiselle from Armentieres" of this war: a ditty called the Orders of the Day.* The other night I was obliged to render them all for the Major and the troop officers and since most of them were most uncomplimentary about the officers, they went over with a bang.

NORTH CAROLINA, OCTOBER 1941†

I am writing this in a churchyard during a lull in the day's activities, while our platoon is resting prior to an all-night session of maneuvers. Actually, in many ways, these maneuvers have not been as strenuous, or as much fun, as those in New Hampshire. I don't know quite the reason why, in either instance, but it seems to be a fact. You still get very little (or, at least, very scattered) sleep; and precious little to eat that you don't pay for yourself. However, I suppose one is more accustomed to it all and since one maneuver is very little different from another they tend to become monotonous. We have had a few hair-raising drives on these dusty roads at night. It is worse than any black-out driving as you literally can't see a thing except white clouds pouring into your windshield and your eyes; but, for the most part, there has not been much excitement. The countryside, as you know, is drab, monotonous; the dust is terrific, and the weather, from my standpoint, magnificent—clear and hot most of the time. The farmers are praying for rain while the soldiers pray for clear weather. As long as it stays clear you can endure anything, but to be watersoaked would be well-nigh unbearable!

All in all, we're having a pretty good time as such times go. Last Sunday was fun with Bobby‡ and I saw Cabot for just a minute.

*See pages 12 and 13.

†In October the 101st cavalry went to North Carolina to take part in the army maneuvers which were held in that state.

‡Robert Bishop.

10

Driving home will, I imagine, be hell. But no doubt we will survive. Will try and get a motorcyclist to post this.

The morale of the 101st Cavalry hit a new all time low today.

First of all, although we got into camp Thursday at dawn from maneuvers, (a dawn that was as cold as any I have ever felt) and were not going out until Sunday evening, they decided not to let us go off for the week end until Saturday noon, because it appears the authorities thought the camp looked messy during our absence. How we could have helped that, the Lord knows, as there was a cloud burst that lasted all one night, which must have raised havoc with the tents, while we were suffering on our own a hundred miles away. However, there you are! Then to cap the climax, came the announcement, that from henceforth no one could leave camp in uniform except in a military vehicle—in other words, as civilian clothes are not allowed in camp at all, no one can leave camp except for one of those mass USO outings. You can't go in a bus, a taxi, a private car in uniform, so where are you! Some people are thinking of hiring horses or bicycles! Of course the order may be rescinded or modified in which case I'll let you know.

If there is a new subterfuge to beat this new horror of a rule, trust us to find it, but this time, I fear, we may be stumped.

Maneuvers are really much duller here than they were up north. You either sit for *hours* (eighteen or twenty) doing nothing at all or drive around getting nowhere, except, of course, being captured. There are about three planes, no more, no less, a handful of old-fashioned tanks, and no one at any time seems to know where they are. One day when our car was captured we must have seen at least a dozen Majors, Colonels, etc., all trying to find out where their command posts were and not one of them having any idea at all. God help us all if we get into a 'shooting war' under these conditions.

No.1

Your food is a life saver. I don't know what we'd do without it.

I can barely stay awake now as we went to bed at 12 midnight Wednesday and got up at 2:15 A.M. to get back to camp yesterday and I was on an R.J.O. detail the better part of the next night.

EN ROUTE FROM FORT DEVENS TO CALIFORNIA, DECEMBER II, 1941
(*Four days after Pearl Harbor*)

Well, it has finally happened—the event we have anticipated for so long! Like everything else in this war, it came in a totally unexpected manner. And I find it hard to believe even now that we really are in this conflagration, even though I am at this moment seated in the turret of a rickety caboose with a tin helmet on and a rifle and pistol both fully loaded with ball ammunition.

It is a curious thing, but I know it is, in my case, a fact, that the dramatic impact of such an occurrence is immensely less forceful when you are more intimately connected with it. You might have imagined that the army camps were seething with excitement, but such was far from the case.

We heard the first news of the bombing when we were lolling around the barracks, trying, not too successfully, to straighten up our things after maneuvers. Although everyone knew what it meant, everyone with any sense, at least, there was no undue excitement. Jack Sturgis and I, who were in the middle of rehearsing a revue we planned to present Friday night, decided it would be wise to go to Boston that night before passes were cancelled. So we did so, going to the Ritz where we dined with some friends and headed back to camp at midnight. The Post Exchange had not yet reopened, so we had no papers, spent the morning cleaning cars, equipment, etc; then gathered in small groups to listen to the President's address to Congress.

Just as he was reaching the climax of his address, a burst of flame shot out through one of the radiator flues! There was a wild dash for fire extinguishers and we put out the fire and got back to the radio just in time to hear him ask Congress to declare a state of war.

No news of any kind from the army, no pronouncements, the inevitable rumors, but none of them much sillier than those heard every day. A "line-up" at 1:30. The top sergeant announced that from hereafter AWOL would be punishable by death or imprisonment! No reports yet re the twenty-eight-year-olds or about furloughs, though everyone sensed that the rules regarding both would be changed. A heightening of interest, a kind of sense of relief that the waiting was all over with, but no emotionalism characterized the reception of the news of the war. Everyone was in excellent spirits; no one seemed perturbed at the prospects of indefinite confinement. Of course, they realized perfectly well the seriousness of all the implications. But army life teaches one to take almost everything in one's stride; we had still hardly recovered our first wind, much less our second, from maneuvers. And it all seemed still rather remote.

That night all passes were cancelled. There were still no newspapers. But the thespians—Pete,* Buck Gordon and a few others from our platoon—went right on rehearsing, changing several of our scenes owing to the new change of events.

The next day, Tuesday, the most dramatic events, concerned, not the war, but our show. Three of our cast were put on details the next day and I had to spend hours getting them off. The furlough situation was altered several times during the day, but still no word from the army, the Colonel or the Captain, announcing that we were at war. But we knew that we were!! We rehearsed until 10 P.M. and then came back to the barracks to listen to the President's speech. Half the men in the barracks were already asleep but about six of us sat around the radio while we were undressing.

Half way through the speech, one of the most idiotic members of the troop came rushing into the barracks in a breathless condition. The captain was out of his head with excitement in the office, he said. All platoon sergeants were to report at once. Something drastic was going to happen! And, in about ten minutes, it did. The sergeants returned. Forty-two men had to be selected at once to go on a secret assignment to the coast, ten from each platoon, leaving, with full equipment, in half an hour.

There were not many more than ten people present from each

*Peter Nicholas.

platoon, as some were already on furlough and a few were out to dinner. So they were soon selected. We hurried back into our filthy uniforms, did up our bed rolls, rifles were assigned, ammunition doled out and an hour later we were in trucks ready to head off we knew not where. It was frigidly cold. And by 5:30 A.M., when we finally drew up at a freight depot somewhere outside of Boston, every one was so cold that they could hardly get out of the trucks. To our infinite joy, we discovered that there were two Pullmans, instead of box cars for the guard, so we piled in finally, the guard details were set up and off we went, to return, we hoped, in 12 days—6 days there and 6 back—but nobody knew just what was what.

We were doing something,* anyway, which was better than doing nothing, though it would have been nice to be able to catch up on our sleep. I can't go into any details now of the trip except to say that so far it has been uneventful and not too strenuous. The guard shifts are now worked eight hours on, eight off, eight on, eight off, which is pretty good as when you are 'on' you don't have to do much except when the train stops. . . .

I think I'll stick with this outfit. Reports are that they are going to push us on very fast, that we were selected especially by the War Department for this job owing to its importance. So I think it best to see what happens.

EN ROUTE FROM FORT DEVENS TO CALIFORNIA, DECEMBER 13, 1941

We have just crossed the Rockies past Cheyenne and are headed on to the coast. I see no harm in disclosing this information as anyone along the Lincoln Highway can have, and has, seen us; and by the time this reaches you all danger of sabotage will be over, anyway. A caboose, by the way, is a thoroughly delightful place in which to ride. There is a turret with slats on either side from which you can lord it over the whole countryside and see right along the track over the top of the train. Last night I was on the shift in the engine itself, which was quite interesting, though decidedly not as comfortable, or as

*Guarding an ammunition train.

16

warm, as the caboose. We are divided into 2 shifts, with a picked guard (including M. C. E.!) to handle the caboose and the engine, and the rest to cover the whole train whenever we come to a stop. On our off time, we sleep, in two Pullmans, thank God! and eat in a baggage car from our own field kitchen. Surprisingly good food, by the way, considering that we brought it all with us from Devens.

We get very little news, though we usually manage to get the porter to pick up a paper for us somewhere along the line. Still you feel frightfully out of touch with the world and almost anything could happen without your knowing it.

EN ROUTE FROM FORT DEVENS TO CALIFORNIA, DECEMBER 14, 1941

We have gotten frightfully delayed en route, even though we were supposed to have precedence over every other train on the line, so that it looks now as if we won't hit our destination until Monday. The load on the flatcars is so heavy that we are continually buckling a wheel and the crates themselves break the wire clamps that hold them down, which means repairs at almost every long stop. Otherwise the journey has been uneventful to the point of acute boredom. And while no one could call it arduous work, the shifts are long and the meals at distant intervals—breakfast at 4:00 A.M., lunch at 12 N., dinner at 8, we'll all be glad when it's over and our cargo is safely deposited, wherever it is due to go; and where that is, none of us knows for certain, even though we have a fair idea.

One thing the army training certainly does for you is to prepare you to do anything without thought or delay. We got the order to be ready to go to the coast with full field equipment—tin hats, gas masks, etc.—at about 10:35 P.M. and by 11 o'clock were all assembled in the Day Room dressed and ready to go. Eight months ago it would have taken us two hours at least and the confusion would have been indescribable. As it was there was no more hubbub than if we were going on guard. It's the constant doing of a thing over and over, at all hours, under all conditions, that teaches you to do it like an automaton. You get the order, when you're just undressed and getting into bed: "Full

17

field equipment and enough clothing for a trip to the coast and back. Report to the supply room to draw ammunition and load machine guns as soon as you're ready. On the double now!" And you don't think: "Oh my God! I'm going to California!" You jump into your clothes, roll up your pack, pray that you haven't left behind any vital piece of equipment (and, by this time, you ought to be shot if you do) and hurry to the supply room.

I imagine that war is a good deal like that in the effect it has on the men. They haven't time to think but just to do what they're told and most of the time they haven't the faintest idea where they're going or why. The important thing in the training is to make the men as impersonal a machine as you can. . . .

Well, so much for military training!!

We are in Nevada now, having shifted from the Union Pacific to the Southern Pacific at Ogden, Utah, and a God-forsaken looking state it is, too, just about as bad as Wyoming, which is saying a lot. But then I never, as you know, have been a rooter for the great open spaces! Or for mountains! And you get a plethora of both out here. I hope California will be an improvement.

Washington and New York, I suppose, are in a wild state of turmoil, with radios blasting like mad and rumors a mile thick. The rumors that concern us most at the moment are those which have to do with our stomachs (whether we're going to have bologni for lunch) or our sleep (a twenty-four-hour guard the moment we hit California). But I guess it was ever thus!!

I had a long talk with Murray Richards while we were on guard in Green River, Wyoming, last night, as to what we should do and neither of us could come to any decision. Now that they're calling men up to 45, I suspect they'll relax the age requirements for officers. If they do, I'd much rather stay on active duty in the line. I couldn't see myself getting a desk job in Washington at this stage of the game. But, after all, with the country at war, it's pretty unimportant what happens to one individual.

San Francisco is wonderful! The most fascinating and exciting city in this country. I wouldn't have missed seeing it for anything and the only tragedy is that we have had no chance to see it except at a distance and, one night, in the dark. Of course I suppose the war heightened the whole picture and lent a touch of drama to an already dramatic setting. But both men and nature have conspired to make the bay with the city rising behind it one of the great sights of the world.

We arrived here Monday at about noon, pulling in slowly down to the waterfront. As soon as we reached the docks, the troop was dismounted and one man was assigned to each flatcar, and we coasted slowly down by the wharfs looking very military and bristling with rifles, pistols and tommy guns. The train was then split into three sections and each section was taken to a different pier, where the material was to be loaded on to boats for shipment, I presume, to the Philippines. Our section was taken to a pier just in front of the fish markets and the fish wharfs. It was a beautiful clear day, with the city rising up behind myriad colored boats at anchor and, on the water side, grey, grim looking liners; further out, cruisers and destroyers; and far in the distance Alcatraz, Angel Island and the Golden Gate Bridge—a marvelous color, red,—towering between the mainland and the island.

After standing on guard for about an hour on the cars, we were relieved by local troops, put into army trucks and taken to the Presidio army base right in San Francisco, on the waterfront near the Golden Gate Bridge. There we picked up our two Pullmans which had been put on a siding, just inside the gate, and then sat down to await orders. No one knew how soon we were coming back, or whether we would get any time off. Finally orders came through that we would be switched on to the Challenger the next evening at 8:45 P.M., and so they gave us passes for the night. We got off at about seven o'clock and went to the Fairmont Hotel, had a bath, and then went out to dinner at a place that was supposed to be, and was, excellent. Owing to the blackout, the place was deserted and we were the only inhabitants.

We had to be back at the Fort at nine A.M. the next day, and there we sat until a few hours ago. Fortunately, a few of us were able to get out and go to the St. Francis Yacht Club, which was right next to the Presidio, for dinner. There we watched the first convoy go out, the first to leave this country—first a cruiser, then three liners and destroyers—just at dusk, a very dramatic scene. Today, we sat around again, waiting for orders, and finally pulled out by one P.M. and came to San Jose. Tonight we are to be switched to a train known as *The Daylight* and then we head, we hope, straight home, though it will probably take us hours to get through Chicago.

FORT DEVENS, JANUARY 6, 1942

Believe it or not, I am just off to Boston on a twenty-four-hour pass. All the rest of the regiment has been denied night passes for the next ten days at least. But this special post guard of eight men, of which I am one, *grace à Dieu,* is still permitted twenty-four hours off every other day, as we are on so-called "detached service," coming under the jurisdiction of the Post O. D. instead of the regiment.

All *very* gratifying, as good Queen Vicky would have said. Especially as every one else has practically perpetual details, there being so few men here; and another contingent of ten men has been sent off on some special guard duty, to Albany this time.

Everything here is very disorganized—a mass of rumors but no definite news and the morale very low. There have been almost 400 applications for transfer made formally through RHQ; there are any number who want to get out of this outfit at any cost, and all is pretty topsy turvy. Four more people, three sergeants and a corporal, were sent to Officers' School last week, which may or may not be an encouraging omen, though the general opinion is that men over 28 are not wanted in active service. I still think, however, that the best thing to do is to wait for a time before taking too definite steps to get transferred.

However, I dropped a line to a friend in Washington telling him to be sure and let me know if there was anything I could do here, in the way of making an application, etc., towards working into the Air Corps G.2. But there I'll let the matter rest for the time being.

I can't begin to tell you how much I enjoyed my furlough, especially the really swell New Year's Eve party.

FORT DEVENS, JANUARY 21, 1942

I talked to the Captain today and he is hopeful that I won't need any more documents than the one I already have (to transfer to the Air Corps).* He is going to discuss the problem with the authorities down at RHQ, and, if they agree, I'll go right ahead and put in the application. He doesn't want me to do that, however, until he is sure that all is O.K., as it is much more difficult to get an application passed once it has been turned down. At any rate it takes a great deal more time.

All in all I should say things look promising, though I'll believe I have the transfer only when it is signed, sealed and delivered and I am off to Westover Field!

Such is the army red tape that anything can happen.

I don't agree with Lippmann at all. I think FDR's doing a very good job, considering the immense difficulties.

FORT DEVENS, FEBRUARY 24, 1942

I should be on my way to Westover Field even before you get this letter. But knowing the Army and this regiment, it's quite on the cards that I shall still be here come the summer. Actually I can't imagine what could have happened to my transfer, though I have my suspicions that our own RHQ has in some way bungled the situation. If nothing happens today, I shall speak to the Captain. That will have given them two weeks grace from the time the transfer left Westover Field.

Except for the futility of it all, however, I don't mind, as life is still perfectly pleasant here. But as long as I am getting out it seems silly to waste all this time.

*A document from authorities at Westover Field requesting his transfer to the Air Corps.

21

Well, here I am! In the U. S. Air Corps.

My papers finally came through at eleven o'clock. I was able to get away from camp about 1:30. Jack Sturgis drove me to Ayer in the half ton truck. There I phoned Colonel Maugham's office to find out when he wanted me to report. He said he would send a plane right over, which he did! and I left the Fort Devens airport at about 3:30 in a four-passenger plane piloted by a Lieutenant with another Lieutenant as a passenger.

Style for a private! (As I rather think the Lieutenant himself thought.)

Well, I have no news as yet. They found a temporary bed for me for the night, but I won't know anything about anything until tomorrow, when I have to report to the sergeant major and then later, I suppose, to Colonel Maugham.

I can hardly believe that I am actually here after all the talk and delay, etc. But I'm sure I'm headed in the right direction. From now on I imagine that the rest will be up to me.

It was something of a wrench leaving the 101st, even though I am delighted to be out. They are such a nice crowd and we really had a lot of fun, even despite the snafu.

But everyone will be leaving there before long. And then life would be hell.

WESTOVER FIELD, MARCH 5, 1942

As I have just told you on the telephone, it is probably a very good omen that I have, as yet, not been officially assigned to any section: that I was just left off hand in the supply room by the sergeant and told I could help out there if they need any typing done. It makes for boring days, with nothing really to do but to sit on a box looking at

*Transferred from the 101st Cavalry to the Air Corps.

the supplies (!). But a year in the army has inured me to almost any boredom. And the main thing of importance is that it looks as if Col. M. told the sergeant just to give me any old thing to do on the assumption that it wasn't worth getting me regularly assigned because I would be out of here so soon.

It really is killing to find that everyone here is dying to get into some other—*any other*—branch of the service. These, of course, are the opinions of the non-flying *enlisted* men. Apparently no one in the army is satisfied and largely, it seems to me, because they don't think they are learning enough and rebel at the inefficiency they run into at every turn. Fifty percent of the discontent is, of course, the normal bitching without which no army would be either normal or healthy. But I'm afraid it goes a little farther than that in the case of most outfits today, and is caused largely by stupid handling.

Well, let's hope this letter isn't censored!

WESTOVER FIELD, MARCH 10, 1942

I have no news myself worth recording, except that I am sure if I stayed here even a month, I would be made a sergeant. I'm already doing a corporal's work and I'm sure it wouldn't take any time to shoot right up. But even though I think the same is true of almost any unit except the 101st, I don't regret that part at all, as I not only had more fun but learned more as a Pfc than I would have as a sergeant anywhere else.

They write me from Devens that they are breaking up the Regiment even more. Half our troop and the whole of another is off to Bangor to do M. P. duty. I really don't know what the army thinks it is doing. It all makes absolutely no sense.

Could you call R. and ask her to send me a copy of *Players at Work* and one of *B'way, Inc.,** if there happens to be an extra one hanging around the office. The top sergeant wants to read them!!!

*Both written by M. C. E.

23

I don't know how shortly I'll be transferred to Bolling Field. I had to fill out a complete form applying for Officers' Training School and then send it with my physical exam attached to 1st Corps Hdq. at Boston. At any rate it's done and I've taken the physical. I suppose I'll take the IQ. in Washington, though what IQ. it is, I can't imagine, as I have already taken the regular IQ. they give for officers' training at Devens and got a score of 134 which is in the "excellent" category.

FROM CADET M. C. EUSTIS, CO. D,
1ST QUARTERMASTER SCHOOL REGIMENT
CAMP LEE, VIRGINIA, APRIL 6, 1942 *

We rose at 5:15 this morning,—I greatly fear that is to be a precedent—and started off the day by marching to breakfast, a hateful procedure, at 5:45. We eat about a quarter of a mile from our barracks, and use mess kits instead of china. At seven we were assembled and marched off to the parade ground to be "welcomed" by the Colonel. Then an hour or so of foot drill followed by policing of the area, and then, miracle of miracles, some free time to straighten up our equipment. As I had already done that yesterday, I am writing to you instead.

I think, in fact, I know, the school is going to be hard work with little or no time off except for Sunday. The courses cover field work as well as Q.M. and, as far as I can determine, I shall be at no disadvantage from lack of business experience and at some considerable advantage from experience in drilling and in field maneuvers.

Bobby† and I were terribly lucky. We arrived at just the right moment and so got into the barracks instead of tents. The officers all seem to be very nice, especially our Captain.

*As no vacancies were available at any Air Corps Officer Candidate School, he was sent by the Air Force to the Quartermaster O.C.S. at Camp Lee to get his commission before going to the Air Corps Intelligence School at Harrisburg.
†Robert Bishop.

I really think this school is going to be first rate, though definitely hard work, as you can see by the 6 A.M. to 9 P.M. hours.

The old timers tell us that Field Operations, neatness, and general deportment and presence count just as much, if not more, than classroom work, which is also encouraging. And they all report that the work is interesting, the officers top notch and the general atmosphere extremely pleasant.

We do still have K.P.!! But it's the only detail and you get it about once a month. We live in officers' barracks, two to a room.

This will be harder work than anything we've undertaken so far, but at least it should lead to something. . . . It makes all the difference in the world having Bobby, as, with one friend, the break-in period is 100% easier.

I have been rushed before in my Army life, but never have I seen anything to equal the schedule to which we adhere in the Q.M. school. You are lucky if you have time to brush your teeth! I shouldn't be writing to you now, but I am just seizing a moment during study period, as much to relax my brain as anything else. Actually, if you did even three-fourths of the work you were supposed to do, you wouldn't sleep at all!

The assignments in each course, — Fiscal Accounting (Ouch!), Procurement, Subsistence and Field Operations (the only one I like) —are sufficient to keep you going all day. So you just have to pick and choose and hope for the best.

The general impression seems to be that they know you can't possibly take in everything you're told to, that they don't expect it, and that they merely want you to get a quick comprehensive (if somewhat confused) idea of the whole picture.

But thank God, I'm not going to be stuck in Q.M. for the duration. That's an idea, incidentally, that is slowly turning Bobby's hair grey, as he's afraid he may be stuck.

So far I have not yet been called on for a three minute speech at the beginning of class, but the time is bound to come. If you can imagine me giving an extemporaneous talk on fiscal accounting you'll know what to expect! I'm not any too sure I can imagine it, except in a nightmare.

CAMP LEE, MAY 1942 TO M. E. F.*

I tried to get you on the 'phone today just to tell you how very appreciative Bobby and I were of the Herculean effort you and David made for us and how much we enjoyed the weekend at Williamsburg. You can't imagine how much it means to be with civilized people and to get away completely for a time from the stultifying army camp atmosphere.

The news is simply awful today. Almost worse than the actual fall of Tobruk is the enormous amount of material that was captured, probably all our latest and best type of armaments and armored vehicles. I'm afraid we have allowed ourselves to be lulled into a false sense of optimism and security, without realizing what a really titanic struggle lies ahead.

CAMP LEE, MAY 1942

Bobby and I went down to the Byrd's for supper, which was very pleasant—just Mr. Byrd as Mrs. Byrd was in Fairfax, and we wandered round the place before supper.† A great pleasure to get in such civilized surroundings even for a brief spell. And it *is* a lovely place with the most beautiful magnolias I have ever seen—something, I fear, that belongs pretty much to the past.

This gas rationing hits so close and so painfully hard on almost everyone we know that there will be a widespread tendency to criticize and to complain. And I don't think one should. We've all been crying for the Administration to get down to brass tacks, saying that we (the American people) wanted to do everything we could do, that *nothing*

*Mrs. David Finley.
†"Upper Brandon" on the James River.

26

was too much; and then, when the first act occurs which really asks for any sacrifice, a wail goes up which can be heard from Maine to Florida.

Of course, it is going to be inconvenient. Of course, it is going to revolutionize American life. But it seems to me that it's like the old and typical American way of thinking we can have our cake and eat it, too. We say we're willing to do anything to win this war and we really mean—anything which doesn't affect us personally.

I know the easy "out" is to say that everything is so badly run by the New Deal that one has every right to complain. But the fact is that all those complaining are doing so not because of New Deal bungling but because their own pocketbooks, their pleasures and their personal conveniences are being affected. And with all the bungling and bureaucracy, a lot of which is inevitable in such a gigantic task as we're taking up, I think you must take off your hats to the President and the New Deal for doing an amazing job in stimulating production, organizing an army—in short, leading us on a path where we're going to win this war, unless the civilians, and through them Congress, bungle the job for largely selfish reasons.

Casualty lists are going to begin pouring in before long and I don't think any sacrifice that's asked of those at home is too much for them to take and take cheerfully. You remember how we all blamed Chamberlain for not doing anything to bring the war home to the English people. And now we blame Roosevelt just because he is farsighted.

I think moreover that those "spiritual values" Arthur Krock talked about in his Sunday article that should accrue from this war won't do so unless people accept it one hundred per cent and do so cheerfully.

CAMP LEE, JUNE 12, 1942

We had our final exam in Salvage today. Only two more exams and then we are finished with our courses. Wednesday next, we go on a three day bivouac,—and finish up the odds and ends of our courses the next week. Then five days to prepare for graduation and then, pray God, the pool at Oatlands.

The news from Africa is terrible, isn't it? I'm afraid they may lose Egypt, which would be a fearful blow, though maybe our troops will turn the tide. We've got to do something drastic soon, as every defeat adds months, if not years, to the total length of the war. And I'm afraid we've allowed ourselves all to be lulled into a false sense of optimism and have become complacent as a result.

I read one account which said that even now Alexandria was gay and completely unwarlike. The Raffles bar all over again? Let's hope not, but it looks ominous. Will the British never learn? Or the Americans either?

I don't think one person out of ten has the faintest idea of the task that lies ahead, or wants to think of it, if they do have an idea. Too many people still think in their heart of hearts that all we have to do is to produce goods—produce, produce, produce—and that Germany will, by some magic formula, collapse internally. When and if that does happen, it will only be because they have been beaten *on their own ground* and in the field of battle. And that's not going to be done in a year or even two. At least I'm afraid it won't be.

CAMP LEE, JUNE 30, 1942

The assignments came through last night and, sure enough, mine was directly into the Air Corps with orders to report to the school in Harrisburg. Although I was sure it would go through, it was a great relief to see it in black and white, for, as you well know, anything can happen in the army and nothing is positive until it is on paper. So Harrisburg it will be, and I imagine I'll have to work like the devil there to make up the lost week. But it will be worth it.

Today we had our physical exams. Tomorrow we have the "dry run" of the parade; the next day, the parade proper and the day following, graduation and our commissions.

I can't tell you how lovely it was at Oatlands. All the lilies and delphiniums were out and the garden looked as beautiful as I have ever seen it.

I shall probably go right through to Harrisburg Friday, which is a bore but can't be helped.

HARRISBURG, PENNSYLVANIA, JULY 8, 1942*
TO M. E. F. AND D. E. F.

My second day of duty as a commissioned officer in the Army of the United States was a most interesting and rewarding one!†

Here are some of the highlights!

Reported at a basement office, delightfully cool and oozing with dampness (the office, not the officer), at 7:45 A.M.! Went immediately to another basement where the laundry was being turned in and given out! Lost 69 cents of G.I. money in the process of receiving money from about ten very important shavetails, much too important to stand in line in an orderly fashion! Made this up out of my own pocket and returned just in time to fill the Coca Cola machine outside my office, a fundamentally simple procedure but one which was made infinitely complicated because my boss, the Legionnaire Captain, insisted on playing with all the dials and got the mechanism all out of joint!

"Now for a spree." We then went to town to take some money to the bank and buy a few odds and ends, including a dozen red roses to be sent to some Harrisburg beauty at 11:15 promptly—these from a British Major teaching at the school! Needless to say, I picked out the roses.

A few bills to be paid, on our return, but no paper, envelopes, paste or paper clips. The Captain said he would get these from the commissary at once. This took an hour and four trips, because each time he came back with only one item, having forgotten the rest!

It was then too late to write the letters, as the morning inspection had to be made. This was intensely exciting work, consisting of turning on every light bulb and water spigot in every room and bathroom in four big buildings and flushing all the toilets to boot! It was almost

*After receiving his commission as 2nd Lieutenant at Camp Lee he was sent to Harrisburg to the Air Intelligence School.

†Arriving too late for the school then in session, he was assigned assistant to the officer in charge of the upkeep of the building.

29

like a game of hide and seek, too, because the Captain was so absent-minded he could never remember what floor he was on and he would solemnly inspect the same floor two or three times, convinced he had never seen it before!

He suddenly decided that we must collect all the spare sheets stored away in countless closets and put them in the laundry room. This necessitated a return trip through all the buildings and we also found a mattress which I had the privilege of carrying down four flights of stairs to give to a Major who was so fat that he was falling through the springs of his bed!

A great humanitarian, my Captain.

The sheets brought us, eventually, to the laundry room again, and from thence to a basement playroom filled with slot machines. On these the Captain dotes, so he spent a good half hour and many of my nickles and dimes trying them out. I learned a great deal about slot machines, which will always help me in the future!

Although it was past lunch time, and the dining room doors close if you don't get there within ten minutes of the hour, he had to bring down several other officers we encountered to try the slot machines, so we eventually had a nice cold lunch with the waiters—'much better, really, you know. You don't have to wait. You can just eat and run to business.'

After lunch I typed out a list of the 'discrepancies' noted in our tour of duty. We played a few minutes more with the Coca Cola machine, putting it permanently out of order this time; and then got some new electric light bulbs to replace those on the blink. Since the Captain was not tall enough to reach the light fixtures, who but his assistant did the work?

This, my friends, is a factual account (to date) of my second day at Harrisburg. However, the day is still young, as it is only four o'clock and the Captain likes to work until nine every night. The reason I have time to write this letter is that he has gone out to take a sunbath to celebrate the fact that he has an assistant to help him and can now get a little well-earned rest. If he did the work he had to do and did it systematically, he could do it all in about three hours, but I've never seen such a man for getting sidetracked and it's a grave question how long I shall be able to retain my sanity working for him.

Seriously, I have not exaggerated the picture one little bit—except, perhaps, by a turn of a phrase here or there for the sake of building the laughter. There's nothing to do but just to 'take it,' as they say, though by army regulations they actually have not got the right to make an officer do the kind of work that no sergeant would ever think of doing. But it does seem to be something of a waste of time. I did think when I became an officer that I had at least, and at last, put behind me those 'details' that add so much to the merriment of an enlisted man's life. But I've been wrong before in my judgments as to what would happen in the army and I certainly was wrong again. It is a little difficult, under these circumstances, not to get a bad inferiority complex, but fortunately I can still laugh at things, something of an achievement in itself after a year and a half in the 101st Cavalry.

HARRISBURG, JULY 10, 1942 TO M. E. F.

Shortly after I had come into this basement office this A.M., a small, unobtrusive looking man, with Colonel's eagles on his shoulders, strolled in and stood looking around in a benign fashion. I asked him if he wanted to see my boss (fortunately the Captain was out) and he said: 'No' and asked me what my name was. Upon being apprised of my identity he said that I was the person he wanted to see. I realized then that he was not one of the students, as I had at first suspected, but that he was the Colonel of the School.

To stop beating around the bush, this is the gist of what he said: that he had heard from Washington from two sources about me and that he wanted to explain what the situation was. He said he hadn't the faintest idea who I was when he heard that a second lieutenant had arrived from Quartermaster School; that he had imagined I was just another one of the boys who had traded on their education and social contacts to get themselves a commission and that he thought it would be a good thing to start me off as assistant janitor for that reason, also because of my quartermaster training.

He said now that he wanted to explain to me that he had the greatest respect for men who had enlisted in the ranks and come up 'the hard way' and that they were just the type he wanted to get into the school; also that my background and training fitted me very well for A2 work. It was impossible for me to get into *this* school but, of course, I should be enrolled in the next (so the only important problem is settled once and for all) starting August 10th; that in the meanwhile he did not want me to be discouraged; that there was lots of work to be done to improve the service (janitorial) department! He evidently knows as well as I do how badly it is being run, wants me to stick it out for a month and do the best I can.

Although nothing was said about giving me any different kind of work to do—in fact the direct inference was exactly the reverse—I suspect that I may easily be shifted to some other kind of job in a little while, or else given more authority in this one and a chance to straighten things up a little, which, God knows, they need.

At any rate, the chief stumbling block, that of getting into the school, is overcome and the picture is a hundred times rosier than it was. It may even work out in the long run to be an advantage. I can get a good many pointers on work in the school during the next month. I can even do some advance work on some of the courses; and, if I do a good job as janitor and don't complain, it will probably start me off with several credits in my favor.

So, *en avant, mes enfants* for bigger and better displays of efficiency in the janitorial department!

HARRISBURG, JULY 12, 1942

I'm not lying when I say that I think things may have turned out for the best. I really do believe it, though I'll be frank to say that I didn't for the first few days, until the Colonel came to see me and my position was clarified. Now I think that the month lost will be a gain. I'll be able to do a lot of advance work and get a head start on the rest of the class and I will also know all the instructors and know my way round, which is always a help.

Actually Harrisburg is a very nice town, even aside from the nice people in it. And the situation of the school is charming with a big lawn looking right out on the river. I haven't lived with so much 'green' since I joined the army.

I think that the work is going to be fascinating, too, from what I can see of the schedule of classes, very thorough and hard work, but nothing like as boring as the Q.M. School.

As far as I can see you have no positive assurance that you will be sent overseas at all. And you run the same risk as at the Q.M. school of being stuck here as a teacher.

Well, we can only leave it to fate and see what happens!

I am very comfortably settled in a single room, high enough to look out over the buildings across the street. Today I hired a radio as I thought it would be nice to get the news and am listening to a delightful concert right this minute.

It seems too queer for words to be one's own boss for a change, to get up when you want to, instead of when a whistle blows and to live in a hotel. What luxury! Of course there is the added responsibility to see that you *do* get up. I have a double check, with an alarm clock and the hotel calling me up. And I go to bed early anyway so I am usually awake. Also I have pretty easy hours. I don't have to be at school until 8:30 every other day and seven the other mornings, but after getting up at five for three months—what is that?

HARRISBURG, AUGUST 11, 1942

I am officer of the guard tonight and have to be on duty until midnight when I make an inspection of the buildings, so I am taking the time to catch up on my correspondence.

Today was our first day of classes—yesterday was taken up with registration, assigning of quarters, etc.—and for the next six weeks we will be hard at work with seven hours of classes a day, and a considerable amount of homework to boot. I am glad now that I have the experience of the Q.M. School behind me as, boring as the actual courses may have been, I at least got back into the way of studying, which was one of the hardest parts of the whole course.

I got a nice pat on the back from Major Baird, the executive officer, yesterday, who told me that the Colonel had been most appreciative

33

of the good work I had done in 'a very difficult situation' and was altogether unnecessarily complimentary. It doesn't mean anything but it is better to start out at the school on that basis than as a complete nonentity.

But I know I shall never regret having come up from the ranks, even though I could have got here via Washington with no effort at all. When we actually get out in the field, the training I have had will pay dividends of a thousand per cent. And that's worth almost anything. Better by far, say I, to be a second lieutenant, who really is an officer than a Major who is only an officer because someone stuck a gold leaf on his shoulder!

HARRISBURG, PA., SEPTEMBER 18, 1942.
POSTED AFTER EMBARKING FOR OVERSEAS DUTY.

Although this will reach you later, you can see by the date line the time at which it was actually written—on the "lobster trick" of the school problem which so discombobulated the last day at Harrisburg!

The Colonel has just paid us a visit during which he took me aside and whispered, "You're going to Egypt" and then shook his head, smiled and put his finger to his lips. He came back a moment later and told me the assignment was "a reward for virtue" as my marks had been "excellent."

I don't need to tell you how thrilled I am at the prospect of finally—after several false starts—getting into a real theatre of operations, as war zones are known in army parlance. And honestly, I have always had a yen to go to the African theatre. The climate will suit me a 100% better than England. The assignment will be far more interesting. Altogether, I am more pleased than I can say, as, frankly, I never believed I would get such a good break. I thank God, now more than ever, that I have behind me the experience as an enlisted man, as I shall at least know the rudiments of my job.

We have all known for the past two, or even three years, that this moment had to arrive sometime and have undoubtedly prepared ourselves to face it, without mincing possibilities of an unpleasant nature. Now that I am actually about to embark (how, I haven't the faintest

34

idea) I feel curiously enough, that there is little to say, except the obvious. The "obvious" is often the truest thing one can say at times like these. We know that there is risk involved (though, in this war, that risk is spread over practically the whole globe); and we know that there is a possibility that we might never see each other again— (though isn't that a possibility every time we step out of the house?). But isn't that about the sum total of the situation? except this, which is probably the most obvious statement of the lot,—that this is a job which is worth doing, whatever the consequences.

I don't, as you know, feel partial to heroics, be they true or false. I don't think it is heroics, however, to say that Hitler has made it impossible for people to lead normal, civilized, decent lives. And so the only thing to do is to go out and fight him.

If one should be killed in the fight, well you have to die sometime. And I can think of worse ways of dying, by far.

I do feel sincerely that this is a war which is worth fighting. That being the case, the thing to do is to go out and fight and get it over with as soon as possible, to have as good a time and do as good a job as you can while you are engaged in this "task," as the army calls it, and always to hope for the best.

BOLLING FIELD, D. C. OCTOBER 27, 1942 *

Just a hurried line before we take off. It was perfectly awful having to say goodbye, but it was an event we had both been expecting for many months and all things considered I think we got through it pretty well.

I hear there is a chance we may be able to telephone from the staging area, but I wouldn't count on it as it seems unlikely to me. We may, however, be able to write.

My heart is still full as I think of leaving you . . . But it has to be, so we must make the best of it.

*Before going to the port of embarkation.

IX AIR FORCE, A.P.O. 696, NEW YORK, N. Y.,
OCTOBER 30, 1942

It looks now as if we are going to pull out today. Whether you will get this letter before we land or not I don't know. I hope so. We had a "foreign service" medical exam this morning, an absolute joke as we all traipsed up to the hospital and they did absolutely nothing but look at us and say OK!

Thank goodness we're not going to wait around here for days doing nothing; we've done that long enough; and while it was a joy at Washington it would be hell here.

Well, I have been given a platoon to command and have to go now, and inspect their equipment. I will have to be their godfather, fifty enlisted men, at least until we reach our destination, which I think I shall rather enjoy. . . .

HQ. HQ. SQDN., IX AIR FORCE, A.P.O. 696,
NEW YORK, N. Y.
OCTOBER 31, 1942

It is not giving away any military secret to tell you that we are leaving camp in about an hour and that I haven't any more idea than you have what our destination is. It will, obviously, be some port of embarkation, but which one I just don't know, any more than I know the type of vessel on which we will set sail. Some day I'll be able to tell you the whole story and let's hope it won't be too long from now. . . .

Am just being summoned to take care of my platoon so I must stop.

36

IN TRANSIT

••

NOVEMBER 11, 1942 TO
DECEMBER 18, 1942

The day shall not be up so soon as I,
To try the fair adventure of tomorrow.
KING JOHN, SHAKESPEARE

Saturday we entrucked at camp at about 2:30 in the afternoon, pulled out an hour or so later, and motored in a column to the dock. Getting on the boat was the worst feature of the trip so far. Had to lead my platoon about two hundred yards down the dock, carrying my "val pack," musette bag, brief case and overcoat. About half way down I really didn't think I'd make it. My bag was so heavy and so clumsy, I couldn't get a grip on it. Had to stop, panting, to shift it to my other hand and was relieved to see most of the enlisted men were in just about as bad straits. Called a halt to let us all, especially the officer in charge, catch our breath! Then staggered forward to the gangplank. Got the EM (enlisted men) on board, and then went over to the officers' gangplank, where I received a card assigning me to Stateroom U48, and then labored up the gangplank, more dead than alive.

U48 was a de luxe cabin for two on the Upper Deck, which shared a bath with another double room. I say "was" advisedly, for there now are fifteen berths in triple decks in our room and ten berths in the smaller one— a 2′ x 2′ closet, no hooks anywhere—one toilet, bath and washbasin for twenty-five men (running water for bathing restricted to 7 to 8:30 A.M.—4 to 5 P.M.!) .... We are all 2nd lieutenants in the cabin, 5 from our unit, the rest from scattered units.

We wonder for a while how we'll ever make out in such cramped quarters; but cease to think of the problem after seeing the EM's quarters—162 men in a room not as big by a long shot as the drawing room, nearer the library in size—with about a seven foot ceiling— bunks in four tiers—corridors about two feet wide between every two bunks—the kind of thing you might dream about in a nightmare!

Every square inch of space on the boat is filled with berths—the only lounging space left is the officers' mess on the top deck, formerly the bar, and the movie theatre for meetings, etc. No question of any lectures on plane identification, thank God! It is a good boat, and a fast one, though not super-size. . . .

Soldiers are coming up the gangplank in the dusk, one after another in a seemingly endless line, their blue barrack bags on their shoulders, packs on their backs. The lights are dimmed but there is no blackout while loading continues. No one knows when we sail, no two people think we're going to the same place. The line keeps plodding up the ramp . . . although the boat already seems jammed to the gills. . . .

Trying to get down to the EM's quarters, three decks down, is a two-hour job. The passageways are jammed. No one knows where anything is. You wonder how they will ever get order out of this chaos.

A snack supper is served at the officers' mess at 10 P.M. It takes about an hour to get to the head of the line. A brief tour of the sundeck. The last batch of men stream up the gangplank. Cartons of food are hoisted over the side.

"No smoking on deck, please" . . . No smoking . . . Blackout . . . and in the distance the dimmed out city.

Down in the bowels of the ship, the EM are lying naked, exhausted, sprawled on their bunks—a silent mass of sweating flesh. . . .

Your own cabin seems what it once was—a de luxe cabin. And you breathe a silent prayer that you are an officer!

Sunday. I grabbed an upper berth because there's about a foot more head room and much more privacy. You can't sit up, but you can lie with your knees up and not touch the ceiling which you can't do in the two berths beneath.

Went down the first thing to see how the EM were making out, and because I'd been ordered to. An alert—just for the officers at 5 A.M.—and all officers had to go to their battle stations. Being a platoon leader, my "station" is down in B11 with my platoon! Have a devil of a time getting down to B11 in the blackout. . . . The only lights are a few red lights in the corridors. Have to dress in pitch blackness (all flashlights had to be turned in the first night) and find our way by some kind of mumbo-jumbo back to the bowels of the ship. The men are still dead to the world, having been told the night before to pay no attention to the alert as it was only for officers. The three platoon leaders and the squadron leader sit for an hour and a half waiting for instructions, which do not arrive. . . . Finally we send an emissary up for information and find that the alert is over and that we'll get our instructions later.

Go out on deck at about seven. We are in the open sea in a fog,

can't see more than one hundred yards or so . . . and we are riding, if not at anchor, at least motionless. Try and get some breakfast, and get some without too much standing in line. . . . Back to B11 to see how the men are making out. . . . They are a swell bunch of men, no complaints save the usual and perpetual bitching. They haven't eaten for about fifteen hours or more. The mess lines for breakfast are hopelessly clogged and yet they take it all in their stride and are joking and laughing as if they were back at camp. Take it from me the American enlisted man is just about as good a specimen of humanity as you can find.

The promenade deck is all boarded up and some EM are sleeping and quartered there, without any bunks or mattresses even. The boat deck and the top deck are the only ones clear and the decks forward and aft.

At about 9 A.M. we start moving and as the fog lifts find ourselves almost out of sight of land with a convoy of three destroyers, zig-zagging back and forth. Shortly we pass a huge convoy of thirty freighters coming in from the other direction, riding high, with sub-chasers darting round and destroyers fore and aft—a dramatic sight in the rather gray light, with the gray ships, a blue gray sky and the low, gray coast in the distance.

Spent most of the rest of the day buying food at the PX for the men. The mess lines are hopelessly clogged. Some groups stand in the passageways for four hours without moving more than a few feet. Most of them give it up and go on deck or lie in their bunks. "It's always this way the first day out," a naval officer tells me. "As soon as it gets systematized it'll be OK." And he is right. By the next day the lines are going much more smoothly and in two days it takes only nine minutes to get up to the mess line.

We settle down quickly into the ship's routine. The worst feature, I think, is that you sweat so much your clothes are constantly drenched and you haven't many clean shirts to get into—also with water rationed to one hour and a half in the A.M. and to one hour in the afternoon you haven't got much chance of washing either yourself or your clothes. There is *no* laundry, I might add. Nor is there any bar! Smoking is restricted severely; you can never smoke in your cabin and only in certain rooms. The EM only eat twice a day, the officers have a coffee hour at lunch, which helps out, not that you really need much food. . . .

Am continuing this letter on the sun deck which is terribly windy, so excuse any illegibility. We have now been on board just about a week and I must say the time has flown, chiefly because we've been so busy. The mails close tonight so I'll try and jam in as many details as I can in a half hour or so.

You may remember that Col. Koenig told us to expect anything once we got out into the field. Well this officer has had a job which taxed his "Intelligence" almost to the breaking point! And may yet send him to the ship's sanitarium, if there is such a thing!!

To be specific, four days ago Col. Blair called me to his office (he is now executive officer of the whole ship) and told me he wanted me to open a barber shop for all the troop personnel on board within two days. We had no equipment of any kind and the barbershop had none, no running water either, but he had a list of a few barbers in different units. The rest was up to me. He didn't want to be bothered, just to be given the set-up to O.K. once it was set up.

You may think writers or actors, or even your own family, are temperamental, but until you have dealt with a lot of barbers you haven't any conception of what temperament is. I almost went mad trying to line up a group of barbers who had their own equipment, but finally, by walking about fifteen miles up and down the boat, I collected seven men (I have three barber chairs), fixed up everything, got the Colonel's O.K. and was all set to open. Everything went well, or comparatively well yesterday (though two men never turned up at all our first day,) but hell broke loose today! One barber got hurt feelings because my head barber told him he didn't know how to cut hair (a true statement, God knows), so he said he was going to quit; then his friend said he'd quit too; and my head man had a rash which I'm sure is just prickly heat, though I'm ready to believe the worst. That meant I had to find three new barbers this morning. Unfortunately I can't as yet order them to stay on the job, since they are just doing volunteer work, though they get good pay. Three new barbers, another frantic morning, and finally I got them. Now I have to arrange an appointment sheet for every unit on the boat for the rest of the voyage! An easy job, if ever I saw one!!

Well, never let anyone tell you that the army isn't a complete education. I think I'll be equipped for every kind of job when I get out, from head man in the men's toilet at the Mayflower to garbage collector anywhere you want to mention! Still, I'd rather have this job than many others that are being handed out, and if I do a good job at it, I think it will not hurt my career!

We had some rather amusing ceremonies on deck yesterday, but I was too busy to do more than just look in on them. Then, presto!— back to keep my barbers in line. I'm scared to leave them for a minute for fear there may be a free-for-all with razors, though actually they're all damn nice!

The mails close very soon so I've got to stop. The food is surprisingly good. While some people feel they'd rather stay across the ocean than face a return voyage, it honestly is not so bad. Crowded as possible, yes. And uncomfortable in its way. But I've seen worse (where, I don't quite know!) and the sea air is swell, whenever you can get the time to get on deck.

I'm sure I've left out much that I wanted to say, but my barbers have drained my imagination and besides it's "coffee hour". . . . P.S. I washed all my underclothes in three canteens of water just now.

This *is* the Army, Mrs. Jones.

ABOARD SHIP, NOVEMBER 1942

I don't know any single thing that contributed more to the morale of the enlisted men than the gift of books and games contributed to our unit by the Camp and Hospital Service, District of Columbia Chapter, of the American Red Cross. I have spent a large part of each day down in the quarters of the enlisted men. There is never a time that I don't see men sprawled around on the floor playing games or perched in any old cramped position with a book. Moreover, they appreciate this gift more than I can say and take great pride in keeping all the books and games in good condition. No one who has not seen for himself the conditions under which the enlisted men live on troop transports can even vaguely imagine what such a gift can mean to them. The boat itself, to be sure, has a few books and old magazines to hand out. But nothing to speak of, and if it had not been for your gift the problem of affording recreation to the men would have been much more difficult.

I might add that we were the only unit on the ship that received anything from the Red Cross, as no kits were handed out at the Port of Embarkation. Whether the Red Cross could make this a regular service I don't know. Space is so limited that it is extremely difficult to get any authorities to consent to taking along another box. . . .

We have just heard via the radio of the news of the landing of American troops at Algiers and Spanish Morocco, also of the British success in Egypt. Wonderful, isn't it? I have a feeling we may really be getting them on the run.

Have to go down now to pay off my barbers!

ABOARD SHIP, NOVEMBER 1942 (LATER)

Today they had Divine services and many Masses in the movie house; and for some incredibly Navy-ish reason restricted all smoking on deck while the ten o'clock service was going on inside. We were all supposed to meditate, I suppose, and meditate I did, about where I was going to dig up another barber to replace the one who has, or says he has, a rash!

The men in my cabin are all 2nd lieutenants and hence years younger than this veteran; but Devens accustomed me to youth, so I am not a bit perturbed.

It is hard to believe, sitting out here in this peaceful scene that all the world is busy trying to exterminate itself. You could almost imagine yourself on a luxury cruise, until you went below decks.

We carry life jackets with us all the time, not as wearing as you might imagine, and have to have our steel helmets with us whenever we are on deck. But you soon get accustomed to the paraphernalia and impedimenta of a so-called 'full field equipment' and we only have to wear everything at 'abandon ship' drills.

44

We had a gala Thanksgiving dinner last night, very good but not good enough to prevent my wishing I were enjoying the same meal at home.

I have nothing but the deepest respect for the Navy and the Army in the way they have handled the men on this boat and in the organization that has been set up. The food has been excellent at the officers' mess; and, if the cooking has perhaps left something to be desired in the enlisted men's mess, they have at least had plenty to eat, which is not a small feat on one of the longest nonstop trips that any liner has ever taken.

The men have adapted themselves remarkably to conditions; there has been, comparatively speaking, no sickness; and I look upon the entire organization as something of a triumph. I am "on duty" now from 7 A.M. to 11 A.M. every morning in the compartment in which our men are located.

We just got a "flash" this morning about the scuttling of the French fleet at Toulon—too good to be true—and the news from Stalingrad is wonderful. I am extremely puzzled about Admiral Darlan. I always thought he was as bad as Laval, if not worse, and here he turns around and offers us the whole of French Africa. Won't it be grand if the whole of France lines up with us, though, of course, it can't do it just yet? I think I'd rather be present at our re-entry into Paris than at almost any event I can think of, not that I'd mind being on hand for the march down Unter den Linden. And this time, I hope, by all that's holy, that we *do* march into Berlin and make Hitler watch us do it. I wouldn't be in Adolph's shoes now for a good deal, as I think a frightful vengeance is going to overtake him and his kind, if we let the right people dictate the peace.

TAJ MAHAL HOTEL, BOMBAY, DECEMBER 2, 1942

I suppose you will be flabbergasted at seeing the heading to this letter. But no more so than I am! It is not exactly the direct route to our destination, is it?

All the officers and men were granted shore leave today, thank God, and I can hardly believe I am back on dry land and sitting in a de luxe hotel, and it is really de luxe. Who would have thought it two years ago? Or even, for that matter, two months. . . .

We are going inland tomorrow to some rest camp, so called, and will stay there until there is a boat ready to take us where we are supposed to go, unless, by that time, the orders are changed and we go somewhere else! Not likely, I think, but in the army, as you know, *anything* is possible.

One look at India and you realize that there is a great deal to be said for the British policy, as I feel convinced, judging from the Indians I have seen, that they are in no wise ready for self-government.

Bombay itself is in a lovely situation, on a beautiful bay with hill crests spotted with huge royal palms on all sides, a good deal like Rio in some ways, except not so dramatic. The city is much more European than you would expect; the waterfront, save for a glimpse of some towers and minarets, might be almost the Riviera and the trees and houses like the Rue de Rivoli with colonnades.

We got off at twelve, took a fiacre to the hotel, stopping first at the cable office to send a cable, which I hope you will receive, had lunch and then took another fiacre to go sightseeing. The man couldn't speak a word of English and took us for miles in the wrong direction. Finally we gave him up and took a taxi instead, but at least we saw Bombay!

The Indians are the filthiest people, the natives, that I have ever seen, even worse than the natives at Algiers. They lie, or squat, on the sidewalks, wrapping and unwrapping strands of their turbans, which are dragging in the gutters. They carry everything, as you know, on their heads, huge baskets that must weigh a ton. We drove up to Malibu Hill where you get, what Baedeker calls, a fine view of the city and the harbor. It is beautiful weather, hot in the daytime but cool at night.

There are lots of uniforms everywhere and about twenty barrage balloons over the harbor, but somehow you don't feel that you're in a warlike community, which, fortunately, of course, you aren't. No one can say you don't "see the world" in this day and age, can they?

46

It is all so fantastic, it seems like a dream rather than reality. I am seated in a room about 8 x 15, with a high, peaked ceiling, a small bathroom (no running water) in the rear. My "bearer," a charming young Indian by the name of Annam, is preparing my bath, getting the hot water with which to fill my tin tub, about 3' x 2', oval shaped! He will then shine the "master's" shoes, get his bed ready, with the mosquito net adjusted, put the finishing touches on my clothes for supper, and then will vanish until, at eight tomorrow, he reappears with my morning tea, and gets the master ready to face another day.

We are living in low shacks, which look rather like small cowbarns, with tiled roofs and long open porches on one side, about ten rooms to a shack, and two men to a room. Each room has its own bearer and he gets paid at the rate of forty rupees a month, about $13.20 or $6.60 apiece, per officer.

A hundred yards or so away is the Officers' Club and mess; breakfast 8 to 9:30; lunch, 1 to 2:30; dinner 8 to 9:30 "or a little bit arfter," as the British 'leftenant' explained it to us. There is a nice lounge where you can get Australian beer, ale and whiskey from 7 P.M. on. Tea is served again in the afternoon at four o'clock in your room, just before the bath.

It seems incredible in this total war to be sitting calmly in a place like this, with you at home probably imagining us in all kinds of hell holes. The British have been most hospitable and very helpful in every way. Even the enlisted men have tea brought to them in the morning and their beds are made and the barracks swept out for them by enlisted men's bearers.

The country looks more like Arizona than any other place I know, except that there are more trees, perhaps, and vegetation. Miles and miles of bare desert land and then, all around, hills and mountains rising abruptly, like towers, or, small hillocks making little bumps and mounds, on the top of most of which are some remains of an old temple, or a watch tower or statue.

About a mile and a half away, still in the camp territory, is the

"Bazaar," the native village, which beats all native villages hollow for dirt, grime and filth and, for good measure, atmosphere.

I hired a bicycle there and am now off to visit a neighboring temple.

INDIA, DECEMBER 6, 1942

The British censor will not permit us to disclose our whereabouts or to name the port where we disembarked, but we are allowed to say that we are in India in a military camp 'somewhere in the country.' Once we reach our final destination we will then, I imagine, be able to tell the whole story.

I don't have any idea how long we will remain in this 'rest camp' in the hills. If I did, I couldn't disclose the information anyway! But it is a very pleasant change after the boat and the service, needless to say, is admirable. The climate, too, is just about perfect. A hot, dry heat during the day, and a drop of about forty degrees at night. The English carry on about the sun as if it were some kind of a monster. Mr. Coward, to the contrary, they never venture forth into the midday sun, if they can possibly help it. Troops are not allowed to exercise between 9:30 A.M. and 4:30 P.M. and there are all kinds of bulletins posted to warn the uninitiated Americans of the danger of exposing oneself to the sun's rays. The British all wear sun helmets. Several of our officers do likewise. But I find myself perfectly happy in my regulation garrison cap, the one with the vizor. And personally I don't think the sun is one bit hotter than it was at Camp Devens. I bicycle down to the bazaar almost every day in the blinding glare that exists largely in the imagination of people who just don't happen to like God's sunlight. I'm sure Cabot will back me up on this statement, too.

To start more or less at the beginning of this phase, we stayed in port for three days, on one of which we were granted shore leave, and on the morning of the fourth we entrained for camp. The enlisted men were put in military cars, much the same as some of the third class cars on the continent, and the officers rode in very comfortable Pullmans.

As we got our first glimpse of the camp, which covers an area bigger, I should say, than Fort Devens, our hearts sank. We saw

48

rows and rows of tents on brownish soil, burnt, with not a tree in sight. Pretty soon, however, we pulled into an oasis of green trees and there we detrained.

Our heavy luggage was sent up by truck but we had to march up to our quarters, about a mile and a half away on a very dusty road. As none of us had had any exercise to speak of since we left America, and as our musette bags, over-coats, et al, were pretty heavy, we were all pretty pooped by the time we reached our quarters and were prepared for the worst.

We got a pleasant surprise, though, as you may imagine, and we sat down an hour or so later to a very good dinner in the officers' club, after being properly ministered to by our 'bearers,' who unpacked all our bags, laid out our bedding rolls, brought us tea, etc.

I collapsed in bed right after supper and slept without stirring until I was awakened the next morning by a tinkle of china and saw Annam's black face and white coat, all topped by an elegant red turban, peering at me through my mosquito netting and telling me in very broken English: "Marster, tea is served."

After breakfast, my roommate and I (his name, by the way, is Jim Hausman, and he is a very nice fellow) walked down towards the bazaar to hire a bicycle before the supply was exhausted. Half way down we stopped a horse-drawn Trondy and hired him to take us the rest of the way.

The native village is really fascinating. Such dirt you have never seen anywhere. Goats, the proudest looking animate objects I have seen in India, and oxen, geese and ducks roam round the streets at will or lie sleeping on the sidewalks or in the middle of the road, along with women, children and old men who seem to squat all day in the most uncomfortable position I have ever seen. The sanitary facilities, if there are any, are not used very much. The dirt streets or paved sidewalks on the main streets seem to fill the bill very adequately for the majority of the population and for all the children.

The town is almost like a sideshow at a county fair, with hawkers outside the shops; but the merchant himself is always seated, in a chair, or squatting at the entrance and he seems not one whit concerned with whether you buy anything or not. I went into one of the

49

cleanest and most elegant shops in town, a large sunny room with kodaks in a case, and found the proprietor seated in the center, inhaling with evident enjoyment some very bad incense which was smoking in a pot under his nose. I asked him if he sold cameras. He shrugged his shoulders and said; 'The prices are marked' and closed his eyes. When I saw that a broken down old Brownie of a vintage of about 1900 was priced at forty rupees, or $13.20, I beat a hasty retreat and left him with his eyes still closed, a serene half smile on his face.

All the natives wear white or dirty colored coats and pants or smocks; the Hindus and the Mohammedans wear turbans, the Catholics, who incidentally seem to be of a much higher type, wear no hats indoors and caps or round, squat, colored hats without brims outside.

The bazaar, as I told you, is a part of the military reservation. A larger town, some eight miles away, is off limits for the army, because, as the British Colonel told us, every woman in it has syphilis. Why anyone survives, living in the conditions of filth that most of the natives do, is beyond me. But they seem to survive, worse still, to multiply. Owing to the caste system, which flourishes in the Hindu and Mohammedan tribes, it is impossible for a man ever to change his station or caste of life. If his father is a beggar, he must be a beggar. If his father is middle caste, he must be middle caste, so there is no opportunity for individual endeavor. The British, they tell me, have been fighting this system for years but there is nothing they can do about it, as it is all tied up with religion. The only hope, really, for India to become a self-respecting country capable of governing itself, would, at the present time (and that would take hundreds of years) be for all the Hindus and Mohammedans to be converted to Christianity. Then they are free and so are their wives.

Honestly, if all the people back home, who shoot off their face about the Indian situation, could only come and see for themselves what the British have to cope with, I think they would soon sing a different tune, and also admit that the British have done, on the whole, a remarkable job. Almost all the officers who came over with us, who were of the opposite opinion originally, changed their minds after a few hours on shore; and, when you come into the country

50

sections, your views are even more favorable to the present British rule.

So far, (we have only been here three days) there has not been much military routine to bother about, but starting tomorrow, we are going to take the men on conditioning hikes, and I believe they will also do some firing on the range.

Annam has just brought in my afternoon tea and I shall shortly thereafter have my bath, a most unpleasant occupation as I can hardly fit into the tub.

INDIA, DECEMBER 9, 1942

I took a fascinating bicycle ride today with Major Thompson to a town about eight miles from here. We had lunch at the Golf Club where my tire blew out and had to walk back to the town and get a patch put on it and then we cycled home.

Most of the trip is along the main road from Bombay to Calcutta, a fairly good macadam road that goes down the one green valley I have seen in the neighborhood. It isn't a valley, actually, as the country is flat, but it gives the impression of being one because of the size of the mango trees along the road and the rich cultivated soil on both sides; beyond—the brown desert grass is all you can see, with mountain ranges jutting out in the distance on all sides.

The road is full of ox carts driven by natives who squat on the traces between the oxen and drive them by pulling their tails when they are not flicking them with whips. Burros, the fascinating small donkeys, are driven along the road. Natives walk along with water cans on their heads. Not many cars but a few buses.

The town is as dirty as most towns. They all have a rather French feeling in architecture, like some of the hill towns back of the Riviera; and the shops are all open to the street like booths at a sideshow, jammed with natives.

The countryside doesn't look at all like what I imagined India to be. It is a mixture of Arizona and Wyoming, as far as desert and mountain contours are concerned, with a touch of France thrown in, in the towns and along the roads.

Since we shall have arrived at our destination by the time this is mailed, it is permissible to tell you that we are now travelling in convoy through the Indian Ocean. Three troop ships, plus corvettes, on the largest and best of which your correspondent is burning the midnight oil to write to the "folks back home," seated on a hard wooden bench in a "berthing area" below the water line, surrounded by a motley collection of legs and arms protruding from hammocks which are slung in every which way from the ceiling.

As you may have guessed, I am on guard duty with our troops and am holding the fort on E Deck aft, in case of any emergency or untoward circumstance. We get four hours on duty each day but the hours of your watch change, fortunately, so that actually you are on duty for four hours every twenty-eight hours. Tomorrow I go on at 6 A.M., the next day at ten and so forth and so on.

To go back to where I left off, we left our rest camp at 5 A.M. Friday morning and took the train back to Bombay. We were scheduled to get there at eleven, but since we spent four hours sitting on a siding just outside the city, in one of the least attractive of the suburban areas, we didn't get to the docks till about three. I say 'least attractive,' because we seemed to be in the midst of a leper colony, judging at least from the natives who thronged around the train windows to beg, many of whom had stumps instead of hands, as their fingers had been eaten away.

The camp we were at was called Deolali, about eight miles from the holy city of Nazik, which I described without naming, in my last letter. I confess that I didn't see any evidence of its being any holier than any other Indian town, unless dirt is akin to holiness, as I have so often claimed it was! That is one of the strange things about India. You hear always of the hold religion has on the natives and yet you see less concrete evidence of religion there than any other country I have been in. In Nazik I didn't see a single temple of any sort, though I am told now that there is a small one outside the town, and you never see natives praying or bowing to the East. The most ritualistic event I have seen anywhere in India—Bombay, Deolali, or Nazik—is the washing of clothes in the village stream—in Bombay not a stream or even a river but the municipal open-air laundry tubs, but the effect is the same.

The natives, and, I imagine, the local laundry men, take all their clothes down to the river bank, beat them out in the running water (which often contains dead animals as well as a whole collection of live ones) and then lay them to dry on the big flat slabs of stone that seem to be characteristic of Indian river beds. They then sit around and do what Cousin Tina* calls 'jaw' with each other in an impassive way, getting excited only, when eight or ten stray burros wander out and step over the 'clean' garments, even then, not too excited, as at least one or two animals will already have rolled or otherwise misbehaved on the laundry. What the social significance of these municipal laundries may be I don't know! I do know they are fascinating to watch, with the rocks and rills all covered with different colored bits of material and the rhythmic "beat-beat" as the natives stamp the cloth into the water and on to the rocks.

Incidentally, before we finish with laundry, it is not at all uncommon in Bombay to see a stately looking patriarch walk up to a drinking fountain or horse trough, divest himself of all his clothes, except a fairly inadequate loin cloth and proceed to wash them then and there on the street corner and squat in an attitude of holy meditation on the sidewalk while they are drying.

A strange race, these Indians. Personally, I wouldn't care if I never saw another one of them as long as I lived. I think I echo the sentiments of one of our lieutenants who said that the best revenge we could ever have on the Japs would be to give them India, fish, flesh, fowl and every single Indian.

The potentialities of the country are immense, even the untrained eye can see that; and I am sure that we, for instance, could do a much more efficient job than the British if we really set our minds to it. But *is* it worth it? *That* is the question.

After a snack lunch served on the dock by the Indian port 'canteen'—not bad at all in taste, though served out of some of the greasiest pots I have ever seen, we boarded this Royal Mail Steamship and

*Mrs. Charles Bohlen.

53

immediately got a very pleasant surprise. Our quarters are luxury, compared to the *West Point*. Everyone over the rank of captain has a cabin to himself; the captains are two to a room; 1st lieutenants, three, and 2nd lieutenants, four. But four, in an outside stateroom, with closet space and drawers and very comfortable beds, is not to be sneered at. And we had at least fifteen in the same cabin space on the U.S. liner.

We have stewards, Indian, one for the cabin, one for the bath, practically like a regular liner. There is a nice lounge, two dining rooms *with* waiters. (we ate cafeteria style on the *West Point*), and a bar—soft drinks morning, early P.M. and evening, alcoholic beverages, 5 P.M. to 7:30.

There is a professional barber shop—God be praised! and deck chairs galore. You can smoke anywhere you want on the boat, except in the men's berthing areas. The food is excellent and altogether it is practically like taking a cruise on a luxury liner, and the war seems a long way off.

The enlisted men also fare much better than they did on our last ship. They have about twice as much space, tables to eat at where they can sit down, and hammocks to sleep in which are unslung in the daytime. Their food is much better, too, they tell me, than anything they have had to date.

There are only about 2,300 troops all told on this boat, so the problem is altogether different than on a boat like the last one where there were four times as many. But God knows this is a very much more pleasant way to travel, even though it may not have much relation to total war.

I am rapidly becoming a tea addict and suspect that I may be a slave to the early-morning tea custom before long.

Well it is 4:20 A.M. now.

The weather is still grand but I'm just as glad that we've got out of the dust of Deolali, as I was beginning to cough my head off from the layers of grime accumulating on my throat.

54

About half the boat is ailing from minor complaints picked up in the charming rest camp where we spent a week, dysentery, or a mild form of a skin itch—the British call it Dobie itch, which comes, they think, from the laundry—and colds of one variety or another. I am happily free of any complaint save a cough, which is not much worse than the old friend you know so well.

This boat is real luxury however, lounges to sit in, writing tables, eating without standing in line for hours, all the comforts we had almost forgotten existed. Also, and perhaps most important, plenty of water to wash in all day long.

They say we may be able to telephone home when we reach our destination. If so, I shall certainly be on the 'phone Christmas Eve, if possible, and to hell with the expense.

The weather is perfectly beautiful, not too hot and yet sunshine all day. We play lots of bridge and some poker and read and sun ourselves a great deal. Guard duty every twenty-eight hours for four hours—which is not too irksome.

SOMEWHERE AT SEA, DECEMBER 18, 1942

We stopped to refuel yesterday at a port in the Gulf of————. I don't know whether we're supposed to mention the name or not, so will play safe. Pulled into the harbor at about two o'clock and were on our way again by six P.M. By early morning (in other words, right now) we should be steaming into that colorful sea of Biblical lore.

The shore line, as we approached the port, was fascinating. Great jagged peaks rising right out of the sea, all rock and shale, no vegetation. Then, through the glasses, the first sign of civilization—a small wooden structure, severe and simple like an army barracks and lying next to an old fort on top of a low promontory. We round the promontory and there the city is spread out before us; a cluster of low buildings along the waterfront spreading out fanwise into the grey hills that tower on three sides of it: a few trees along the boulevard that runs along the waterfront: everything else is grey, brown, arid.

55

On the other side of the harbor are miles of desert which seem to melt into the distant hills; desert that looks like pools of muddy water in a brackish swamp. On the water's edge, tents, houses, oil wells and white adobe storage tanks.

"Not all the perfumes of Araby" would lure me into picking this spot for a permanent base. But a couple of British officers who came on board say that it "isn't so bad," once you accustom yourself to it. In other words, it's "God awful."

EGYPT

••

DECEMBER 26, 1942 TO MARCH 31, 1943

Pugnam sperate parati.
(Being ready, hope for the battle.)
AENEID, VIRGIL

Now it can be told, or at least a part of the story. As you probably guessed, our first stop after leaving the U. S. was Rio, for refueling. No one was allowed off the boat, which was tantalizing in the extreme, as we stayed in the harbor over night and the town looked fascinating through the Zeiss glasses. In a couple of days word got around that our next stop was not Capetown or Durbin but Bombay, some five thousand miles out of our way. I imagine you have already received all my letters from India, so I won't cover that ground again. After a week in Deolali, which I enjoyed immensely, we went back to Bombay and got on the British transport. Ten days or so later we drew up to our destination at the head of the ——— Sea. There we were put in trains again and whisked at a crawling speed across the desert to our present destination in the Middle East. We are located, temporarily, in a camp in the desert, all the officers jammed into one long, low barracks, with about a foot of space between each bed. But the quarters are not bad at all and we have running water in an adjoining building and the food is all American 'G.I.,' something of a relief after the British and Indian food, though that wasn't too bad, either. The climate is wonderful, warm in the daytime, cold at night. A trench coat, by the way, is quite adequate protection. And I never cease to thank God that I applied for this theatre rather than for England.

Things are still a bit disorganized so we are uncertain yet what our permanent assignments are to be, whether we will stay in this immediate vicinity or be moved elsewhere. But in a few days or maybe weeks, we will know the best, or worst. We probably won't be able to write what we are doing or where we are going, whatever is decided; but I am optimistic that things will break eventually just the way I want them to. A group of us from the A2 section, plus a Colonel, made a Christmas expedition to Cairo, which I will describe at length anon.

We got our first batch of letters the day after we got here. I got about fifteen, the last one of yours dated the 29th of November. One of our officers got letters dated as late as December 12 in the same batch of mail. These told him that our safe destination cards had reached home the 9th, when we were still three thousand miles from our destination! But I am still glad that they were sent off, as I was afraid you might have placed us in another and more active theatre. We made the quickest crossing from New York to Bombay that has ever been made, they tell me—twenty-nine days, including the stop at Rio. From Rio we went way down some five hundred miles south of Capetown to avoid submarines. The entire trip was uneventful, as far as any submarine scares were concerned. We had almost daily 'abandon ship' drills—and only one unscheduled one when an unidentified boat was sighted, and we turned tail and ran from it as fast as we could! So there was no excitement of any kind, as you must have gathered from the dull ship's log I sent you from time to time.

Now for a brief picture of Xmas Eve in Cairo, a fascinating city, by the way. Despite the fact that the British have been in control here for God knows how many years, Cairo is completely French, in appearance and feeling. If it weren't for the Arabs and Egyptians, you could easily imagine you were in Paris or Marseilles. There are no sidewalk cafés, but that is the only thing lacking. There is the same bustle and confusion, the taxi horns, the crowds in the streets speaking any one of ten different languages, the gaiety and electrical kind of excitement which any French city seems to germinate.

Since the war, of course, the town is experiencing a boom the like of which it has never been through before. You can't get a room in any hotel; the shops are jammed; the sidewalk peddlers and sight-seeing guides do a land-office business; and the restaurants and night clubs are thronged with all nationalities.

We drew up at the famous Shepherd's in the morning and proceeded at once to do a little shopping and to get oriented before lunch.

We had beer and cocktails on the terrace in front of the hotel and then lunched in the gala dining room. We had previously been warned by some idiot that none of the food in Cairo was safe to eat: some man, I feel sure, who had never been out of the United States before and who thought that any food that wasn't G.I. was con-

60

taminated. But we did very well by ourselves none the less, though we didn't, I admit, take the salad.

After lunch we engaged a taxi for the afternoon with a dragoman to take us out to the pyramids, the dragoman being a picturesque Arab in flowing white robes, who was willing, for a prodigious sum of money, to escort us on our journey.

We stopped at the Mena Hotel at the foot of the pyramids for a glass of coffee and then engaged seven camels and started up the hill to see the big show, our dragoman leading the way on a milky white pony. The pyramids are a magnificent sight, as you know. You can't imagine their sheer bulk until you see them. And the whole setting with Cairo in the flat delta of the Nile below them, is perfectly stunning. At the foot of the Sphinx we had our photograph taken with considerable altercation about the price, etc. and I will send you a copy as soon as it is developed.

In one respect Cairo is even more French than Paris, that is, in the prices charged for anything and everything and in the hands held out for tips wherever you go.

There are quite a few soldiers, Australians, New Zealanders, British and some Egyptians, wandering round the sands or humping round on camels and the guides and camelmen yell and scream at each other in Arabic almost as loudly as the camels bray themselves. The Sphinx has sandbags beneath her proud head, which destroys somewhat her dignity but she is still very impressive and we walked all through the temples that have recently been excavated at the foot of the Sphinx.

Had a grand row with our dragoman, after coming out of the Sphinx's temple, as we found that he had loaned out our camels to some Australians to have their pictures taken and we had to wait about ten minutes to get them back. But everyone enjoyed himself, just as in an old-fashioned French argument.

Then back to town, across the Nile, which looks, I hate to tell you, just like the lagoon at Miami Beach, and stopped at Groppi's, the equivalent of Rumplemayers, for tea. The place was jammed with officers and Waacs, Waafs and Waves. Back to Shepherd's after wandering through the streets in the dim-out, practically but not entirely a blackout, the streets filled with honking cars and taxicabs, the sidewalks so crowded you can hardly move, everyone talking at the top of his voice and having the time of his life, apparently.

Sat in the bar and watched the world go by, French, Poles, South Africans, Indians, Egyptians, British, Australian, New Zealanders, Americans, every type of uniform you could imagine. Dined in state, eating everything on the menu, washed down with a nice South African white wine and then out into the night to end our holiday.

The streets are absolutely riotous, the Australians out in force, singing, shouting, kidding the natives, everyone tight, but pleasantly so and in a high good humor. It is like New Year's Eve on Broadway, only much gayer and more amusing. You can't get a taxi for love or money, because, whenever you stop one, the Australians leap into it from the other side and go whooping away. But no one gets mad, everyone is having too good a time.

Hooting, tooting, singing, shouting, all in the darkness of this total war. It is a picture to be remembered. Finally we manage to outwit the Australians by surrounding a taxi on all four sides and forcing our way in and we are on our way!

The 'Merry Xmas'ers' are somewhat subdued at 6:45 A.M. the next morning, as we pull ourselves out of our sleeping bags in the freezing early morn and get our mess kits ready. You can't really believe it is Christmas in a climate like this one but later in the day I go down to the service club and join in singing 'O Come All Ye Faithful,' just as lustily as if I were playing the organ at Oatlands church.

SOMEWHERE IN THE MIDDLE EAST,
DECEMBER 28, 1942

I had hoped that the telephone lines might be open so that we could have one lengthy and frightfully expensive inter-family communication on Christmas Eve. But the telephone lines are closed to everything but official calls, so the next best thing I could do was to cable.

This letter may prove difficult to read, as I am writing it after supper in the gloom of the barracks and cannot see the keyboard at all. I went for a seven-mile hike this P.M. into the real sand desert which lies about three miles from where we are located and then climbed up into the sand dunes and peaks. It was perfectly fascinating. The wind has cut clean knife-like ridges on the top of all the dunes which undulate in wavy motions like clouds. The shadows are constantly shifting, as the sun moves towards the horizon, and a light wind blows fine sprays of sand in whirling patterns in all the valleys. We sat for about an hour on one of the peaks and, beautiful as it is, I can easily imagine how desert madness would set in if you were parched with thirst and starving and tramping, à la Hollywood, in search of water. Distance is almost impossible to judge and, if you look very long at one spot, it seems to move in slow circles in front of your eyes.

The climate is wonderful, about 70° to 75° during the day and cold at night. The farther out you get into the real desert, the greater the drop in temperature.

I went to the Mohammed Ali Mosque in Cairo one day when I was there. The mosque itself is 19th Century but the setting, on top of a hill surrounded by a citadel, is magnificent and the whole thing is extremely effective. Just to one side is the escarpment on one edge of the Nile Delta from which all the stone that made the pyramids was taken. And eight miles off, at the far end of the delta, with the Nile flowing lazily between, are the pyramids themselves.

SOMEWHERE IN THE MIDDLE EAST,
DECEMBER 31, 1942

It is now eight days since we arrived in the Middle East but we haven't as yet settled down to any real routine. We have a fair idea of what our assignments are going to be, but no definite orders have been issued as yet, so anything at all can happen. We come to head-quarters every day and stand around waiting for something to happen. And probably, before this letter is even finished, something will have occurred and we will be down to serious work. If we are with Headquarters, which seems likely at the moment, we work all morning from eight to one, knock off until three and then work until seven. The Army pays for your billets and then gives you $5.00 per diem as well on which to feed yourself, this besides your pay and foreign service pay, so I should do very well, even as a second lieutenant.

I had hoped to be sent up with a group or a squadron, and there is still a chance that I may be; but it looks as though we will be kept here for a time at any rate. I hate the thought of fighting a war from the safe vantage point of an Air Force headquarters. But what can you do but do as you are told? And at least the work should be interesting.

Cigarettes and beer are rationed at the Post Exchange but oddly enough in Cairo, when I went there for Christmas, you could get all the canned American beer you wanted. And all the elite were drinking it in Shepherd's. Ironic, isn't it, when everybody used to look down on American beer, especially canned beer.

It is much warmer now, even in the week that we have been here, and you don't need a coat at night, unless you happen to go out in an open car of any kind. New Year's Eve tonight! How different from the last one when we had that marvelous party at the house. I have no special plans, but something may turn up. There is a dance at the Officers' Club with nurses for partners, but something tells me I shall finesse that one.

Well, keep up with your letters. They have been marvelous and mean everything when you are so far away.

EGYPT, JANUARY 2, 1943

Nothing new yet, as far as the disposition of our men and officers is concerned. But orders should come through within the near future. We sit round the office most of the day but there is nothing for us to do. In the meantime we make the best of the situation and have as pleasant a time as we can. It is hard to believe that a war is going on, in this atmosphere.

Money flows through your hands here and while prices quoted for meals, etc., may seem cheap, by the time all the extras and 10%, etc., are added up you find that a pound here ($4.23) is about the equivalent of $1.00 at home. The town is at least as expensive as New York or Washington to live in, one reason for this being that you can only go to the best places to eat, for fear of the dire results if you got poisoned. And you can't, of course, drink any of the water. So you take quantities of tea, beer and soda water.

EGYPT, JANUARY 5, 1943

I have just returned from dinner at Mr. Kirk's, fourteen men and two women, lots of brass hats and, believe it or not, Mr. Phillips on his way through to India.

EGYPT, JANUARY 8, 1943

Am writing now during the afternoon siesta period, on the balcony of my room, sitting in my shirtsleeves in the sun. And for the first time in several days have time to write without fear of interruption and with no undue pressure on me.

I am, as I told you, assigned to headquarters, and while I could (and do) wish that I were with a Group or Squadron out at an air base, well, I shouldn't have expected that, being in a Hq. Sqdn. The work, at least, is interesting and the type of thing I can do. I keep the situation maps posted in the air room and, in addition, write the weekly periodic intelligence summary. By the time we get things organized better, I think that we shall have more and more to do—and it is more than likely that opportunities to go out into the field will present themselves before long. Meanwhile I should thank my stars, I imagine, that I am not in some awful dump in Burma, or, worst of all, India!

In time, too, we are sure to get things better organized and to get our own jobs better clarified. We were really *de trop* when we arrived —owing to events beyond anyone's control—and it was only natural, I suppose, that they didn't know what to do with us when first we breezed into the office.

I am no longer living in the desert, however, but am very comfortably situated in a room with Dudley.* Whether he will stay here

*Captain K. C. Dudley.

or not, I don't know, as he remained with the organization we had both been transferred to and may be sent out into the field. His head-quarters will probably be here, however, and so we will probably keep our room.

I am rapidly falling into a sound sleep while typing. It is hard to get anything but a four-course lunch and you usually eat it all and then are unfit for anything but bed! It takes time, also, to accustom your-self to the Brioni hours of dining—nine at the earliest and sometimes 9:30 or ten. But if that is the worst I have to put up with for the dura-tion, I shall not complain unduly! Not while I am in a de luxe hotel room, either—even though it isn't de luxe at all by our standards.

EGYPT, THURSDAY, JANUARY 16, 1943

I have to keep the Russian war map posted as a sideline to my regu-lar duties and it is one hell of a job to tell anything from the com-muniques that come out, especially as all the towns, on our map, have the Czarist names! But however exaggerated the newspaper reports may be, there is no doubt that they seem to be ploughing ahead and that Helen* has won her bet about Stalingrad.

There is no shortage of food in the neighborhood where I am, though certain articles are rationed for those who keep house. You can buy a great many American articles at the Post Exchange, though cigarettes are scarce and double the price when you can get them. My supply is still holding out from home, but it won't last much longer. When once that is depleted I shall have to resort to Goldflakes, I guess, or some Middle Eastern mixture.

I am still hoping that I may be able to wangle a job out in the field, so as to get away from an office job. And have a hunch, based on a few cautious inquiries, that I may be successful.

EGYPT, JANUARY 18, 1943, HQ. SQDN.

I bought myself a camera finally, at a perfectly staggering price, and hope to be able to send you some snap shots before long. I could shoot

*Mrs. J. Averell Clark.

66

myself for not having brought my own camera with me. Took some shots in the real desert—nothing but sand dunes to be seen—which will, I hope, be effective. A scene just like a Hollywood movie.

Tell Margey to write me another one of her long letters, and to fill it with day to day news of people and events in her life. That's what interests you when you are miles away, the type of thing you ordinarily wouldn't think of putting in a letter,—a diary type of thing, what you did each day, and all the general gossip and chit chat.

EGYPT, JANUARY 25, 1943

I went on a visit to Cairo last week and had a fascinating afternoon visiting the University, which is situated in an old Mosque, 960 A.D., in the old part of Cairo. It is quite the most beautiful building architecturally in Cairo—a lovely big courtyard with an Arabesque colonnade running around it. But more interesting than the architecture was the University life. The students sit on the stone floor of the courtyard. The teacher squats down, leaning up against a pillar and then they all sway from side to side in little groups, chanting the Koran. It is all very informal. Anyone can wander around. There seems to be no set curriculum and it is almost impossible to tell when a student is praying or when he is being studious. Would that university life at home were as informal!

I also went to the Bazaar and bought you and Margey and Anne some fabulously expensive perfume—though much cheaper than perfume at home. I only got you a two ounce bottle. But it is essence and by mixing it with ten times the amount of alcohol and five times the amount of water you get the equivalent of the French version. I had to sit down and drink Turkish coffee and describe each one of you, tell your coloring,—and then smell, God knows how many samples, before the proprietor would let me make my choice.

Thanks to the handsome per diem allowance of the Government, plus salary, billets, etc., I can live in style on my salary, without even touching my letter of credit or travellers cheques.

I have been lax about writing the past five days because I have been pretty busy on my weekly summary which is now assuming monumental proportions. It is seventeen single spaced typed pages of this size page. I wish I could send you a copy, but needless to say, it is a secret document and so not for civilians like yourself to read! One of the interesting features of working on this summary is that you get all the inside news the minute it comes out. You also get more news from home than you would in any other department, as we see all the press bulletins, also all the foreign broadcast bulletins, plus all the British secret reports. So a good deal of your time is spent reading to cull material to put in the summary. We send out about seventy odd copies of this to all our various units, to the British and to Washington. I suppose some poor soul in the War Department has to wade through it each week and extract interesting items. God help him!

Speaking of careers I wired you that I had been promoted,—it all helps in the army! I would never have got it if it hadn't been for Major Whitridge, now Colonel, who requested the Colonel in our section to put in a recommendation for me. I don't know that I particularly deserved it, but anyway I'm glad I've got it.

I'm still hoping that fate will soon pick me up bodily out of headquarters and send me somewhere into the field.

You might be amused to hear this news report from Shanghai which stated, that at the funeral of a celebrated demi mondaine in the Red Light District, the band played "I wonder who's kissing her now," while the mourners all solemnly removed their hats.

EGYPT, FEBRUARY 10, 1943 TO E. B.*

You might enjoy hearing about the party I went to the other night when I was on a visit to ————. It was given by a British Brigadier General to promote, among other things, I believe, Anglo-American relations. As one of the outstanding Americans in the neighborhood, I was selected as the junior officer to accompany two

*To Miss Ellen Bohlen.

Colonels, a couple of Majors and a Captain or so! I need hardly say that the selection was most unwise.

After meeting a round of British brass hats who were settling down to a little pre-dinner drinking of warm whiskey and water, I was seized by the Brigadier and told that I would have to join a happy little group in a Scottish bag-pipe square dance after dinner. I was then whisked up to meet my partner, a brawny woman in uniform, with one of those absolutely flat British faces sticking, without benefit of a neck, out of a pair of shoulders that looked as if they had shoulder pads on them.

I was then left with this appalling creature and discovered, to my dismay, that she had one of those exaggerated British accents which made it impossible to understand a single word she said.

I promptly mixed myself a double whiskey and considered what I should do about my predicament. I had already told the Brigadier that it was unlikely that Anglo-American relations would be improved by asking me to do a Scottish jig in public. But the Brigadier had said: "Nonsense, old boy, old boy!" and so that was that.

Just at this moment, the woman grasped my arm with the grip of a sergeant major in the Australian Marines and yanked me out into the hallway. We would have a practice round, she said, and promptly threw one hand into the air, uttered a great "Whoop" and started prancing around me. I was so covered with confusion I could do nothing but stand there gazing at her out of my big brown eyes like an Irish setter. This went on for what seemed like hours, first she went round in one direction, then in another, each time uttering a loud "Whoop." I smiled a sickly smile, and instantly she seized the glass out of my hand and yelled: "Now it's your turn!"

That was where one WAAF was wrong. It was *not* my turn. "All right!" I yelled, waving one hand in the air and tripped speedily out of the hall and made for the bar at a fast run.

There was no place to hide, but I was at least able to pour myself a drink before Antonia (I'm not joking, that was her name, the poor misguided creature) came crashing through in search of her victim.

69

I won't go into the full horror of the dance, but I will give you a brief description of the indignities I had to put up with.

First of all, six men were lined up facing six women. Then at a prearranged signal everybody (including this miserable correspondent) said "Whoops!", threw one hand in the air and kicked his, or her, feet in a jig-like motion. Then (rather like a Virginia reel), the end couple pranced out into the center, danced round each other "Whooping" for dear life, and then twirled each other down the full length of the floor, swinging each person round as they passed.

I grew quite gray as soon as I realized that in one moment, Antonia and I would have to take the floor.

She came at me with a lusty yell, and scared me so that, instead of advancing to meet her, I backed up out of the line of fire. She pulled me forth, shouting and swinging her hand and twirled me round so violently that I almost fell flat on my face. Then "Whoops! Whoops! And away we go!" and there we were making the greatest jackasses of ourselves doing a Scotch twirl down the center.

How I lived through the mortification of those three or four minutes during which Antonia and I held the center of the stage, I will never know.

Suffice it, I came through it all with nothing more than a few bruises where Antonia had bumped into me and, a profound conviction that Anglo-American relations had better be left right where they were. A few more Scotch reels, and I shudder to think what the results would be.

They got rid of the G-d- bagpipe and settled down to some more prosaic jazz in a moment and all proceeded to have a very jolly time. I left shortly, again for the sake of Anglo-American relations, and decided that in the future my social activities would be limited to frankly partisan affairs or those not aimed at promoting anything but a spirit of good clean fun, minus, if you please, the bagpipes.

EGYPT, FEBRUARY 11, 1943

B. van Royen turned up here today, among a mass of Intelligence officers flown over from Washington. What we are going to do with them all, God knows. We've got more than we need here already, but still they come! One whole outfit arrived here the other day completely equipped with skis, snowboots, extra-thick sleeping bags and enough Arctic paraphernalia to sink the ship. I hope they enjoy themselves!

I haven't the vaguest idea what is going to happen to all of us—and if I did have I couldn't tell you—but I suppose it will depend to a great extent upon conditions and events, the results of which one cannot even predict at this date. The war seems to be going our way for a change, thank goodness, and a lot of people seem to think Germany is on the verge of cracking. I don't agree with that supposition at all, as I think the more defeats she suffers the more desperate will be her resistance. She knows, or ought to know, this time, that she can't expect much mercy from the people she has subjugated and she will, for that reason, go on fighting to the bitter end. She may put out peace feelers, to see if she can catch us unaware and lull us into a false security and so salvage something from the wreckage herself. But that isn't going to do her any good as, this time, I am confident, we are not going to stop until we have hammered our way right into Berlin, wrecking all the communities along the road. If we do that from one side and the Russians do it from the other, there needn't be overmuch of a German problem for us to solve after it is all over. I hope you don't think this is too bloodthirsty a program. Personally, I don't think it's bloodthirsty enough.

EGYPT, FEBRUARY 13, 1943 TO M. E. F.

Incidentally, re clippings. They are *most* welcome. Please don't imagine that they aren't. But there should be a law that every enclosure of clippings should contain some personal note, even if it is only a few scrawled lines in pencil, to humanize them. You can't imagine how infuriating it is, after you have gone a week or so without mail, to have the boy bring up a nice fat letter and open it to find nothing but clippings! Just a thin page of handwriting is all that is needed to make them bearable.

The most enraging mail I received in a long time, after a considerable gap without any mail, was an exciting looking little package which came with surprising rapidity and looked as if it might contain jewelry or some tricky Xmas gift. I opened it to discover a tube of Lilly's Ephedrine Jelly! I realize full well that I had asked Mother to send it and that she probably went to considerable trouble to do so, but, my, what a comedown!

We haven't received any of our Xmas packages yet but I think there is a good chance that they may come through by Easter. And no doubt they will come in just as handy then.

I can tell you briefly about a British prisoner of war camp I visited last week. The British showed us all around it and couldn't have been nicer. It was intensely interesting. I sat in while two prisoners were being interrogated. One, a very sullen Nazi who wouldn't say anything, just stood at attention, looking rather ill at ease but none the less defiant. I couldn't understand the interrogation as it was all in German (though the officer translated it for us afterwards), but I was fascinated to watch his reactions. The second prisoner was also a definite Nazi type—only about eighteen, with full, reddish lips, a pasty face and he was talking a blue streak, telling everything he knew (which was plenty). The first man seemed to resent our presence in the room. The second was not a bit concerned. In fact we asked him several questions, through the interpreter, and he seemed perfectly willing to answer. We asked the interrogator if he had broken the news to him about the surrender at Stalingrad and he said he hadn't but would do so then. The prisoner merely shrugged his shoulders. He was the type of flabby, effeminate Nazi and he had no staying powers once he had been captured. He seemed convinced that the Germans were going to lose the war and was only anxious to get it over with quickly so that he could get home. Meanwhile he was perfectly happy where he was!

After seeing these prisoners, we went up into the compound where a new batch had just come in. In one room was a German and an Italian officer. The Italian looked as if he might have been a barber from Naples. It was incredible to think of him as an officer. The German was a good looking young chap, cocky and attractive, with excellent manners. He came to a smart salute when we came in (while

72

the Italian just slouched in the corner), and he seemed to be on friendly terms with the officer who escorted us around. He had none of the look of the Nazi about him. You would just place him as a nice young man in any country.

I couldn't help feeling, seeing these two, what a strange feeling it would have been if either one of them (which might easily have happened) had been someone I had known before in Washington. Suppose it had been Gino. What in hell would you have said to him?

We went next into the compound where the enlisted men were. There were about fourteen of them, all Germans I should think. They all snapped to attention as we came and stayed at attention the whole time we were in their barracks. They were for the most part in their teens. They all were pretty sullen looking, with the exception of one lad who had occupied his spare time making a huge cartoon on the wall, depicting their compound with Roosevelt, Churchill and Stalin in the watch towers, looking down and Hitler and Mussolini in the compound looking very miserable. He took great satisfaction out of our enjoyment in the picture and wanted us all to be sure that he was the artist.

That's about all I can disclose about the camp, except to say that the prisoners lived in much better quarters than I have, on occasions, been thrust into. If I were a German or an Italian, I should think the best place I could possibly be was a prison camp. I gather, in fact, that that is increasingly true of the prisoners of late. The Italians have always, almost to a man, been delighted to be prisoners. The Germans never, though recently they are far less sullen, and much more willing to talk. Their greatest fear seems to be that they will not be home in time to protect their families from the avenging fury of the multitudes of conquered races which will sweep over and despoil Germany. They seem to have no illusions, I gather, about what will happen to them if they lose the war and a few—a very few—who were openly anti-Nazi actually claimed that they deserved everything they would get.

Have you done anything, by the way, about peddling my songs. Obviously, nothing at all!

I went completely haywire yesterday and bought myself a camera for the staggering sum of forty pounds—some $170! It is a Russian Leica, however, and a really good camera. I was getting sick to death of taking pictures with the old cartwheel of a German camera I had bought when I first got here. Also I couldn't get any film for that camera and you can get all the 35 mm film you want. It is a frightful extravagance, but I can afford it, thanks to what the government pays me, and I can really take some pictures from now on. Incidentally, I got thirteen pounds for my old camera in exchange, which wasn't so bad. You can expect to get a flock of pictures from now on, provided the censor doesn't abstract them all from my letters.

My magazine gets more and more ambitious each week. I have put a lot of drawings in it and may eventually be able to arrange to get photographs. There is intense rivalry between all the various groups that get out reports in this area to see which is the best. The RAF report is, obviously, the best of the lot as they have access to all kinds of material that we don't have. But ours isn't bad considering the handicaps under which we work.

Colonel Whitridge told me that he had heard from his wife that she had seen Margey at the Red Cross conference. He is second in command of our section and as a result I see a lot of him. About once every two weeks or so we go off on an afternoon of sightseeing together. There is not terribly much to see but we manage to find something or other which is usually of some interest.

I ran into Porter Chandler* yesterday while I was on a visit to Cairo. He was back from the field, hadn't had a bath (except in six table-spoonful of water) for six months and was in very good form! I had lunch and dinner with him and found him very entertaining. He is the Intelligence Officer of a fighter squadron—a perfect assignment,

*Colonel Porter Chandler.

I think, and was with them all the way from El Alamein to Tripoli, so he was very interesting.

The news from Tunis, which you undoubtedly have heard more about than we have, is not good at the moment, but I suppose we had to expect reverses, though perhaps not such a staggering one right at the start. I always did think, however, that it would take time to drive the Axis out of Tunisia, as they are going to make a "do or die" defense there to try and prove to us, in one humble opinion, how costly an invasion of the continent would be. Then they will start to make peace feelers, which won't, thank God, be accepted.

I'd give my eye teeth to transfer to the armored forces and get back to my old friend, the scout car. Maybe I can work it but I fear it is most doubtful. Though anything I suppose *can* happen in this war. If I ever should be able to work it, I'll try and let you know by cable. If I ever mention Pete Nicholas' name in a cable, say that I have met him or am joining him, you will know what it means, as I naturally associate Pete with a scout car and so, I suppose, do you. But I know it is all a pipe dream, so don't anticipate receiving any such message.

Honestly, I thought the Indians took the prize for being the dirtiest, the most slovenly and altogether the most hopeless people I had ever seen. But I am not sure, after a visit to Cairo, whether the "Wogs" (the Egyptian peasants) don't beat them. There is a certain quality of humor about a "Wog" which an Indian, perhaps, lacks. A wog is not only utterly ridiculous, but he is aware of the fact, nine times out of ten. But that still doesn't prevent them from being perfectly infuriating people whenever you want to get anything done.

I was staying at Shepherds when Porter was here and I had him to my room for a drink in the late afternoon. This is the type of thing that occurs, not occasionally, but *every* time you have any dealings with these wretched wogs. I rang the bell that said "Waiter" and, having some acquaintance with such matters in these parts, took off my coat and lay down on the bed to await results. In about twenty minutes there was a knock on the door and in walked a savage looking black skinned creature in a long white tunic, with a bushy black mustache and a fez on his head. "Ice, glasses, soda water—quick!!"

we said in unison. He stood there with an absolutely blank expression on his face (a typical wog expression, I need hardly add).

As one of the ways to get them to register is repetition on an ever rising note, we repeated our staccato summons over and over. He merely shrugged his shoulders, smiled inanely and then said: "I go get waiter!" and bowed himself out backwards. We rang all bells furiously and in about ten minutes a small little dark man, with a sly furtive expression, a very long elongated face with hardly any forehead, slunk noiselessly into the room, winked and, standing in a perpetual forward lean, said: "Ice, glasses, soda!" and suddenly left the room at a run.

Presuming that meant he was going to procure same, we sat patiently and waited. Ten minutes more and nothing happened. And then Dudley, who was with me, could stand it no longer and said he would go and get some himself. Porter and I decided there was no use waiting and so used the tap water and went without ice. In about ten minutes Dudley returned, bearing a bucket of ice and some soda water tucked under his arm, which he had forcibly extracted from some protesting idiot in the serving pantry.

We had no sooner settled down than there was a timid knock on the door and then, with a swish, the little man burst in carrying ice, soda water, glasses, although Dudley had specifically told him not to at the serving pantry. He beamed with excitement and answered all our remarks telling him we didn't want it, with guttural exclamations. He then proceeded to put down *his* bottles and pick up the ones we already had (exactly the same thing). We finally shooed him out, a quick rustle of his robes and he was gone. Peace again. Then a heavy banging on the door and a shout outside and in walked a great big man we none of us had seen before bearing "ice, soda water, glasses." He spoke in fluent broken English and was very much (so he thought) the major domo. We were laughing so hard that it was no use protesting, and so we let him leave them, even though we already had twice as much as we needed.

And so it goes, everywhere. They follow you on the streets, trying to sell you everything from canes to dirty postcards, and it doesn't make any difference how many times you shoo them away. You usually have a long procession following you as you go down one of the main shopping streets. One of the favorite tricks is for the shoe shine boys to follow you along, implore you to have a shine and then, after you have refused about nineteen times, throw a lot of black mud, or manure, on your shoes and tell you you need a shoe shine (which, God knows, you do.) Maybe there are stupider people in the world. I shouldn't know, not having seen any. The Indians are more unpleasant but certainly not stupider.

EGYPT, MARCH 8, 1943

Last week was a very busy week for me. Colonel W. and Captain M. had gone off on a week's tour of inspection, leaving me alone in the War Room. Then, on Monday, Colonel C. was rushed to the hospital with appendicitis, so there I was left holding the bag. To my horror, I found that I had to give the G2 report to the staff meeting at noon every day; in other words to tell all the brass hats what was what in the war situation on all fronts. As you know, I am not by nature a public speaker and I was somewhat appalled at the prospect of making a speech to about forty odd Colonels and Generals, etc. But it wasn't as bad as I feared it would be and, much to my amazement, I heard myself sounding off as military tactician, prophesying probable moves that the enemy would make, etc. You would have been amused to see me, though it's doubtless just as well you didn't as I should have been petrified.

I expect to go out on a tour of inspection myself sometime in the next two weeks or so and am looking forward to shaking the dust of headquarters off my feet and to inhaling some of the pure desert air for a change. With any luck I may be able to get right up close to the front line, unless that has disappeared into the ocean by that time!

Our new ribbons arrived from Washington last week so I now have two instead of the one measly yellow one you saw me wearing. When this is all over we will probably have half a dozen others, including, we trust, the victory ribbon. None of them mean very much, however, if you haven't actually been in a combat operation.

Please tell Anne to congratulate Grenny on his promotion. . . . Tell

77

him also, for God's sake, not to let them put him back on the staff as there is nothing drearier than staff work, unless perhaps, it is quartermaster duty.

EGYPT, MARCH 1943 TO M. E. F.

For your information, in case anything ever comes of it, I am enclosing the application I have made to be transferred to the Armored Force.

As you will have sensed from my letters, I have bridled strongly against fighting this war from a comfortable desk miles away from the firing line. When the idea first came to me of how swell it would be to get back to a scout car again, or even better a jeep, I dismissed it as being absolutely out of the realm of possibility and thought no more of it. Then I happened to be talking to a Major, who had been in the Cavalry himself, and he said that he didn't see why it was impossible at all. I told him he would if he had anything to do with a transfer himself. But he said that in a combat theatre everything was quite different and that he saw no reason why it couldn't be managed.

I accordingly took the bull by both horns, sat down and wrote the "military letter," a copy of which I enclose, and proceeded to go to my boss with it. Before that I had discussed the situation with Col. Whitridge, who is now second in command (in my section) and he urged me strongly to go ahead with my plan. His hunch was, he said, that it wouldn't go through, but he thought it was well worth trying. He agreed with me that there is little chance of Hq. ever getting into any real combat zone, and he thought that anyone who wanted to and was competent to do the work there, should be given a chance to do so.

Col. Crom whom I bearded in his office at eight the next morning, was extremely nice about the whole thing. He said he quite understood how I felt and sympathized with me. He said that, even if he didn't approve of the idea himself, he would feel that he would have to pass on any such request to go from staff to active field work. But I gather from what he said that he did approve and that he would pass on my request with his endorsement. (His approval by endorsement, just went to the Commanding General this minute.)

Frankly I don't think anything will come of it, except by a fluke. It presents so many appalling mechanical difficulties, paper work, etc., which many people would hesitate to embark on for only one officer. If it were a whole group, that would be one thing. But one man! I don't know. And the Colonel himself said that he thought that would be the chief stumbling block.

Still you never can tell. The impossible has happened before and it may happen again in this particular instance. It would be quite ironic, wouldn't it, after having gone through all the hell I did to get into the Air Corps, to then go through just as much to get out of it. . . . Anyway the die has been cast and there is nothing to do now but wait and see what happens.

I have had quite a number of qualms about it, feeling that perhaps I was not really qualified to work in an armored force. But I am convinced that I really know the reconnaissance end of it to a T and see no reason why I shouldn't be able to click either in that end or as a G-2. You always run a risk, of course, in all transfers of getting the wrong end of the stick and finding yourself mess officer or worse. But that's a chance you have to take, whenever you leave the known for the unknown. I know about the known, that I shall never be completely satisfied sitting at a desk, even if the work I am doing is extremely interesting. The unknown will simply have to take care of itself. I am frankly not expecting anything to happen, so I won't be broken-hearted in any sense if my request is turned down. In fact I think its only chance is that it's such a strange request that its very oddity might make it click.

If it doesn't go through, it will, I feel sure, hasten my chances of getting into the field with an air corps group or squadron, as the Colonel at least realizes now that I, in no uncertain terms, want to get out of headquarters. So no harm can possibly come of it, whatever happens. The pleasure of getting back to a scout car again would be something almost beatific! I really loved everything about maneuvers and the real thing would be even more exciting, even though considerably less hilarious. I really am fundamentally much more interested in ground than in air maneuvers. I'll take the latter if I can't get the former. But an armored force for me any day.

I realize, obviously, that I am exposing myself to considerably more danger in such a unit than at headquarters. As far as that goes you couldn't be in less danger anywhere in the world than where we are right now. But you know that I have wanted to get into actual action from the beginning and I'm not going to give up trying until the war is over. Incidentally, even if this thing should meet with approval all along the line, the war might be over before the necessary paper work was concluded.

[Later]

My application for transfer has been approved by all the powers that be in this theatre, including Gen. Brereton. It was flown last week to the other theatre and God knows what will happen to it there. But it may, with luck, get back here (when the war is all over) with their approval as well.

MARCH 1943

COPY OF REQUEST FOR TRANSFER

1. I hereby request that I be transferred from A.2, 9th Air Force, Headquarters,   to one of the Armored Divisions, now operating in the capacity of either (1) an officer in a reconnaissance unit or (2) an assistant field G.2.
2. This request is made in the belief that I could be of more value to the service at this time in the Armored Force in   than in A.2, 9th Air Force. It is not made for "my own convenience." There are several Intelligence officers in this theatre available now to take over the duties I am performing here, whereas there may be a shortage of trained officer personnel in the Armored Forces in   due to casualties in the recent engagement.
3. I was an enlisted man in the Mechanized Cavalry—Troop E. 101st Caval. from Sept. 1940, until March 1942. During that period we were on active field maneuvers for five months, three in New England and two in North Carolina.

4. I was a scout car driver, assistant gunner and car commander in this unit. I also attended a special G.2 school given by the 1st Division at Fort Devens, in which I was in charge of a unit setting up G.2 Observation Posts during maneuvers of the 1st Division, and went through a three weeks Cavalry Intelligence School. In April 1942, I went to O.C.S. at Camp Lee, Virginia.

5. In view of this experience, I believe that I am qualified to serve in, as an officer, a reconnaissance unit of the Armored Forces, or else an assistant field G.2. I have had no experience with tanks proper, but every Armored Force has reconnaissance units, with half tracks, scout cars and jeeps, all of which I am familiar with.

6. In case the contention is made that my training at the Intelligence School at Harrisburg qualifies me particularly for work in the Air Corps rather than a ground unit, I would like to point out that much of the training given at Harrisburg is equally applicable to work with ground forces.

Morton Eustis, O. 1575303.
1st Lieut. A.C.

EGYPT, MARCH 29, 1943

I sent you a hasty note yesterday, telling you that I was off on a tour of inspection of all our groups and squadrons. Well, I am still "off" but not on a tour of inspection but on what is known in the army as a "permanent change of station." I am no longer in the U. S. Air Corps (!) but have been transferred to the ground forces and have been directed to proceed at my earliest convenience to a Replacement Depot in another theatre and report there for assignment to the commanding officer. I am going by plane, taking off on Wednesday morning early, with only a bare 100-lbs of baggage—the rest to follow, I hope, by delayed priority (which means I will probably receive it in about three years' time).

Although I cannot tell you where I am heading to, I can tell you that the plane ride there will be extremely interesting, particularly as there is a stopover, of one or more days, at a Mediterranean town that figured prominently in the news a few weeks ago.

Well, as I hinted to you, I put in a formal application for transfer to an armored unit (as an officer either in a reconnaissance unit or as a field G2) about seven weeks ago. It was cleared through here fairly rapidly, receiving the approval of everyone from Colonel Crom to General Brereton himself, and then it went by air to the theatre to which I had applied to be transferred.

I honestly didn't think there was one chance in ten of its going through, and I don't think that Colonel Crom did either; but, by miraculous good fortune, it went through and I received my orders yesterday. Evidently they had had to go to Washington, as it said, by War Department Order!

What is going to happen to me, the Lord only knows! I am to report to a replacement depot way back of the lines and there I suppose I will find out what my fate is to be. Probably I will sit there for at least a month waiting for an assignment—things always seem to go like that in the army. I also run a chance of getting some God awful assignment, perhaps in a Q.M. Bakery or Laundry unit (thanks to my experience at Camp Lee), as anything at all can happen when you transfer.

But that is the chance I have to take, and I figure that, at the worst, I will have a job that is at least active—in the point of view of being in the field—though it may not even be that, God help me!

The one worry I do have is that I may have some difficulty in catching up if I find myself with a unit that has actually been engaged in combat and has had extensive training before that. Well, there's nothing to do but to do the best I can and hope that that best will be good enough.

EGYPT, AFTERNOON OF MARCH 29, 1943

I will probably have time to burn once I reach the Replacement Depot, as I can hardly believe that they are waiting with bated breath to receive me and to rush me to the front line! Even if they have a definite assignment, they are more than likely, I should think, to keep me at some training base for a few weeks before letting me get near a combat outfit.

I have given up all hope of getting into the present conflict in that theatre, as it looks now as if it will all be over shortly after I get there, if not before, at the rate things are going now. But presumably there will be another one in some other country before the summer is over and, with luck, I may get into that one.

What your reaction will be to this move of mine I can't tell. I suppose, in one sense, you won't like it, as it will, theoretically, at least, put me into a more dangerous type of work. I was in grave danger of dying of boredom at my present post, however, so at least that is put off. What is more, I don't really think there was any future in this headquarters, no matter what type of work we turned to. Headquarters is always headquarters—miles behind the line, seething with politics and never enough work to do. The only thing you get out of headquarters work, as the Colonel himself told me, are promotions and ribbons, and I don't give a damn about either one of these. I know, if I'd waited here, I'd have been a captain in May or June, and a Major in October or November. I wouldn't have deserved it but that would have had nothing to do with it. Promotions, at headquarters, are more or less automatic, irrespective of talent, ability or the will to work.

I stand a good chance, in fact, of getting a demotion, instead of a promotion, by this transfer, as my promotion was only an Air Corps promotion which is not necessarily recognized by the Army of the United States. . . .

I have been scurrying round all day tying up the loose ends and cleaning up my desk, etc., and feel like a new man with the prospect of shaking the dust of —————— forever from my feet, eyes, ears and nose. It is the dustiest place, incidentally, I have ever known, far worse than the desert which is a clean, invigorating type of dust,—and bad for sinus, even though it is a dry climate.

I have come to the conclusion anyhow that the Air Corps is O.K. only for those who fly. They really do a job. The rest just sit round. Except for those on top.

I shall be curious to know what Bob Walsh's* reaction is. I do hope he will approve. Because he must know, if anyone, how many Intelli-

*Major General Robert L. Walsh, A. C.

gence Officers there are all over the globe, and I am sure that he will understand my wanting to get into active service, in whatever capacity.

I know *you* will approve, *au fond,* even if you may not admit it. Believe me, it was the only thing to do. It is a case of *chacun son gout,* and this, here, is not my dish of tea.

EGYPT, MARCH 31, 1943

It is 5:30 A.M. and I am just putting the finishing touches to my packing before leaving at 6:30.

It is quite a step, you know, getting into the plane and heading towards an entirely new career, which may be pleasant or may not! But nothing venture—and anyway I'll be doing what I want to do.

I don't want you to think this was an ill-advised, hare-brained scheme. I thought it out very seriously.

Here is what Col. Whitridge said in his letter of recommendation:

"1st Lt. Morton Eustis, 0-1575303, has been in this section for the last three months where he has done excellent work. He has had charge of the war maps and has been largely responsible for the Periodic Intelligence Summary. In all his duties he has shown initiative as well as conscientiousness and intelligence.

"He has requested that he be assigned to duty with troops; this office regrets that he is leaving, but we feel confident that he will give a good account of himself in any job he undertakes: he has had considerable experience with ground troops. I hope it will be possible to promote him in the near future."

NORTH AFRICA

APRIL 2, 1943 TO JULY 2, 1943

Keep alive in our hearts that adventurous spirit,
which makes men scorn the way of safety.

WARTIME PRAYER

This is the beginning of the third day (sounds awfully Biblical) of my trip to my new post. And I don't imagine I will actually reach my final destination till the day after tomorrow or maybe the day after that, as the last stage will have to be by car.

It is now 9 A.M. and we have just taken off from the airport and are travelling across a range of low desert mountains, quite fascinating to look at.

The first day was about an eight-hour flight with one brief stop for fuel—nothing to eat during the trip (which didn't bother me) and miles and miles of desert underneath us. When you fly over desert land and see how incredibly barren it is, you begin to have an over-whelming admiration for General Montgomery's feat of fighting across 2,000 miles of it.

We arrived at the airport at about five—to find it was only four in the new meridian. I finally collected my belongings, got a jeep and took them up to the Hotel DeGink which is for transient officers and men—a de luxe accommodation, I need hardly add! There is one reception tent and then you are assigned a cot—upper or lower, as the case may be, in another tent.

As luck would have it, I ran into Lieut. Bill Marvel at mess shortly afterwards. He was ass't. Intelligence and Operations officer, in charge of all the supplies that came into the field. He had been there about a month and he moved me over into his tent which was in a rather secluded spot in a nice peach orchard, and gave me an extra cot. In the early evening we went over for a beer to the RAF mess on the other side of the field.

Although 80% of the traffic in the field is American, the English, needless to say, have taken all the fine Italian accommodations which were left more or less intact—villas, clubhouses, gardens, etc., and appropriated them for their own use, while the Americans bask in tents in the dust across the way! There was no beer on our side of the field but the English had plenty (American canned beer, I need hardly add), not to mention whiskey, gin, brandy, rum and wine.

We had a pleasant couple of hours chinning with the British and

87

then came back from the floral villas to Mother Nature and had a very sound sleep.

In the morning, I took the camp bus (filled with effervescent enlisted men off for a day's leave) into the nearest town, as I had a couple of things to do for the Colonel at Headquarters there. Spent a couple of hours sightseeing and taking pictures—remarkably little damage despite all the bombing—and then met Bill for lunch at the RAF Officers' Club in town, a huge Italian modernistic building, where we got a delicious meal served by dapper Italian waiters, to the accompaniment of an Italian string orchestra playing Italian opera in the balcony. The British certainly do not neglect their comforts, whatever their other faults may be!

We stopped on the way back to camp at a hot sulphur bath, formerly a de luxe Thermal establishment, but now the water just spouts out into a field and someone has conveniently piped it into four old bath tubs and some makeshift showers. I had a marvellous bath in a tub just vacated by an enormous black Sudanese and lay there *en plein air,* steaming in the sulphur water. It was very pleasant.

I took several pictures which I hope the censor will not consider indecent as they were certainly picturesque—officers and enlisted men of all nationalities and colors dressing, undressing or stripped in the middle of a green field and getting one after the other into bath tubs in which there is an incessant flow of water as hot as you can stand it. Where they picked up the bath tubs God knows, but it is all very informal and delightful.

Although there are very few shops open, the town now seems comparatively normal, and the local police is once more handling the traffic. I saw a batch of Italian prisoners being taken off to camp, with their poor wives wailing and weeping on the other side of the barrier. One nice Italian peasant woman was sobbing as if her heart would break; but still, poor thing, she's lucky her husband is a prisoner and going to a really nice camp for the duration.

In case you picture me seated in a luxury passenger plane, let me give you a brief picture of the scene. It is a troop carrier, stripped of everything on the inside, with a row of steel chairs that look rather like toilet seats along each side. Cargo is stowed in every nook and cranny and the passengers, about ten of us, loll around, lying on bedding rolls or mail sacks, sitting on the steel floor, in every which position. Eight of the ten, which include three British naval officers, are asleep.

Well, I'll lay off for a while now.

But I want you to know that *whatever* happens at my new post, however *infra dig* an assignment I get, I'll be happier than I was at Headquarters. I already feel ten years younger after two nights of sleeping in a tent, and, even if I never see the firing line, I'll at least be doing more active work than formerly.

NORTH AFRICA, APRIL 3, 1943

Shortly after finishing the last installment, we ran into rough weather crossing the desert mountains—quite beautiful, by the way, very much like miles and miles of the Grand Canyon—all different colored reds and browns—and one by one people began to turn pea-green and then be sick. There was only one bucket which an English naval officer conveniently appropriated, so that a man (RAF) directly opposite me had to be sick right on the floor at my feet. Then an American captain, who had been lying on some bed rolls suddenly threw up, also at my feet, after a particularly savage lurch. Bad weather doesn't affect me as you know, but the sight of others being sick is pretty hard to take and I was mighty glad to get some fresh air when we stopped to fuel at a mountain airport shortly afterwards. It was freezing there and no sooner had we stepped, gratefully, into the fresh air, than the air raid alert sounded, and three planes zoomed over one of the mountain tops. The controller yelled to duck, though where he meant you to duck to I couldn't imagine, as there was nothing but a tent handy, so I just watched and waited for the fireworks. Unfortunately it was a false alarm—I guess I'll never see an air raid!—as they were French planes and the general equanimity was soon restored.

We took off shortly and in about an hour and a half arrived at the next day's stop. I can't tell you how beautiful it was suddenly to come over the desert mountain range and see a perfectly beautiful plateau

89

along the sea, all cultivated in neat rows, as only the French can culti-vate—with lovely Spanish type houses with tile roofs and the clear blue sea with white crests along the edge.

At the airport I found I couldn't get accommodations until the day after the next day to my next stop, and got an army car to take me into the city. I couldn't help thinking of that famous occasion in 1923 when I took the boat over to meet you and almost drowned in the mistral while you and Margey and Babs waited for me, expecting me on the big boat.

I had a hell of a time getting billeted and finally was assigned to a hotel known as the Central Touring. I arrived and had to walk up eleven flights of stairs, then found myself in a nice little box-like room, with a balcony overlooking the harbor, but unfortunately it was already inhabited. I protested but the boy said there were always two in every room and that all was *en ordre*. The bed was barely a ¾ size, but it was getting late so I didn't see what I could do. I argued with the Madame downstairs, who assured me they always put two officers to a bed, and then I went across the street to a rather swanky looking café. Who should I find, seated at the bar, but Major Larry Poole! He'd come back from the front because he'd been bitten by a dog—not mad—and army regulations insist that if you are bitten by a dog, mad or not, you must take the fourteen-day cure for hydro-phobia. This was his thirteenth day. Larry was in excellent form, had been doing all kinds of brain surgery at the front, and I had a most enjoyable evening. We dined at an officers' mess; food is very scarce and everything shuts hermetically at 7:30 when the blackout starts. We sat on the waterfront for an hour or so because an air raid alert practice had been announced, which didn't take place; and then I came home to meet my bed companion, a young flier on leave.

I found afterwards that I had absolutely *de luxe* accommodations. Dudley Wood, whom I ran into the next day, said he'd tried for ten days to get into the Central Touring and had only just succeeded. Three in bed were quite normal, with one or more on the floor.

In the morning, I had gone up to Headquarters to find Dudley— later I lunched with him, and am meeting him in an hour for a beer at the one bar in town, then, going to dine.

What is going to happen to me, the Lord only knows. At present no one here has much of an idea, as my papers, as I expected, had not arrived and my actual orders only assigned me to this replacement depot.

The adjutant said that what would probably happen would be that I would have to come up before a reclassification board and then be reassigned to some ground unit, God knows what. How long that process will take I haven't any idea—maybe a week, maybe several months!

I am now living in a tent on some cliffs overlooking the sea with five other lieutenants, and starting tomorrow have to attend a so-called officers' school which is just something to keep us busy — close order drill in the morning and hiking in the afternoon, also classes each night except Saturday. It won't be thrilling but at least it will be a healthy life and will get me in shape after my life of inaction at 696, which will be a good thing if I am going to be assigned to an active unit.

I really am happy at the prospects that lie ahead—whatever they are, they are better than my desk job. And, good or bad, they'll be something interesting. Even this life will be active and healthy. In fact it's just like maneuvers all over again, eating in mess kits, living on the ground.

I was shifted to this Battalion yesterday and to a much nicer tent with a group of very amusing officers, who also moved in yesterday. Today four of them were sent out, leaving two of us in the tent—very de luxe. Am writing on my bedding roll in a rather cramped position —hence the wabbly writing.

I had a long talk with the adjutant yesterday and he assured me he would write to headquarters and try to get my papers located, so that I could be assigned. I don't expect anything will happen for at least two or three weeks, but I don't mind, as I can get into condition here and we will be training troops every third day and having classes at officers' school the other two, which should teach us something and is a good preliminary before going with a combat unit—if and when that ever happens.

I feel like a million dollars, which I didn't in Headquarters, thanks to the perpetual sinus, and am altogether delighted that I made the move I did, even if I don't get a very good assignment. I am begininng to think the Lord never intended me to sit at a desk, as I feel so much happier and healthier when I am outdoors. I think possibly when the war is over that I had better become a farmer at Oatlands (with your permission!) and write on the side and do manual work on the farm!

But first we've got to get this job settled once and for all. I hope the people back home realize how much Roosevelt is admired by the rank and file of the troops. They are solidly behind him and admire him as a leader of vision, who has the guts to take chances and cut corners to get things done. I only hope that Congress doesn't knife him and the peace treaty in the back. And even if things at home are rather in a mess, people should remember what a really tremendous job is being done here and all over the world. But I guess in Washington they can't see the forest because of the trees.

NORTH AFRICA, TO E. I.* APRIL 12, 1943†

I'll try to give you a brief picture of a show I saw somewhere in NATOUSA, the army designation for the North African Theatre of Operations, U. S. Army.

The scene was a building taken over by the Red Cross as a recreation centre. It was formerly an auditorium, and had evidently been modeled on the Radio City Music Hall. I had expected a film and so I was surprised to hear someone say that there was an American Red Cross Revue this afternoon. By 2:30 when the show was scheduled to start, the all-soldier audience was clapping vociferously in unison. There was a burst of laughter when over the loud speaker came a

*Mrs. Isaacs.
†Reprinted from *Theatre Arts,* July 1943.

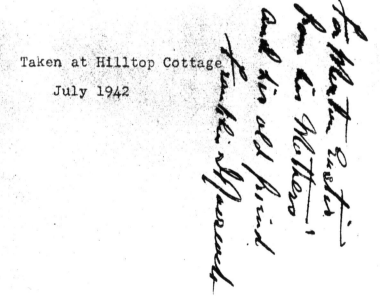

Taken at Hilltop Cottage
July 1942

Photograph given by the President to Lt. Eustis on the eve of his departure overseas, October, 1942.

It was found in the pocket of his blouse, when it was returned to his family after his death.

soprano voice singing in broken English, "I'm dreaming of a white mistress." The cast was trying out the loudspeaker, unaware that it was also connected into the auditorium.

It was an all-French company: about six show-girls, a pert young mistress of ceremonies, who couldn't speak a word of English except for the phrase, "How's cooking?" with which she introduced every number, flipping her skirts and giving an eloquent bump. There were the usual vaudeville acts, a little frayed around the edges: an acrobatic team—two women and a man dressed up like shiny seals (they got a big hand)—a magician, a "twister" artist who could really twist, the leading lady—singing, this time, "I'm Dreaming of a White Christmas" to roars of applause—three really funny comedians (two men and a girl) of the deadpan variety.

The show wouldn't have got much of a hand at the Old Palace. But there was something about it in this setting that made it strangely appealing. For this soldier audience, many of whom were just back from the front, several of them wounded, was one of the best audiences I have ever seen. They were eager to be entertained and distracted, not too raucous, and good-humored and friendly to a degree. The boys knew perfectly well that it wasn't too "hot" a show. But the Red Cross was doing the best it could to fill up their spare time. And the French cast was obviously giving its all.

The audience gave its all, too. A young soldier next to me had obviously been shell-shocked. He jumped a little whenever the bass drum was banged and he sat strained and tense before the lights went out. Before an hour had passed, he was relaxed and was laughing his head off. And when an acrobat picked up one of the girls very close to her centre of gravity and twirled her in the air, he yelled out delightedly, "Not too close, son. Keep it clean."

For two hours he forgot Maknassy and the Kasserine Pass, the shrapnel that burst at his feet, killed his best friend and imbedded itself in thirty-two places in his back. (I learned these details about the kid later from one of his officers). And when the cast sang the "Marseillaise" and the "Star Spangled Banner" at the conclusion of the show, he stood proudly at attention and never even winced when the drummer banged out the closing bars of the National Anthem.

93

If theatre people back home could see for themselves what a show like this means to soldiers just back from the front or waiting to go, you'd have a flood of top-notch artists volunteering their services to come and entertain the troops. A few have already done it, I know, and lots more are working in camps at home. But just think what an Ed Wynn or an Eddie Cantor, a Fred Astaire or an Ethel Merman could do with and for such an audience.

Well, even without stars, the American Red Cross Revue was a resounding success! . . .

NORTH AFRICA, APRIL 12, 1943

It being the Sabbath, we have the day more or less to ourselves. And so, having eaten a healthy repast of baked beans, sweet potatoes, carrots and canned peaches, seated on terra firma in the African sunlight, I am now propped up on my air mattress, with a box as a back rest, and taking up my pencil again.

In bad weather, this place would be an unimaginable hell hole as you do everything out of doors except sleep. But fortunately the rainy season is over and so it is very pleasant.

The "Casino" in the village is now the home of the permanent cadre operating the camp and the baccarat room (which is perched almost overhanging a five hundred foot cliff), is the kitchen. There are still a few French families (peasants really) living here. Otherwise the army has taken over.

Every morning and afternoon the A/A batteries along the coast send thousands of shells into the air at "sleeve" targets towed behind airplanes. It is quite a sight to see the sky suddenly full of black clusters of smoke and I'd hate to be in a plane trying to pierce that barrage.

The only occupant of my tent now is a 2nd Lieutenant from Pittsburgh, a very nice fellow and he expects to get his orders to go out at any moment which will leave this 1st Lieutenant in sole possession of one tent pyramidal, as the army calls it. But I expect other officers will move in before long.

We had a very interesting talk last night from a general who had

94

just come back from the front. He said the American troops were lacking in only one thing—experience—which has to be learned the hard way, alas, but that they had all the guts, courage, and drive in the world. He told of one battalion commander who was badly wounded by shrapnel in the leg one morning but who insisted on staying with his battalion all day while they were under heavy fire and died as a result, from his wound. Another officer here told me of the case of one sergeant whose leg was literally blown off by a shell, except that it was hanging by one cord. The sergeant ripped out his knife, cut the cord, and hobbled along on the stump giving orders to his battery that eventually resulted in the destruction of the enemy battery and in our winning the day's battle. The American soldier may have a lot to learn, but no one can say that he hasn't got what it takes to make an army. I only hope if I ever get under fire that I will show one-tenth the fortitude and coolness of some of the boys up there now.

Everyone here who has been up there says that you're scared absolutely sick the first time that you're dive-bombed or shelled, but that gradually you get accustomed to it, particularly as you realize how rarely you get hit, especially if you don't lose your head.

Well I may never get near it all but, if I do, I'll try not to get hit, you may rest assured! I'll also try to keep my head.

NORTH AFRICA, APRIL, 1943

Am writing seated, not too uncomfortably, on my air mattress in a tent. It is a lovely situation on a high cliff overlooking the sea, more beautiful really than the Grande Corniche drive and just as high. You can see for miles along the coast which makes a deep bend, and about twelve kilometres away a town nestles along the coast and winds up into the hills. As to my status, it is, as I expected, indefinite. My papers have not come through as yet so no one here knows what to do with me. But they'll come through in time and meanwhile I can vegetate very pleasantly, if in a primitive manner, on this rocky crag. Although there are people here who have been waiting three months for assignment (!), I am not depressed and have a hunch that things will

95

straighten themselves out fairly quickly. Whether or not I'll get into the Armored Force, which I applied for, the Lord only knows, but even the Infantry would be better than sitting at a desk. Although we're nowhere near the front, the war is much closer here, as there are lots of wounded men around. Some of their stories are very interesting.

NORTH AFRICA, APRIL 13, 1943

I wish you could see me now. I am sitting precariously on the edge of a cliff overlooking the sea and a broad harbor miles beyond. Through your glasses I can see clearly an old French Fort on a crag some twelve miles away. Below it is a monastery with a town built on the edge of just such a cliff as the one I am seated on. It is really as beautiful a view as you would find anywhere in the world. And I don't believe nine people out of ten we know have even heard of the place. Aside from its occupation by the American army, our village is famous for only one other thing. It is reputed to be the place in which Mrs. Simpson met the then Prince of Wales! What on earth either one of them was doing in this God forsaken spot, don't ask me, but they are said to have met for the first time in the Casino where we have our nightly classes. *Tempus fugit,* does it not?

I have the afternoon off, by dint of a little luck and quick thinking on my part, and so I strolled up to this secluded spot to lie in the sun and write my daily piece. Honestly, I haven't done badly by letters since I left headquarters—almost one a day!

A man from the 1st Armored Force has just come into our tent. I am going to pump him and see if he can't think of a way to get me into his outfit, as he says he knows some big shot at headquarters near here. If I could only get to see him, I might be able to be assigned to them, which would of course, be just what I should like.

But I am not pinning any hopes on it.

I shall just continue to bask in this lovely sunshine and await my fate, whatever it may be,—probably an assignment with a Negro regiment or with a Q.M. Sterilization and Bath outfit!

Well, it's my own fault, whatever happens, so I shall bear it with equanimity. It is getting to be time for retreat, so I must get back to my tent.

Today I met a lieutenant in town from one of the armored divisions and I am full of hope again that my chance to get into the Armored Force still is good, as he says they definitely need officers.

Tunisia was swell, wasn't it? Let's hope the next drive will be just as successful.

We had a three day mistral which almost blew down all the tents and made life rather uncomfortable; but we survived and today it is fine again. A lot of new officers came in today. Poor things, they all expect to be assigned right away, little knowing that they will probably sit in this garden spot for months! Along with a certain first lieutenant in the Air Corps!

Last week on some leave I was able to visit in —————————. It is quite nice and jammed with troops, French and American, but no British except for some Naval Officers. They have a ceremony every day at retreat in the square in front of the post office. An American band and a company of M.P.'s parade, then lower the French, English and American flags while all three national anthems are played. The French went wild after the Marseillaise, cheered and yelled *Vive De Gaulle* in unison, so that they almost drowned out "God Save the King"; and they kept up shouting for De Gaulle after the whole ceremony was over and the band had marched away. It is a healthy symptom, this enthusiasm for De Gaulle, and I only wish our State Department had a little more of it. Giraud is fine, too, but after all De Gaulle is the one who carried on the fight when everyone else had thrown up the sponge.

The Red Cross has an Officers' Club and three service clubs and restaurants in the town and does a really remarkable job. Free movies every afternoon and night. All the shops and restaurants are open, though many things are rationed. Meat is absolutely unobtainable except at the Red Cross, but you can get good French omelets and some green vegetables. The bars stay open until eight but you can only get wine and beer, a rather sweet muscatel made in Algeria and very bad beer. There are a few night clubs, which also close at eight but they are not too exciting. The hostesses are all the elite of the town.

It is nice, I can tell you, to be in a town that is run by the American Army instead of the British. I don't know why it is that the Anglais can be so infuriating at times but it is, alas, true. Well, if I have done nothing else in the army, I have at least seen the world at its expense. All I need to do is to come back via the Southwest Pacific (which, pray God, I do not do) and I will have circled the globe.

NORTH AFRICA, APRIL 24, 1943

I was interviewed today to know if I wanted a special service job writing scripts to be broadcast from here to the troops. I said "no" quite firmly, though even if I had said "yes" I couldn't have got the assignment as my status is still that of a man who has no status. I was merely picked for interview by someone who thumbed through the classification cards for anyone with writing or technical experience in radio.

Meanwhile the weather continues fine; the program of activity is just as "basic" as ever. God's in his heaven, All's right with the world!

NORTH AFRICA, EASTER DAY—APRIL 25, 1943

How different both Christmas and Easter were this year from last. Then we were all together, on both occasions, as I recall it. Now we are separated by thousands of miles. I am sitting in a tent with my feet propped up on a wooden box, the writing paper perched on my knees. On Xmas day I was in an American camp in the desert. Easter finds me in another American camp overlooking the sea, for the morning, at any rate, as I may get a pass to go into a neighboring town for the afternoon! And perhaps, with luck, next Easter may find us all re-assembled at 1534 with one Lieutenant back in civilian clothes. That may be a trifle optimistic but why not be optimistic on Easter Day.

I have just come back from Easter services which were held in the roulette room of the Casino perched on top of the cliff—the same room, perhaps, in which Wally first met Edward! I am ashamed to say I only stayed for the first two hymns and then beat an ignomini-ous retreat—the same as I did at Xmas services in the Middle East. The army Protestant service seems to be a conglomeration of all Protestant services known to man, and the service opened, not with "Jesus Christ Is Risen Today" (one of the chief reasons why I went!) but with a number called "Praise Him! Praise Him!", which sounded like something concocted by the Holy Rollers. The prayers too, although there were a few familiar ones, were not of the Episcopal type and there was a great deal in the way of mass responses. The Chaplain led the hymns as if he were conducting a symphony orchestra and needless to say, there were no chairs—so my religious zeal waned with perceptible rapidity and "Love Divine All Love Excell-ing" found one 1st Lieutenant going AWOL from his Easter ob-servances.

The two men from the Armored Force who were in my tent went back to the front yesterday—the lucky devils.

You might be interested in knowing how we fill up our days before being sent to combat units to which, presumably, all the officers and enlisted men here will be sent, so I will give you a rough outline of our daily activity. I will make no comments myself.

There is an officer's class and we are supposed to be with that every other day when we are not with troops, but both follow the same training schedule. Actually, our battalion has no enlisted men at present, so we do it all with the officers, if we can't think of any way of getting out of it.

We start with "Close order drill," by squads, 07.30 to 08.30. Then "Disciplinary calisthenics" 08.30 to 09.30, just very elementary exer-cises. 09.30 to 10.30, "Memory drill," 10 minutes; "Position of the soldier at attention," 10 minutes; "General orders," 10 minutes; "The hand salute." In each case you recite to the officers, or men, the *exact* wording in the manual and they repeat it after you. In the hand salute they have added the following which we are required to say with all seriousness: "An alert soldier is a live soldier. The salute means that I am alert. My salute means that I recognize in you a person who has authority to give me orders. It means (salute) I am here to carry out your orders, Sir. (Two) . . . When do I salute: Always . . . Even though a soldier is on the battle front with his finger on the trigger and an officer crawls up he still salutes, not by raising his hand or moving it from the trigger of his rifle but in his mind and through his eyes flashes "I recognize in you a superior officer, I am here to carry out your orders, Sir." We have to give this to men and officers who have actually been at the front! 10.30 to 11.30 mass athletics, 35 minutes personal contests, wrestling, etc., as prescribed in F.M. 21-20, Par. 76. 15 minutes hand to hand fighting with men paired, 10 minutes rest: 13.00 to 15.00 marching to music—held on drill field; 15.00 to 16.30 physical hardening, 4 miles, run $\frac{1}{2}$, walk $\frac{1}{4}$, run $\frac{1}{2}$, walk $\frac{1}{4}$, etc.; 17.00 to 17.30 retreat.

The morale among the officers is, needless to say, excellent, though quite a few of them feel they would like both to give and to receive training which was more useful for the work they will soon have to undertake.

There is still no more news re. my status, except that the Air Liaison Officer told me yesterday afternoon that he had called Natousa Headquarters and that they had no record of my case either. I am still however, not sorry that I made the move. I seem to be fated to have this kind of thing happen to me—witness the time at Westover Field, and the "assistant janitor" period at Harrisburg. So I have grown acclimated to it and am philosophical enough to believe that sooner or later the break will come.

NORTH AFRICA, APRIL 1943[*] TO E. I.

You might be interested to hear about the double-feature show we had at camp last night—one starring Josephine Baker—in person,

*Reprinted by permission from *Theatre Arts*, October 1943.

the other a host of featured players manning the ack-ack guns and an unidentified number of Jerry planes.

The first show started as scheduled at 8 P.M., on an improvised wooden stage at one corner of a dusty drill field 'somewhere in North Africa.' Several thousand soldiers sat on the ground in a semicircle around the stage. Most of them had been sitting there for almost an hour, watching the sunset, reading or just chewing the fat. A gramophone attached to loud speakers provided tinny music.

I can't give away the location of the camp—that would be 'military information' though I'm quite sure the enemy knows just where we are!—but I can at least tell you that from the field in which we sat you could see the landscape for miles around and that the setting, geographically speaking, was extraordinarily dramatic.

It was a clear night. The sky had a golden tint. Back of the distant mountains it was already turning grey. The pyramidal tents which dotted the landscape stood out in black relief.

On the stage a Negro soldier swing band was tuning up. Miss Baker was getting into costume in a tent just back of it.

"Bet you we'll have another air raid tonight," a soldier behind me remarked.

"Bet you we won't," his friend answered.

"One hundred francs."

"O.K."

There had been an air raid the night before—not actually aimed at our camp but near enough for us to get a good, grandstand view.

A sergeant M. C. started off the show by introducing the orchestra and giving the audience a brief program note on Josephine Baker's background. Miss Baker, he told us, had been very ill for a year and a half at some North African resort. The moment she was well she insisted, against her doctor's advice, on making an extended tour of all the American camps in North Africa, donating her services to the cause of entertaining the troops. "So let's give Josephine a great big hand."

Miss Baker, in a flamboyant costume of vertical purple and red stripes, with a flowing skirt and puffed sleeves, swept onto the stage and up to the mike. She looked the audience over, smiled mischievously, gave an impudent wiggle, kicked a foot in the air, disclosing a shapely leg through a slit in the skirt; then, as a gasp of pleasure rippled through the audience, she stood delightedly waving at 'the boys.' The 'boys,' needless to say, roared their approval.

Her first number was an American ditty as sly and insinuating as the curves, bumps and contortions of the dusky 'Vedette' herself, 'La Grande Vedette Americaine,' as she was billed in the heydey of her fame in Paris. I remember seeing her at the Casino de Paris with Maurice Chevalier—before the crash of '29—the toast of the fashionable world.

Here she was years later, on a platform in one corner of a dusty field in Africa—no older apparently, no less dextrous in putting over a song, in punctuating every line with an appropriate twist of her body—standing them up in the aisles (literally and to roars of disapproval from the soldiers seated in the rear) and holding the audience with as much ease as if both she and they had all the facilities of a comfortable theatre at their disposal. I doubt, too, if Miss Baker ever had a more genuinely and vociferously appreciative audience, and her evident enjoyment of the furore she was creating was as infectious as the lilt of her strident voice and the brazen strut with which she sidled about the stage.

Two more encores, one French and one American, two more swing interludes by the band, then Miss Baker reappeared in a tight-fitting, low-cut evening dress of green and gold—cheers and whistles of delight—and told us she was going to sing a song describing the plight of the American soldier in Africa who knows but a few words of French and is unable to express his feelings to a French girl—*tres Mignon, mais oui!* The song, *Darling, je vous aime beaucoup,* had a catchy, rollicking tune with gay and idiotic lyrics. It 'wowed' the audience, and Miss Baker broke into an encore, leaving the mike and parading before the footlights.

"Uh huh! You win!" the soldier back of me exclaimed.

"There she goes!" another voice broke out.

A stream of red tracers was shooting up into the sky a few miles away, making a pattern that just framed the stage. It might have been

102

a number specially staged for the grand finale. The air-raid siren wailed out in the distance—near at hand, the camps' bugle. The footlights went out. A voice over the loud speaker—"Air raid! Air raid! Disperse into the fields at once."

"Damn it all," a soldier said, "this is the second show those damned Jerries have broken up. Come on, let's go."

The soldier audience dispersed quickly and quietly into the adjacent fields where they lay down, their heads cocked up so they could see what was going on. Another officer and I found a spot just below the crest of a hill from which we could view the whole scene. We sat there leaning against some branches of low scrub, watching the 'second feature.'

The ack-ack was spitting from all directions, the red tracers converging over the target area, where they exploded in a flash of white light. The muffled, steady 'rat tat tat' of the machine guns was broken occasionally by the crack of a larger calibre gun, the steady effect of the tracers suddenly altered by a burst of heavy black smoke as a heavy shell exploded.

The whole scene seemed unreal and curiously remote. You watched it with complete detachment but with the same type of fascination, though doubly intense, that you viewed the infinitely less dramatic show in the World's Fair Lagoon.

A full moon, rising in a golden ball, lit up the incredible setting.

Then, as suddenly as it started, the show closed. The 'all clear' bugle sounded at the camp. Josephine Baker took up where she left off! *Ca c'est Paris* in La Baker's best style—a few more songs—then 'God Save the King,' the 'Marseillaise,' 'The Star Spangled Banner' —and that show also was over.

NORTH AFRICA, APRIL 28, 1943

I had an interesting talk with the owner of a restaurant last night. He had just returned from the Riviera before the occupation here and he said conditions there were terrible. Hardly any food, except on the black market at fabulous prices, five hundred francs for a loaf of bread, one thousand francs for potatoes. He said the Germans just took everything. He said France is now 85% behind De Gaulle and 100% pro-Ally. People wave out of the windows at the British and American bombers. Even though they are killing French people as well, the Germans had finally to pass a decree that anyone waving from a window would be shot. No one paid any attention, so they put snipers in the streets and shot anyone who opened his window. He says the English and Americans will get such a reception as they never dreamed of when they get into France; but, he warned, if we wait too late, the people may be so starved that they are past helping. Already T.B. is rampant, especially among children. A terrible picture, isn't it, and I hate to think of Cousin Lydia, John and Anita. But it all goes to show there's no punishment too bad for the Germans. I only hope we don't get sentimental about them once again.

NORTH AFRICA, APRIL 30, 1943

Am writing at the Officers' Red Cross Club again. No one will ever know what a superlative job the Red Cross has done in setting up these recreation centers all over Africa. In this town alone, they have an enlisted man's club, an Officers' Club, two restaurants with excellent food—20 cts. a meal for enlisted men, 40 cts. for Officers—free movies, afternoon and evening variety shows. It's really a remarkable achievement. And the first place any enlisted man looks for is not the nearest bar, but the Red Cross Club.

NORTH AFRICA, MAY 2, 1943

Today is the second consecutive day of steady and unabated rain—the sixth of bad weather. The vaunted African sunlight, which I wrote about so glowingly when I first arrived here, is apparently as fickle a mistress as the one who supervises the transfers of men from one branch of the Armed Forces into another! In beautiful weather, the camp, though primitive, is more than bearable. In rain and wind, it is an appalling spot! Seas of mud everywhere—and everything has to be done in a raincoat with a helmet on, as all kitchen and latrine facilities are in the open. It has been raining too hard to make even going on a hike a bearable thing—the only other thing to do is to huddle in the tent, read, write and play poker. Yesterday, in desperation, we played poker all afternoon and until midnight. By night we play by the light of two gasoline candles, improvised out of wine bottles by cutting the cork in half, hollowing it out, then using a rope for a wick, reinserting the cork, and filling with gas. No one seems to know why it doesn't explode, but so far it hasn't, and it gives a flame about the equivalent of a candle. I lost 1,850 francs in the P.M. session, some $37.00, and won about $4.00 in the evening. So much for my activity yesterday. Today, being Sunday, I slept until nine, had my daily breakfast of a dynamin tablet (breakfast is at 6:15 but most of the officers don't bother to get up for it) and then lolled around reading the Sunday Herald-Tribune (of March 28th!)

NORTH AFRICA, MAY 5, 1943

I had no sooner finished mailing my letter of this morning than I got a message to report to Classification. There I was told that my status was finally cleared up (thanks to the Major at Base headquarters who telephoned Natousa yesterday and finally got matters cleared up) and that they could now assign me. Lo and behold, it turned out, to my horror, that owing to the fact that I was over age in grade, I could not be assigned to any combat outfit. It was a strict order and they could not waive it. The best they held out was an MP outfit (perish the thought!) or some headquarters not very far from here. I was furious; but there seemed to be nothing to do but to say: "OK. Do the best you can," and then hope that later I could finagle something myself. I personally had thought that the "over age in grade" rule went out sometime in July, but evidently I was wrong. Well, thought I, you have made a mess of things, getting out of a job which at least was interesting, to end up just as an M.P. in some town hundreds of miles from the front or with a bad job in some other headquarters. But what could I, or they, for that matter, do?

So I composed myself as best I could and lay down for some more bunk fatigue. Then I had a brain wave. Why shouldn't I play my trump card (I'm afraid it will make you blush) and, if it *was* impossible to get into a combat unit, at least get into G-2 work, where my fluent knowledge of French and of France could be of some use? So I rose from my bed and went back to Classification. In the circumstances, said I, surely you can use some one who can speak fluent French, who's lived half his life in France, to more advantage than just burying him in some God awful little town to look after a bunch of drunks? I've been to four intelligence schools, three in the Ground Forces. I've been doing active G-2 work for six months. There *must* be some opening for someone with these talents! The minute I mentioned French and G-2, a Colonel who happened to be in the room perked up his ears. Just the man we want, he said, or words to that effect. It appears a request had just come from Headquarters Natousa for three officers who could speak French fluently to work there. How fluently could I speak, translate and write, they asked me? A little rusty, perhaps, on writing, I admitted, but O.K. on the other. You're sure, they asked. Sure, I replied. And so the long and short of it is, the Classification officer said I'd almost surely be assigned to the G-2 section at Allied Headquarters and told me to "stand by," as I might be summoned in a day or two.

Well, it's not what I came here for but it's 100% better than what I might have got. Also, while I'm simply exchanging headquarters in one sense, I'm at least in the key position of our most active theatre, and, owing to my French, might easily get into some very interesting work instead of being buried at a desk.

You may wonder if I had any qualms about my French. Very few. I speak so much better French than most of the other officers I have seen; a barmaid, in fact, told me I spoke better French than any American officer she had seen in this theatre!! And with a dictionary I can do a lot. I admit that the writing would be somewhat difficult but then I doubt if I'd have to write much and I *can* translate.

Well, anyway, it's so much a brighter prospect than any I had this morning that I am almost jubilant on the rebound.

And from there, too, I might always get myself assigned as a G-2 to an armored unit.

In order to have something to do to pass the time between roll calls, I amused myself by devising an acting version of *Macbeth* for Lynn and Alfred. I hope they get it, (I didn't make any copy), as I think it was a superlative job! I made fairly free with the immortal bard in cutting, transposing and rearranging scenes, but added no Eustis words save one harmless line. "Go get thee hence!" I also added a brief scene after the sleep walking scene in which I pulled Lady M's "Naughts had—All's spent" speech from an earlier scene and let her emerge, again, this time awake, and pluck a dagger from the wall to prepare the audience for her suicide and to improve on Mr. Shakespeare!

NORTH AFRICA, MAY 15, 1943

Am most excited as I told you in yesterday's V-mail letter, at the possibility that my trip tomorrow may result in getting me assigned at long last. Why I even entertain any hopes on such a wild chance I don't know, but it is just so wild that it might work. As I told you, I ran into a lieutenant from one of the Armored units, who told me there were several vacancies in the officer personnel in his battalion and advised me to go and see his Colonel personally and ask for one of the assignments. If—and it's a big if—I can persuade him to take the time to write a letter to the C.O. here requesting that I be assigned to his outfit, then I think I'm all set, whether I'm "over age in grade" or not. But, to look on the dark side, it seems extremely unlikely that he will suddenly make a request for an officer he has never laid eyes on before; in fact, it is quite likely he will even refuse to interview me! Well, I'll know the worst or best tomorrow. But no harm can come by trying, even if it is a slightly irregular military procedure for a lieutenant from the Air Corps (I still have Air Corps insignia) to go and ask a Commanding Officer of an armored reconnaissance unit for a job.

Still, if you don't ever take long chances, you're apt to sit in a

Replacement Depot for the duration—a fate which would be far worse than the proverbial "worse than death."

Well the African Campaign is over. Where do we go from here? is the question of the day. You'll probably know the answer, too, before we do!

NORTH AFRICA, MAY 18, 1943

Yesterday was my red letter day! My coup was successful, and, barring several quite possible accidents, I should be assigned to the Armored force in a week or so.

This is how it all happened. I told you I ran into a Lieutenant from the 2nd Armored Division in town the other day, who advised my taking a trip out to where they were in bivouac, there to see the Colonel in person. It was a distinctly unorthodox course of action— a Lieutenant going up to a perfectly strange Colonel and asking for a job—but desperate conditions require desperate remedies and so I decided to take a chance.

Bright and early yesterday morning, accordingly, I set out across the fields with a Captain who also wanted to clarify his status with the Armored Force. Without any by-your-leave, we by-passed the gate and headed along the road. It was a trip of about forty miles and we hitch-hiked in about four different vehicles, a garbage truck, a water truck, a troop carrier and finally a peep. We had to walk about ten miles of the way in the broiling sun, but it was a most interesting trip and we saw a lot of the countryside.

The Colonel I wanted to see was the C. O. of the 82nd Armored Reconnaissance Battalion. They were bivouacked, with full camouflage, in some low scrub on a hill, in pup tents with all the scout cars and half tracks camouflaged or concealed.

We wandered up to the Message Center tent and I went in boldly and asked the Lieutenant if I could see Colonel Disney. He said "Certainly" and took me over to the Colonel's tent where he was seated alone at a little folding desk. Without any formality or nonsense, he asked me to sit down and tell him what I wanted to see him about.

I told him my case as succinctly as I could, showed him my orders

108

and my letter of recommendation from Col. Whitridge, apologized for my unorthodox way of skipping channels and going direct to the top without any authority whatsoever. He asked me a few questions, was extremely nice and put me completely at my ease, said he'd be "tickled to death" to have me and asked me what he should do. I told him I thought if he made a request in writing from the C. O. of this Depot that that would be all that would be necessary. He took down a few notes, said that he would send it off at once. I stood up, thanked him and saluted. *Un point c'est tout!*

A little while later, at Division headquarters, where the Captain wanted to go, the Lieutenant, who took me over, drove up in a peep with the letter already written and took it up to Division headquarters and asked them to rush it up to Corps so that we could get it through as quickly as possible. Then he asked us back to lunch and said he'd send us back to town in the recreation truck which was leaving at 12.30.

Everyone couldn't have been nicer, including the Colonel himself. His name, by the way, is Lt. Colonel Paul A. Disney, and he has been in the Cavalry for about 8 or 10 years. He comes from Massachusetts, he told me, is not much older than I am, if at all, and is just the type of C. O. I should like to work under.

We didn't discuss at all the type of work I would do. I don't care what it is, so long as I get into the unit, but I imagine I will probably be put in charge of a platoon of four scout cars or half tracks—back again in the mechanized cavalry!! Away, forever, from Headquarters and replacement depots.

The work will not be easy. I have no illusions about that. I saw the training schedule and it is hard, tough but *sensible* work. They teach us to fight both in and out of the vehicles. We fire live ammunition and it is real business with no horse play. I'll have a lot to learn too, as it is more than a year since I left the cavalry; but it's what I want and I feel confident that I can do whatever job I am assigned to.

Wish me luck, both in getting the assignment and in getting on well when I get there.

Just a hasty line before retiring or going to my grandstand seat to watch the Jerries in case they decide to come over again tonight.

I should like to be able to report that everything was progressing smoothly in my quest to get assigned but I fear that is far from the case. Well, I am philosophical. I have done all I can. The only recourse left to me is to get permission to fly to headquarters and see if I can't straighten out things myself. It will be nine weeks then, and I really think I have a case. Especially as an outfit really wants me.

I am writing by the light of one candle, which is almost out, but I shall struggle on until it does go out. If St. Anthony was responsible for my meeting with the Colonel of the Reconnaissance B-n, I hope he will follow up the case and bring it to a successful conclusion. Meanwhile, except for being bored, I am in the best of health, and am gradually closing up like an oyster—an animal and vegetable life only!

NORTH AFRICA, MAY 26, 1943

Two days after my letter telling you I expected to be here for the duration, I am off and to the unit I wanted to go to! It seems unbelievable. Here is how it happened. I went and saw the Colonel here and told him the whole sad story. He agreed that it might be weeks or even months before the situation was cleared up at Natousa, but said he could cut corners and assign me to that unit on "detached service" and then make it a permanent assignment when and if the situation was ever straightened up. Of course, he said he might have to pull me back and assign me to something else if Natousa didn't agree or decided I was still in the Air Corps. But he was hopeful and I shall not even think of that horror at this point. My address will be —I hope *permanently!*—82nd Armored Reconnaissance Battalion,* A.P.O. 252, New York. Please let everyone know.

From today on, I shall really be roughing it, as if it were a permanent maneuver, living in pup tents, making night marches and really

*2nd Armored Division.

doing combat training, and I am delighted at the prospect. I only hope I do a good job as I've got a lot to learn and relearn.

NORTH AFRICA, MAY 27, 1943

This is too good to last, obviously! But at least I feel ten years younger getting out of that Replacement Depot, even if it may only be for a brief spell in case they decide to pull me back. I only hope they will forget all about me, as they seemed to do so easily while I was there.

I arrived here this P.M. after dropping off some enlisted men at a hospital and was told that I was going to be assigned to Hq. Co. I checked in with my orders and then set up my pup tent and unpacked. By the time that officers' call at the Colonel's tent took place, I'd just about got settled. I have all my equipment, incidentally, including my foot locker, thank God.

I didn't see the Colonel personally but had chow and then came back home prepared to blow up my air mattress. The executive officer then came to tell me that the Colonel had decided that he'd send me for two weeks' indoctrination to C company which is located about —— miles away and then pull me back here.

That suits me to perfection. I want to get down to brass tacks, find out what it's all about, and the best way to do that is to be actually on duty with a company. Then when I come back to Hq. Co. I'll know, I hope, how the wheels click.

There is a swell view from the open end of my pup tent, in which I write, but I can't describe it alas. It is more extensive and panoramic than the one I left, if less sensational.

Don't expect as much mail from now on as I'm going to be a working man for a change, but I'll write as often as possible.

Meanwhile, please get all your saints working to try and keep me here, and not let Natousa pull me out. This is a swell outfit and I want to settle down with it permanently, provided they want to keep me.

The mosquitoes are buzzing round like dive bombers now, so I must fix my netting. . . .

Shades of 101! Last night and all this morning, from 6 A.M. on, the men are feverishly preparing for a lay down inspection: the grousing sounds exactly the same as it did in the old days in the Carolina maneuvers. And with all the old familiar vehicles scattered around in the low scrub palms you might really be back in the Carolinas, though I doubt, there, if you would have seen an Arab in flowing white robes mounted on a grey donkey about half his size driving a herd of black goats through the bivouac site. Nor did you get such extensive views there with almost no trees in sight.

I haven't any idea what our plans are; if I did, I couldn't tell you anyway, but I only hope, whatever they are, that we get under way before the 1st Replacement Depot has a chance to pull me back into confinement!

If I get nothing else out of this war, I certainly ought to get material for a good play or maybe a good book of memoirs. The trouble is that most of the best episodes would be unprintable either for military reasons—criticism of some sort of higher authorities—or because you could not reproduce the soldier's vocabulary, which consists, as you can imagine, almost entirely of unprintable words and phrases! Still I think you could write an amusing lighthearted picture of army life, which is what the public would want after this is all over. No serious war plays, I fear, until ten or fifteen years have passed.

Well, we'll leave all that to the future, but save all my letters, even the old ones from 101, as they'll help to bring back memories of one sort or another and I might want to use the material either for a novel or a play!

8.45 A.M. I am seated in the broiling sun, on my foot locker, which is parked on four rocks, to keep it off the ground, outside my pup tent. Inspection isn't till 9.30, and as I am duly prepared for same, with all my "full field equipment" in good shape, I hope, I am passing the time fighting off the mosquitoes and writing.

Speaking of mosquitoes, we are forced, as you must have read in the papers, to take a yellow atabrin pill four times a week—Monday, Tuesday, Thursday and Friday—to offset malaria, though I doubt if there are any malarial mosquitoes around, at least I haven't seen any as yet. The atabrin doesn't affect me badly at all, but it makes some people miserable. However, they say you get used to it like everything else in the Army or, for that matter, life.

We get very little news from the outside world, but I trust that we and the British are still pounding the hell out of the Jerries and Eyeties from the air. They're going to be sorry, methinks, that they ever started this war.

Must line up the platoon for inspection.

NORTH AFRICA, MAY 30, 1943

I resume what amounts to my diary—censored, of course—at 8.40 A.M., seated on my foot locker in a twenty minute lull before we march up to a special Memorial Day service at Battalion headquarters.

I think the best way to write is just to put in snatches when I can and thus fill up a full letter.

Yesterday, after evening chow, everyone who wanted to go was taken down in trucks for a swim. It was a beautiful evening and most of the division, it seemed, was on the beach. The water was the nicest I have been in yet, and it was a great restorative after an exhaustive inspection of men, materials and vehicles.

I'm hoping now that I can persuade the powers that be to leave me in this company rather than to pull me back to headquarters, as I like the officers and men and think the work would be more congenial than in headquarters. However, that's a small matter provided Natousa doesn't decide to pull me out of the B'n altogether. On that score, I'm not really very worried. They're so swamped with paper work that I don't think they'll ever get around to thinking about my case again. I spoke to the adjutant at Division headquarters yesterday and he thought it was a good bet that I'd stay on detached service with the B'n for the duration, which is O. K. by me. Just so long as they leave me alone, whether from forgetfulness or good will, it's all the same to me.

Most of the company officers are southern or western—one from western Virginia, one from West Virginia, one from Texas, one, I think, from Arkansas—and southern accents predominate among the enlisted men.

Today I'm going to have a big house cleaning, and get rid of a hell of a lot of junk that is weighing me down, leaving only the essential items. I may keep my foot locker and store it with heavy winter clothes, send my cottons and tropicals home boxed and trust to luck my foot locker reaches me if we are still here in winter time, wherever we may be. But I am going to strip myself down to what amounts to a combat pack without any frills.

10.35 A.M. It's too much trouble, if nothing else, to be encumbered with a lot of stuff when you haven't any place to store it except one half of a pup tent and have to be constantly ready to move.

Before I'm through I shall have left possessions all over the Globe!

I left some junk in Deolali, India—gave it to my bat boy: a foot locker and more remained in the Middle East after I left. I gave my British battle dress away and left a lot of other stuff in the tent at the 1st Replacement Depot and I still have more than twice what I need. I don't know how it is, but at each place you seem to pick up a lot of bulky junk which you feel you just can't part with.

Today is going to be a real African broiler. It's only 9.30 sun time and there's not a breath of air. As there's no shade for miles around, the alternative is to sit in the sun and get your lips so chapped that they break out in gory cracks from one side to the other, or to crawl into the pup tent and have a turkish bath. Of the two, I think I'll choose the former at least until after lunch.

The Memorial Day service was curiously impressive. The B'n assembled in a wheat field and sat in a semi-circle on bales of hay, facing a row of company regimental and national standards.

The Colonel gave a brief address in which he spoke of the heroism of those who had died in Tunisia, of the necessity always of fighting to preserve our national heritage. His speech was accompanied by the far off rumble of guns booming, and machine gun fire on the nearby ranges.

Then the Chaplain took over and conducted a brief service.

It was very simple and unemotional—a few hymns, "Holy, Holy, Holy!" among them,—a short sermon—another hymn and the bene-

114

diction. A few hundred soldiers sitting singing hymns in a wheat field in Africa during a lull in a training program—saying the Lord's Prayer as a prelude to heaven knows what.

Neither the Colonel nor the Chaplain tried to gloss over the fact that combat and all that it meant lay just around the corner. But they accepted the fact calmly and without any verbal fireworks or false emotionalism.

That men would die was S. O. P. The important thing was that those who lived should not let down those who had given their lives, either on the field of battle or by their actions later on.

I'm afraid I have let my sense of drama make me become a bit rhetorical and pompous. But the scene was affecting, chiefly because it was simple and matter-of-fact and left so many things unsaid.

The same soldiers who had been cursing everyone and everything during the horrors of a full field inspection the day before now sat with their helmets off, listening in silence to stories of what the troops that had gone before them had done and to what was expected of them.

Oh well—you can see what I mean to convey.

Small, simple ceremonies can often mean more than all the pomp and majesty of cathedral services or vast parades—a curiously unexpressive sentence!

But the sun is getting me down, so I'll call a halt until later on.

[Later]

As you have never seen me in my "full field" uniform, which one is supposed to wear in combat (and never does, because you resemble nothing as much as an over decorated Xmas tree), I'll give you a brief description: O. D. pants, shirt, leggings, boots, helmet with lining, pistol belt with pistol, canteen, canteen cup, first aid packet, two ammunition clips (for pistol), gas mask (on left), ammunition pouch for tommy gun, slung on right shoulder—around the neck, field glasses, goggles and dust evaporator (have forgotten name of this, but you stick it over your nose like a small gas mask),—in the pockets, cigarettes, knife, lighter, a package of K rations (if you can steal one), and lastly, but by no means least, a musette bag full of toilet articles, extra socks and underwear slung on your back.

How much it all weighs I don't know, though I toted it round for nigh on three hours yesterday. But I do know that the minute you get near the battle field, according to those who have been there, you rip most of it off and proceed in a more normal costume!

I keep on talking about combat as if it were imminent when actually it will be months or more, I strongly suspect, before we get even a whiff of enemy gunpowder.

The breeze has come off nicely this afternoon, driving away the mosquitoes and making it quite pleasant to sit in the sun.

Later I expect to go for another swim, and then, when darkness falls, to crawl into my pup tent.

And so to bed.

NORTH AFRICA, MAY 31, 1943

Last night, after an early chow, 4.15 P.M., another officer and I, Lieut. Jordan—the one from Virginia, took a peep and motored fifteen miles or so to a neighboring village to leave some laundry with a nice French woman. We bought a couple of bottles of muscatel for good measure, and then joined the boys on the beach for a swim about seven. It got rather coolish, as the sun went under a cloud, so we just took a dip, came home and had a few glasses of wine before retiring to our luxurious quarters.

This morning after breakfast, as I was straightening up my tent, I chanced to see a spider about two inches in diameter sauntering non-chalantly across my sleeping bag. I then noticed a collection of black ants crawling on the floor, (ground) and discovered that there were hordes of them making merry under my rubber mattress.

I instantly thought of Margey (why, I can't imagine!) and wished she were here to put on one of her "bat, spider, bee, frog or bug" scenes.

I realized that caution dictated that I should give my quarters a thorough cleaning but I had to take some enlisted men on a range detail in a few minutes, so I left the ants and spiders to themselves while I took a quick shave out of my collapsible canvas bucket.

I have never felt better, and haven't even a trace of sinus, despite the fact that we are living half the time in a sea of brown dust that makes Carolina seem like a health resort. The cure for sinus seems to be fresh air and lots of it, whether it be dry or wet, cold or hot.

Incidentally, the helmet liners which we wear day in and day out are marvellous sun helmets and are the lightest and most comfortable hats I have ever worn. You don't know you have anything on your head and yet you're protected from the back of your neck to your eyebrows.

I feel completely at home here now. It is so like the 101st that it is almost as if I had never left it but just changed my status in it from an enlisted man to an officer.

It is a happy go lucky, informal life in bivouac that you don't get in any other type of service. Nothing is formalized. All the life of each section centers around one scout car, or three cars scattered around in dispersed positions.

We hear all the short wave programs from England and America on the scout car radios in the evenings and altogether it is—why, I don't quite know—an extremely pleasant existence.

I have even given up thinking about the possibility of being yanked out of here by Natousa and am convinced that I am here for the duration, whether on "detached service" or permanently assigned. I have accordingly ripped off my Air Corps insignia and arm patches and now have the red and yellow triangular patch of the 2nd Armored Division, with a blue tank and a streak of lightning through the center, on my left shoulder, while the regimental insignia (a shiny brass shield) is on my shoulder lapels between the bars and my neck. When next you see me, what with the two ribbons, augmented, I hope, by then, I shall be a dazzling sight!

I returned early from the range detail, collapsed my tent and got rid of the bug life.

My back is getting sore from sitting in this cramped position on my foot locker and my lips need another treatment, so I think I shall call it another day. I shall now collapse amongst the bugs and read till chow, which, by the way, is very good. It was just the opposite at that nightmarish spot from which I came.

I am writing in my pup tent with the aid of a flashlight—with a mosquito bar, thank God, shrouded round me and tickling my head.

I am, in fact, drinking in solitary grandeur the remnants of a bottle of vino left over from last night. I have just drunk a toast to you and David and one to the success of my project, which is to remain on in this particular company.

I talked to the Captain just now and asked him if he could use me in his company. He said certainly, that he was an officer under strength, as it was, and that he'd like very much to have me.

Tomorrow, I am to speak to the executive officer of the Battalion and see if he can't arrange with the Colonel to have me assigned here permanently. If that mission succeeds—and things are going my way now in such a phenomenal manner that I think it will—I shall be in charge of the forward reconnaissance section of the company—with four peeps under my command, in one of which—the second—I shall ride, with a radio to communicate to the scout cars further back.

This above all! If you had asked me one job I should prefer to *all* others in the Army, it would be to have a peep of my own and be in charge of a section of peeps.

Nothing could please me as much.

Also, once I get in this outfit, if I do! Natousa, will have a hell of a time catching up with me. For I have a hunch—based on nothing but intuition—a certain feeling in the air—that this company won't be in touch with headquarters very much longer. (Time out to kill several mosquitoes that had the effrontery to enter these sacred portals!)

I like this particular company. It is like the old 101st—bitching all the time, but by far the best fighting aggregation in the battalion—tough, don't give a damn and with a real sense of humor. And the officers are of the same type. I know I shall like them and get on with them.

I doubt if anyone has *ever* had such a queer status as I have (no one still knows what it is) but if I go into combat with this outfit, I'm going to remain with it, Army regulations or no Army regulations! I really can't help feeling this time—the whole tale is so fantastic—that our old friend Antonio of Padua must have had something to do with it. There were so many coincidences involved. If I hadn't gone to take a turkish bath just when I did—and I didn't particularly want to at that moment—I'd never have run into the officer who put me wise as to what to do to see the Colonel. If I hadn't gone over the hill, if a hundred other things hadn't dovetailed, I should still be at the Replacement Depot. Thank Mother for his intervention.

P. S. *Tuesday*

The Major says he's sure it's OK for me to be assigned here permanently. I am simply delighted.

Had a perfectly swell time today—the most interesting since I have been in the Army—on an all-day range problem. The platoon leader was absent so I had to take over and plan a whole battle operation to capture a valley and a Djebel, beyond which, was held by a mythical enemy. Each platoon worked out its own method, while the others watched. We used everything we had in the way of ammunition and arms and staged it just as realistically as a real battle.

I put a thirty and a fifty (machine guns) in concealed dismounted positions on the crest of a hill on one side of the valley—one 30 on the other side—a 75 further back to cover the advance of the gunners and a mortar just behind the machine guns.

With the machine guns, 75 and mortar delivering a terrific barrage on the enemy positions at the head of the valley, I sneaked my foot troops under the cover of brush up one side of the valley and then had them take up a firing position and deliver a surprise, and, we hope, a knockout blow with rifles, tommy guns and one machine gun.

I stayed with the gunners on the right hill and watched the show through glasses, delivering occasional instructions, for all the world as if I were a full fledged Hollywood director.

You can't imagine how fascinating it is to work out a problem of this kind and then watch it unroll before your eyes, without any rehearsal. Also it's no joke when you're working with live ammunition, as one slip can kill off a lot of men. Your 75 and mortar are firing from rear positions—as in battle, and their shells land just ahead of the forward infantry and the machine gun bullets are whizzing over their heads as well.

Fortunately, I had a beautifully trained platoon. All I had to do was to plan the tactics and they knew just how to execute them. If they hadn't, God knows what would have happened!

But it all worked out really well, and I honestly think we had the best plan—as several spectators told me—and I *know* we put on the best show!

I can't help feeling that if more attention was paid to this type of training—which the men all love—and less to right face left face and policing the area, that we'd have a much better trained Army. Of course you couldn't put rookies through this type of problem— they'd be killing themselves off like flies—but once they know how to handle guns, there are an infinite variety of problems you could work out which would really teach them how to handle their weapons, and that is, after all, fairly important.

Tomorrow we go on an all night problem, scouting and patrolling and the like—so you can see we are really getting the works.

Well, congratulate me on my good luck. I shall give St. Anthony a handsome present when I return.

P. S. I add this postscript and you can use your judgment as to whether to show it to Mother or not, to tell you that I realize obviously that I am in an extremely precarious branch of the Service. I believe only about 50% of a similar group in Tunisia survived. But I knew that all along, and damn it, it's what I wanted to do. And if I do have bad luck, well, *c'est la guerre.*

Incidentally, I think in a way you're safer in the peep section than farther back—even though you are the first element to reach the enemy lines. Because you're so maneuverable for one thing and you are such a small target; also the enemy often lets you by to get the bigger fry beyond. I think you do stand a very good chance of being taken prisoner because you haven't even a machine gun to defend yourself with, but I think the men just behind you are really in a more dangerous spot.

Well, all I'm worried about is not whether I'm killed, wounded or taken prisoner (though I don't *want* any of these three alternatives to happen!) but how well I acquit myself when I come up against the real thing.

I have a hunch I'll be O.K. because, even though I am high strung, I have a great sense of drama and also can be terribly impersonal about things. For instance, in the air raid, I never felt a moment's— not even an instant's—twinge of fear, and yet fully half the personnel were scared to death and some of them actually panicked. That, of course, was something else again, as we never were in any real danger except from some plane which might have decided to dump its bombs or strafe us just for the hell of it.

But no one can tell until it happens just how he will react. I think the thing that would upset me most would be seeing my friends killed and mangled at my feet—but they say you become accustomed even to that—that you learn to think of them not as individuals but as numbers.

I have a hunch that I'm going to see this thing through and come home *on my feet*—but no one can tell of course. There's so damn much luck connected with this whole game! But even if the worst should happen, I still wouldn't be sorry that I took the stand I did about leaving Cairo.

I could never have looked myself in the face if I hadn't made an effort to get out of that soft berth, difficult as it was to accomplish, God knows.

Some day, when I am lying in a slit trench, with stukas diving all round me, I may be sorry I'm not back in Shepherds Hotel—but fundamentally I still will be glad.

I'm happier now than I've been since I've been overseas—I feel at last I'm doing what I wanted to do ever since 1940. And if you're built the way I am, well, what else can you do?

Each person must decide for himself what he must do in a situation of this kind. I decided three years ago and not until last Monday did I come anywhere near realization of my aims.

If I do succeed in killing any Germans—and God knows I hope I do—I'll check off the first one for you and the next for David!

Now for the great news. The Major told me he thought it could certainly be arranged for me to stay here and said that if I did I would be extremely lucky, compared to the rest of the battalion. Evidently this Company is considered the crack reconnaissance company and as such may get special favors.

NORTH AFRICA, JUNE 4, 1943

Before going on the problem this evening, I decided to get rid of everything I didn't need and go, in just the same manner as to a real combat instead of a problem. I packed very cleverly, putting a little bit of everything in each container, so that if I lose one I'll have all the essentials in the other. I don't have to worry any longer about possessions, thank God, and you can't imagine what a relief it is. Don't think, too, that I haven't got plenty left. I still could get along comfortably with a third of what I have, and probably will before I am through.

I am looking forward a great deal to the two day problem that starts in two hours. To describe it would be a military secret, but I can say I think it will be the most interesting one we have gone on yet.

I have no other news. I am sitting in my peep awaiting early chow. I wish you could see the peep! Although there's only a driver and myself—and, in combat, there will be three—it is piled high with equipment, ammunition, guns, extra gas and water tanks, etc. How we'll ever squeeze a third person in, with another bed roll and barracks bag, I can't quite see. But we'll do it somehow! Probably by strapping all the bedding rolls on the hood.

My peep is named "Colt," if that means anything! My driver is a young kid by the name of Austin.

Every time I go out on a march, I always thank God, as I did in 101st, that I'm not in the infantry. There are so many comforts in a vehicle—so many places to store extras!

Well, I must inspect the platoons' cars and line them up so I've got to stop.

We got back from the two day problem on Friday afternoon—most interesting it was, too, though I can't elaborate much further—and the next day our company moved bag, baggage and vehicles to a new bivouac site away from the B'n. That afternoon, Lt. Morton and I got permission from the Captain to take a peep and go into town to make some necessary last-minute purchases. I got three pairs of new coveralls—the grey-green kind—as that will be our regular uniform in the field and in combat, and two more O. D. pants, which I needed badly. I am now ready for any eventuality!

The town was so crowded, you could hardly walk the streets and they have closed the restaurants and bars at all hours except between 5 and 7:30 P.M. We had a snack at the Red Cross Club, however, some wine and brandy (mixed!) at the Officers' bar, and then had supper at a little café where I had made friends with the proprietor. He let us stay there till 9:15 and served us an excellent meal, though without meat; and we headed back to our barren, rock-bound bivouac site at about 9:30. The next few days all training has been called off and we are doing a job of maintenance on all the vehicles, checking supplies, ammunition, etc. Tomorrow, to celebrate this lull in the daily round of activity, I am going over to visit the battalion dentist. Better to get it over with now while I can, I figure, though I dread the idea. I'd rather face a machine gun any day then a dentist's drill. With the former you've at least got a chance; with the latter, you're doomed from the start.

As a coming home present, I would suggest, if any are available, a Contax F2 camera, but without a light meter attached. I can't think of anything, short of seeing all of you again, that I should like better to find awaiting me. I only wish to God I had one with me now, but there's no use crying over spilt milk. Maybe Lt. O'Connor* will still be able to send me my Russian Leica, though I doubt, now, if there'd be much chance of its catching up with me. Still and all, I'll have other things to do besides taking pictures!

I like the company, and my job in it, more every day. The three

*Lt. T. J. O'Connor.

platoon leaders—Lt. Morton, Lt. Jordan and Lt. Chase couldn't be nicer and the Captain—Capt. Johnson is a fine fellow, too. So, barring some ugly work on the part of that she-witch, Natousa, I'm all set for the duration. There's a swell bunch of enlisted men, too, who know their job to a T and are itching to get into action. It's so much more satisfactory to be with a company than with headquarters. You really get a chance to do some constructive work and to see the results of that work from day to day.

Also, there's a kind of camaraderie in a company, with only nine officers thrown together all the time, that you don't get in larger units with many more officers. And there are also no big shots, and everybody has a job to do which he can't shirk.

I got only two hours' sleep on the two-day problem, but I was just as wide-awake at the finish as at the beginning. What a lot of rot it is about over age officers not being able to take it. All of them may not be able to, but the ones that are in good physical shape can stand up just as well as the younger men, if not better.

The 1st Replacement Depot seems aeons away from me now—so much has been crowded into these past two weeks. It was a nightmarish spot but even then it was worth it to get this.

I am sitting propped up on my sleeping bag at the mouth of my pup tent, with the wind whipping this charming African dust all around me. There's not a tree in sight, not even a low bush to give any shade, so, needless to say, I am sitting in the sun!

I'm sure it was St. Anthony who pulled this deal for me! It was too good for it just to have happened.

NORTH AFRICA, JUNE 10, 1943

I have been so rushed the past few days that I haven't had a moment to write. We decided at the last minute that we didn't have enough fire power on our peeps and I took upon myself the task of seeing if I couldn't beg, borrow or steal some machine guns to mount on the vehicles. We couldn't requisition any more through the usual channels as we already had our quota. I bethought me of my old friend, the Air Corps, and decided to try and chisel some guns out of them. I accordingly put back my A. C. insignia on my uniform and went over to the airport and the Air Force Ordnance. To make a long story short, I returned with ten machine guns and 15,000 rounds of ammunition! All of which I got without even having to tell a lie or sign my name to a piece of paper, though I was fully prepared to do one or both of these things! To be sure, the guns are British instead of American, but they are darn good guns; we can get the ammunition needed at any airport or from any British outfit and everyone seems to be delighted with them.

NORTH AFRICA, JUNE 12, 1943

Did not have time to finish Thursday as was up to my ears improvising some mounts for the guns and getting new racks (designed by M. C. E.) for the back of the peeps. I got these put on by a Navy Engineer shop in a nearby port. I can't tell you how much I have enjoyed circumventing army channels and standard army procedure and getting things *done!* These racks are being put on all the company peeps and so are the gun mounts.

In the P.M. I took another scouting trip with my driver to get some more ammunition, as I didn't think we had a safe cushion for an operation in which we mightn't run into a British unit for a week or so. Unfortunately, all the British ammunition in the neighborhood had been requisitioned that very day by some high priority order, so I just stole some scrap iron from an airport dump instead, to make up the racks. I got permission from the Captain to take off again yesterday to a more distant airport, and left at four in the morning with my driver. It proved to be farther than we thought and an extremely circuitous mountain route, so we didn't hit the airport till almost one o'clock and didn't get back to camp till 12:45 A.M. However, we brought back 12,000 more rounds of ammunition and several more magazine drums, so it was well worth it. I may say, however, that seventeen hours in a peep is a little wearing on the derrière! It was a beautiful trip, scenically—quite the most exciting views I have seen in Africa.

I gave the company a lecture on the gun today, based on informa-

125

tion I had pieced together from the British and had them all take it down (the gun!) and assemble it. In a couple of days we shall fire it to test the guns and then, I hope, will use them solely to kill Germans with.

The men, incidentally, are crazy about the guns. They always like a new weapon, of course, and this is a particularly trick one. Also they're delighted to have every peep armed with a machine gun—a great morale 'builder,' if nothing else, when you're driving in one.

Lieut. Chase and I, prior to my lecture, were experimenting with the gun, to try and discover its finer points of operation, during which test the gun went off (as we rather expected it might). Fortunately, we'd taken the precaution to point it carefully to the ground before we started, and we learned all we wanted to know, which was how the bullet was extracted from the drum!

I have just about ten minutes left before the mosquitoes drive me underneath my net at round about 9 P.M. I think we shall remain at this bug-ridden site a few days more. It's just above a swamp and the mosquitoes come down upon us like angry wolves every evening and stay until after breakfast. By which time they are as completely satiated as we are infuriated.

NORTH AFRICA, JUNE 13, 1943

I had a rigorous house cleaning day today, which consisted of doing all my laundry in a tin can over a gasoline jar, dry cleaning five shirts and a pair of pants (in GI gasoline—five gallons of it, just to make you squirm!) and once again sorting and eliminating unnecessary items.

My laundry was not a success. The clothes look just as dirty as ever, though at least they don't smell! But the dry cleaning was superb. I could go into the business any day. All you do is dip it solidly in gasoline, wait a while, rinse it, dip it a couple more times and the deed is done.

Have just come back from an evening swim; the water was wonderful and it is one of the best beaches I have ever seen. The avalanche of bugs is due any moment at which time I shall retire under my mosquito net.

We just got in some new officer replacements—four 2nd Lieutenants—as they are filling us up over strength in order to give all these casual officers some training. Am delighted that I got in here and got well settled before they came. I feel almost like an old timer, even though it will be only three weeks tomorrow since I came. They have been days crowded with activity.

I think I am getting on well in the company and doing a good job, but time will have to settle that. As one general is reputed to have said to a company: "I'm told you're good. I'll believe it when I see you doing a good job in combat."

A mosquito has just raised a hefty welt smack on my temple, so bedtime seems to be drawing nigh.

For heaven's sake don't worry about me over here. I'm just where I want to be, which is the second most important thing in my life at the moment. The first is that I do a good job when and if the going should get tough.

NORTH AFRICA, JUNE 15, 1943 TO M. E. F.

I have just finished giving the platoon an hour's lecture on plane identification, following a gruelling session in which I had to read the "Articles of War" to the new men. My mind is still full of "Shall suffer death or such penalty as the court martial shall decree." In fact, after reading the Articles of War, you wonder how anyone stays alive at all!

I have now a perfectly frightful confession to make to you, which is that your going-away present to me, which I treasured and still treasure enormously, is being buried by me in a slit trench in Africa. It is simply a case of space. I haven't room any longer to take it with me. If I had had any sense, I would have packed it away in my footlocker, but I hoped I could sneak it into my bed roll. I now find that I just can't. We are too crowded for any one person to take up an inch more space than he needs to, and the backgammon board, small as it is, will not roll up. I had so much sentiment about it, remembering Venice, Brioni and, if I'm not wrong, your honeymoon, that I held it to the last but the stern law of physics finally won out. Then rather than give it to any Arab I decided to bury it. Perhaps, if we make a trip here after the war, we can come back to the spot and dig it up and start where we left off, with me winning almost every game. If you saw this spot after the war, it would be hard to believe that we had lived on such barren ground and been on the whole, so comfortable in the process.

The wind is now howling around like a mad thing, swirling layers of reddish dust into every nook and crevice. I don't much like the wind but it's better than the mosquitoes, so I rather hope that it keeps up.

I am completely out of touch with world events, despite the fact that we can get the BBC on our car radios and also programs from America. I know we have taken Pantelleria and Lampedusa, but that's about the sum total of my knowledge. And oddly enough, living this kind of life, you don't really care very much about news. Your own daily *train train* keeps you occupied. The rest of the time you are eating, sleeping and fighting, not the Germans, alas, but the bugs.

You would *love* it here. There's a creepy thing of some sort just crawling up my sleeve!

Time out.

Just an ant, carrying a wasp's legs. Nothing less. Nothing more.

A huge grasshopper has just landed on my knee and is regarding me quizzically—now he has gone.

The only thing I haven't run into—thank God—is a serpent! And I expect that any day now.

Well the mystic hour of five is approaching, when we partake of our evening meal. It will be nine-tenths dust this evening, which will be too bad, as I understand we have fresh meat. But welcome, none the less.

NORTH AFRICA, JUNE 16, 1943

I have improvised a new boudoir for myself, in which luxurious setting, I am now sitting, writing. It consists of a pup tent, or rather half a pup tent, with one half open to the skies held up by my mosquito bar! The left half is tent, the right mosquito netting. In this way I can get light during the daytime and protection from the bugs during the night. Also the tenting is on the windy side and helps to keep some of the North African dust from out of my meagre belongings.

What if it rains, you may say? The answer is, it doesn't, though it probably will tonight just to be perverse.

We seem to be in the midst of another of those abominable periods of *mistral,* like the one I wrote you about at my last post. That time the wind lasted for five solid days. So far, here it has gone on for two.

I am ashamed to confess that I came into my tent after lunch for a little quiet session with Mr. Charlie Chan and fell fast asleep until 3:30. Then I rose, corralled the platoon, which was also asleep, had them give a thorough policing to the area, lay down again and slept until 5:30! I am now back in my nook (it is 7:00) and will probably fall asleep again as soon as I have finished this letter!

NORTH AFRICA, JUNE 17, 1943

I had the bulk of the company on my hands today, as the other officers were out on one thing or another and had a fairly exhausting time trying to think of something to occupy them. I took them on a six mile hike, in the broiling sun, in the morning, and was accused, by them, of setting a pace that was more suited to a P-40 than a man. In the afternoon, I gave them a map reading class for two hours and a half, with the wind blowing the maps every which way, and then called it a day, which, indeed, it was!

9:15 P.M. As the kitchen truck did not make an appearance until 7, and we had to wait still another hour for supper to be cooked, I took the men swimming during the interval. After supper I went up to see one of the officers who had been feeling sick all day. It is turning colder, which is infuriating, as I am without my sleeping bag, and two blankets is not a hell of a lot of protection against a chilly fifty mile an hour gale.

We moved to a new bivouac site this A.M. in a nice and dusty ploughed field! An advantage in many ways, as the ground is soft and it was hard as a rock up on the wind swept hill top. Tell Margey, by the way, that I have marked the spot where I buried her back-gammon board in case we ever come back here *après la guerre*—and God forbid that we should! I fear the Arabs will dig it up, however. They dig up all slit trenches, even kitchen dumps and scavenge for anything they can get.

A man outside my tent has just ejaculated: "Oh, what I wouldn't give for a drink of real ice water, without chlorine in it." A sentiment with which I concur 300%. However, you get on surprisingly well without it.

The King apparently passed within a few miles of our camp but we did not have to go out and swelter all day waiting for him to "pass in review," for which I give much thanks. The "typical" army luncheon, as the paper called it, which was served him, created mild amusement everywhere. Typical for generals and kings, no doubt, but for no one else!

I haven't seen any roast beef since I have been in Africa. Neither has any one else that I know of. But I have seen plenty of "C" rations which, though you get tired of them, are still pretty good, in their own way. . . .

8.40 P.M. Have just returned from swimming where I had to call on my first aid experience to bind up the foot of a man who got a nasty cut from an iron slab. I took him to the infirmary afterwards and they described it as a "major perforation of the dorsum." What nonsense!

Apparently they don't use stitches any more if they can help it—just slap some sulphanilamide powder on it and put a bandage on and let it heal.

What the army would do without the sulpha drugs, I don't know. I imagine they've saved more lives in this war than any other single drug. Every man carries a box of twelve, in his first aid pack, plus a package of powder and we have lots of spares in the car. The minute you are wounded, you eat all twelve, either at one gulp or one every 2½ minutes. You also spray the powder on the wound.

All the officers carry morphine serets as well, with extra ones in the car. If a man is in great pain, we give him one, write M on his forehead with an iodine capsule, plus the time, and then radio back his position to the medics while we go about our mission. We are really well equipped from a first aid standpoint and they tell me all the advance hospitals are first rate. Our own battalion medical department is said to be the best equipped in Africa—better even than the Division's, which is all to the good! So much for this medical interlude which I thought would interest you.

Have been here now either a month or five weeks, I forget which and have enjoyed it more than the previous five months. Hope I'll be able to say the same about the weeks to come!

9.35 P.M. (By flashlight, carefully concealed.)

I have just had a talk with the Captain who was out today in my peep watching some maneuvers. He told me that the General had ridden in the peep and was so fascinated with my British machine gun that he played with it all the time and was delighted with it. We had been afraid that the higher authorities might frown on the use of the weapon of another nation; in fact, the Captain had, for that reason, told us to keep them hidden until we were away from prying staff eyes. But now, I guess, the lid's off! I only hope with eight guns, in actual operation, and with four thousand rounds of ammunition per gun, just as a starter, that we can each knock out at least a hundred Jerries apiece—again, just as a starter.

Don't worry any time if you don't get mail for long intervals. I've been lucky so far being able to write a good deal, but when I'm busier I won't be able to.

I took the company on a ten-mile cross-country hike this morning, wearing "full field equipment" which they seemed to find strenuous in the extreme! Actually it *was* fairly strenuous, as I kept up a fast pace, uphill and down, and, with two ten-minute breaks, we made it in two hours and a half.

We may take it easy tomorrow, as it's Sunday, or we may not. The morrow will tell the tale. Meanwhile, as there are some movies being shown in the field just a few hundred yards from us, I think I shall stroll over and see what the show is like.

NORTH AFRICA, JUNE 20, 1943

Today was on the uneventful side. I took in money from the men to be changed this A.M., which necessitated a hell of a lot of addition, at which, as you may remember, I am very bad. After lunch the whole company marched to a nearby field to hear a talk by the General commanding us. We had a band that played festive marches until the General's arrival and we left to the tune of "Over There"—which reminded me of the afternoon you and I went to see "Yankee Doodle Dandy" in New York.

Have just returned from the usual evening swimming party; it was lovely tonight because the wind has died down and I am now preparing to go to the movies. The ones last night failed to materialize.

Got some more "shots" at the dispensary today—three in one arm— as my typhoid, tetanus and typhus were on their last legs. No ill effects as yet.

NORTH AFRICA, JUNE 21, 1943

At long last I am a man with an official status!!—"Assigned," permanently, as far as I am concerned, at least for the duration, to the 82nd. The order, which came in today from that rat hole, the replacement depot, was dated June 16.

Actually, I had no fears that anything so dastardly as an order removing me from this outfit could possibly come through, but it is a great relief, none the less, to know that the thing is settled once and for all, and that Natousa cannot cast out her grasping hand and push me from pillar to post at her slightest whim.

Well it was a long pull—some five months from the time I first put in the application—but it was well worth it as things have turned out. In fact they *couldn't* have turned out better. For which I give due thanks to our mutual friend, St. Anthony, and enclose an offering of thanks which I wish you would put in his box.

It was so much better to get into an outfit that had not yet been in combat, also to be in it long enough to get a pretty good idea of what it's all about. If I'd been assigned to the 1st Armored, I'd have been a rooky among a group of seasoned troops. This way we all start at scratch; and while I am not, naturally, as well trained as those who have been with the outfit two years, I at least have a pretty fair groundwork and during the past weeks had an opportunity for a strenuous and extremely valuable combat refresher course.

I am reclining now in a bed of rocks—the remnants of a stone wall —and it is rather trying on the anatomy. So I think I shall call a halt to the proceedings.

NORTH AFRICA, JUNE 25, 1943 TO M. E. F.

I don't know how all of you feel about Mr. John L. Lewis and his precious coal miners, but I can tell you that the feeling here is intense —so much so, in fact, that I should guess Lewis has set back the cause of labor a generation by his actions. Because when this voting bloc gets home, it's not going to have any use for organized labor.

Most of the talk you hear—the suggestions as to what should be done with Lewis and the miners—is unprintable. The prevailing opinion expressed by the sober minded is that Lewis and the miners should immediately be sent over here and put, without any arms or ammunition, in the first assault wave of the invasion!!

I'm not joking. That's how bitterly the average soldier—the sensible not the hysterical type—feels about this situation.

When men have been living for eight months in pup tents, if they've had any tents at all—when they haven't bathed in anything but a helmet full of water—when they've eaten largely C rations and put up with hundreds of privations (perfectly willing, mind you, and not thinking they were heroes), it's pretty hard to stomach the fact that a selfish group back home, living in the lap of luxury, compared to them, making huge wages, compared to them, and united with their families and friends, should take this opportunity to imperil the whole war effort.

Although this is the official siesta hour, and the temperature in my tent must be at least 105°, I am breaking a long standing precedent and writing you instead of falling simultaneously to sleep and into a pool of perspiration. I am actually doing the latter but shall postpone the former at least until I have finished this letter.

The latest body blow was six boxes of K rations and six of D which we have to take on our person (supposedly). I have managed to squeeze five K and two D into my musette bag, taking out everything but toilet articles and one change of socks and underwear and will put the rest into my blanket roll. As soon as I connect with my car, I will, needless to state, throw everything into the vehicle, as I don't relish trudging any distance with my musette bag and blanket roll on my back.

Tell M, A, and C, I was so touched with their messages of thanks for the presents I gave them that I have decided to repeat them while I still have anything left in the bank. The money's no use to me, God knows, and if it can give them any pleasure, it will mean far more to me than putting it in a bank to give to Uncle Sam a year later. I accordingly enclose three checks which I trust you'll send on to them with my love. Tell them also the same stipulations hold—they are to be used for *pleasure,* not to pay bills or buy dishwashing machines.

NORTH AFRICA, JUNE 29, 1943

I have just said goodbye to my val pack and am really not sorry to be rid of it. The fewer material things I have with me, the less there is to take care of, worry about, and by *far* the most important, to carry. I am now reduced to a blanket roll and a musette bag, both of which I can carry on my back without undue strain. The rest is on my person!

I went swimming again this afternoon and am now reposing in my sun parlor awaiting that moment—at 10 P.M.—when the sun decides to go down and I can retire.

Not one drop of rain since I have been here—delightful, in many respects, as we are none of us prepared for rain and leave everything out in the open, but it makes things dusty as you can imagine.

I will write, as you know, as often as I can, and don't worry if, at any time, there are gaps between letters. When we get down to active training again, I won't have as much free time as I have had the past two weeks.

NORTH AFRICA, JUNE 30, 1943 TO M. E. F.

I lightened my load again today, I hope for the last time, as I can't get rid of any more equipment, and the only luxuries I am still keeping are cigarettes, four cartons,—three in the bed roll and one in the musette bag.

Here is the dinner I want on my return. I thought it up on the road march this morning.

Oysters on the half shell (if in season), if not little neck clams.
Filet mignon on fried toast, sauce bearnaise,
Fried egg plant, baked tomatoes in cheese, fresh peas,
Mixed green salad with tomatoes and cheeses assorted.
Strawberry ice cream with fresh crushed strawberries!!
My mouth is watering pitifully!!

NORTH AFRICA, JULY 2ND, 1943 TO M. E. F.

I heard today at lunch that the B'n had heard over the radio that Europe has actually been invaded. You undoubtedly know all the details back home, whereas we know absolutely nothing, and don't even know where said invasion has taken place. It is most exciting news, however, though vaguely disappointing as I had somehow hoped we would be the vanguard of any invasion. However, you can't have everything, I guess, and maybe someday I'll be glad we weren't.

I went to a neighboring town yesterday afternoon to see if I could dig up some extra PX supplies for the men. We weren't actually entitled to them but I felt it would be good for the morale if we had a little extra stock on hand. I finally wangled permission to get a full

135

week's supply if I returned at eight the next morning. Then, not wishing to return empty handed to a hungry and expectant group of men in the dust bowl, I decided to get them some beer. Finally located a brewery, but could only get fifty bottles, as bottles are scarcer than hen's teeth in this vicinity, so I also got fifty bottles of muscatel. I figured that would be enough for our present strength of about one hundred and thirty, which was a grave error as it was all consumed within less than forty-five minutes—all except seven bottles which I salted away for the seven officers. However, though they could easily have drunk twice the amount and still remain relatively sober, they were very grateful for the gift. The sand storm, or rather dirt storm, had abated by evening so we had a pleasant time sitting around drinking our first vino in some six weeks.

This morning early, I set off to take the bottles back and got a rip snorting amount of PX supplies, including some fifty boy scout knives which sold like hot cakes for 85 cents apiece.

*Forsan et haec olim meminisse iuvabit** (David will translate), but none the less, I am eager to be out of here and to get into action. It is terribly hard also to keep a company keyed up, in high gear all the time, if nothing happens. However, I am not worrying much on that score. I like the company more every day I am in it. The men are a swell bunch and so are the officers. Altogether I couldn't have done better for myself. And I suppose it goes to show that if you try hard enough, you can get what you want, even in the Army. You can, if you're lucky, that is. It's funny, when you think of it, for someone who enjoys comfort and luxury as much as I do, to actually be 100% happier living in this sink hole, than in Shepherds. But, *c'est la guerre,* I suppose, which changes, if it does not actually distort, all values.

*Perhaps some time it will be a pleasure to recall these things.

SICILY

••

JULY 27, 1943 TO OCTOBER 29, 1943

There may be danger in the deed
But there is honour too.

W. E. AYTOUN

The ban on letter writing was lifted yesterday afternoon. But as I was in the midst of writing a Platoon Journal describing our activity during the invasion, I could not get around to personal mail until this morning. Censorship restrictions are such that we cannot give much detailed information, though we can state, two weeks after the event, that we were in such and such a locality.

I imagine that you, back home, have already read detailed descriptions of our activities, most of them greatly exaggerated, I don't doubt, so everything I will tell you will probably be "old stuff." However, I'll give you as full a description as I can of our part in the Sicilian campaign.

D Day, as you all know, was July 10th. From shortly after midnight the 9th till the next afternoon we watched the advance units landing, from our ship, sitting on the sun deck in comfortable deck chairs and looking on just as if it were a show staged for our benefit. There were a couple of air raids during the night, or early morning, of the 10th but nothing to amount to much. One by one the shore batteries were silenced and by dawn the coast looked very serene and peaceful save for occasional fires and bursts of artillery and for the host of ships spread out in the harbor.

Our unit was scheduled to disembark early on the morning of D Day plus one, as we were acting as a reserve force for the units already landed. At six o'clock P.M. on D Day I was told to collect a detail of 12 men from the scout section to make an advance landing that evening and guide the company on the next day to the assembly area on shore.

I had them out on the after well of the ship prepared to go over the side in 15 minutes, with full equipment, but the boat which was scheduled to take us ashore failed to make an appearance, so we sat and waited. As soon as it was dusk, the air activity started in again. Just at sunset a Jerry dive bomber hit a ship near the shore with a direct hit and it went up in flames almost instantaneously. The reaction among the troops crowding the after well deck was one of spontaneous fury. For the first time I saw that spirit of hate kindled, without which you can't have a good fighting army.

"If I ever get one of those sons of bitches," a sergeant behind me said, "I'll get someone to hold him and I'll just slit his throat slowly —inch by inch— and let him watch himself bleed to death." There were other similar comments, most of them unprintable.

Ten—eleven—twelve o'clock—and still no boat and no information from either the Navy or Army as to what had happened to it. I accordingly bedded down the detail on a hatch and arranged with the Navy to wake us as soon as any transportation appeared.

At three I got the signal to get my men on a boat which was taking off another unit. After some milling and pushing round in the pitch darkness, we went over the side of the ship, down the nets, and boarded a landing craft.

At 05.35 precisely, I stepped off into waist deep water on the shore of Sicily and waded ashore on to the beach. All my cigarettes were ruined, as I had them in my pants pocket, but otherwise no damage was done. We contacted our higher headquarters after walking inland about a mile, in single file, ten yards between men, in case of strafing, and set down our equipment in an orchard right next to a delightful tomato patch. I was sent by the CO on a couple of missions to contact other headquarters and, by the time I returned, the rest of the company had joined us.

(Since two weeks have passed I am at liberty to state that we were in the Gela sector for the first few days of fighting.)

I can't give you a full description of our first day in Sicily. It would take too long, but I'll touch upon the highlights.

It was, in my opinion, an almost perfect indoctrination to combat, as practically everything happened to us that could happen, except that we did not take part ourselves in any active combat but were merely passive observers or targets for enemy aircraft, artillery or machine gun fire.

Before very long, about 10 A.M. to be exact, we found ourselves perched in the midst of a tank battle, with the Germans about a mile off on one side of our hill and our own tanks to the rear of us. We watched the battle for about an hour through glasses and then, with the naked eye, as the German tanks approached closer and closer to our OP.

Finally, as the Jerry tanks were about 300 yards away and our own tanks had moved in just to our right, I got the order to lead the company to a safer position back of the next hill. We traipsed down the hill and up the other side. Just as we were nearing the crest of the hill, I heard machine gun fire and looked back. A machine gun from the German tank was spraying the edge of a little mound about 50 feet behind me. We took the rest of the hill on the double (the ones that were ahead of the gunfire); the others split off to the right under another lieutenant.

Lest you think that we retreated ignobly from the combat (which we did!), let me explain that we had none of our arms and equipment with us, save our sidearms, and so there was nothing else that we could do at the moment.

I halted my men in a railroad cut over the hill, where we had some protection, and could at least take up an infantry position, but several other units joined us and the place soon became too crowded for safety. A plane flew over the gorge strafing us (without any ill effects), so I dispersed my men in a melon patch next to the tracks and we stayed there for lunch which was composed largely of assorted varieties of melons plus a few tomatoes.

I sent a lieutenant and three sergeants to locate the rest of the company, which they found down near the beach, and we were told to stay where we were. Just then, however, the enemy artillery got our range and a hefty shell landed about 100 feet from us. We moved about 100 yards and the next hit was even closer, so, as we were right in line with a railroad track and one of our own gun positions, we decided to make a retrograde movement (the American Army never retreats!) and rejoin the company by the beach.

This we did, being strafed by Messerschmidts a couple of times en route, with no casualties, and dug in the dunes for the next couple of hours, while the Jerries bombed and strafed the area, particularly the harbor, every ten or fifteen minutes. The German tanks had meanwhile been stopped and forced to retreat so we eventually went back to our original bivouac site, and then were put on an all night outpost guard to prevent a surprise attack.

There were a couple of air raids in the evening (spectacular as far as the ack ack was concerned) and an artillery position just back of us kept up a steady shelling of the enemy forward positions from 9 till 1 A.M., so the night could hardly be described as quiet, but it was for the most part uneventful. A mortar dud fell in our area wounding an attached officer just before midnight. I had to check the guard a couple of times after midnight and fell into a profound slumber on the hard ground as soon as I could, to wake in the morning to hear the welcome pounding of our own artillery fire and—most welcome sight of all—to see a large formation of Spitfires flying overhead. It seemed that we finally had control of the air and would no longer be subjected to these constant wasp-like harrassing attacks.

The Jerries never sent over large formations of planes, hardly ever more than five or six at a time and sometimes just one or two, but they made you take cover and were a big nervous strain to the ships in the harbor, although they did, in actuality, very little damage.

Well, so much for "D Day plus one," an almost perfect indoctrination, as I said before, to a period of combat. We got a little sampling of almost everything, except active combat on our own part, and were ready to push ahead feeling that we had our baptism of fire behind us.

We knew what to expect. We knew it wasn't half as bad as we had been led to expect and that your chances of getting hit, even under direct machine gun fire, were slight. Most comforting of all, we found, at least most of us did, I think, that it was not so frightening as you might think to be under fire. For one thing, if the fire is close to you, you haven't time to be frightened. If it isn't, well there's nothing to be worried about.

You have to, I imagine, develop a philosophy that, if you're going to be hit, you're going to be hit and there's not much you can do about it. And I think everyone, consciously or subconsciously develops that point of view—really *has* to develop it—before he's much use in a combat zone. But once you have that, there's not much to it. You do what you've been taught to do instinctively. You do a lot that you haven't been taught, also instinctively, like diving for cover when an artillery shell whistles by and lands not far off (though you're all right, they do say, if you can hear the whistle). And you're too interested, excited and tired the rest of the time to worry about anything except the all-important matter of rations. Let the ration truck be half an hour late or fail to turn up and then you'll really have a riot on your hands! Fortunately we carry enough rations in each car to see us through three days, but even then, it's the first thing you think about when you come back from the front. Get more and better rations. Water and toilet paper, too, are mighty important items. Oh yes, and ammunition, also, but we always, being mechanized, had more of that than we needed.

I will say here that I got through the campaign without a scratch, save for those on my hands from crawling through bushes, scouting. I have a couple of bruises on my back where an enterprising sergeant ran right up it while we were both hurtling into a crevice in the cliffs to get away from a German 88, which had spotted us just after we had spotted it. I have now made up my sleep and feel almost sluggish from too much rest! I am bound to confess, though I know it is the unorthodox viewpoint, that I enjoyed the campaign immensely. It's a fascinating game, particularly when you're the first element out front. And the fact that the stakes are high makes it all the more engrossing.

Now that we're awaiting new developments, we're all crazy to get going again. A crazy point of view, I guess, but there you are!

P. S. I wonder if you ever guessed that we were in the invasion. I never knew myself where we were going, until 24 hours after we had sailed.

SICILY, JULY 27, 1943

The news of Mussolini's downfall came through on the radio yesterday. Fascinating isn't it and all sorts of things may happen.

But to get back to Sicily, which I imagine is of more immediate interest to you, though I'm sure, again, that you know far more of the campaign than I, who took part in it, do.

I'll try and touch the highlights briefly and chronologically, though I can't mention any localities except for the first sector we started out in—the Gela sector—as that's the only one that's two weeks old.

143

Two weeks from today, I can tell you that we were, as of today, bivouacked in the general vicinity of ——————,* but not until that mystic period has elapsed. It's a capital spot for a bivouac that we're in now, however, a nice olive grove with plenty of shade and ground that can be moulded without too much difficulty to fit the human form. I am anxious to be on the go again, however, so I hope we won't relax here too long.

*   *   *

D Day plus two was largely spent getting the company organized. Our vehicles began to drift in one by one and by nightfall they were all on hand, which was a great relief. A mechanized soldier feels about the same without his vehicle as an infantryman without his rifle. You just can't function effectively.

The enemy tanks, incidentally, had been forced to withdraw. Fifteen out of some 40 or 50 had been knocked out and the whole coastal area was now ours.

The next day we were alerted at 11:00 A.M. and moved out at 7 P.M. to act as flank reconnaissance support for an attack by the infantry to the north. We waited a few hours in an assembly area and started out at three in the morning. My scout section had to make a cross country reconnaissance on the left flank. We actually started out from the forward position at about dawn, encountered no enemy and set up an O.P. on a high hill overlooking the town that was to be the pivot of the attack. Actually, as we discovered later, the town had fallen early in the morning and our troops were already well ahead. We were still a reserve force, however, so we were not being used for forward reconnaissance.

Got orders by radio to return to a new assembly area at about three P.M. As soon as we got there the Captain said he wanted to take my peeps and a few of his own on a reconnaissance mission much further north to try and make contact with two of our own divisions and see if there were any enemy between them.

We set out about 6:30 P.M., my car in the lead. I had decided, about

*Palermo.

144

two days after taking over the scout section, that the only way I could function effectively was to put myself in the point peep—the first car in the column. You've got to be on hand yourself to make the decisions, so it's just a waste of time to send another car on ahead first. We went through the town of —————————, which had fallen to the infantry in the morning—one of those incredible towns like those on the French Riviera set on the pinnacle of a high cliff. The roads, winding up to the town were littered with debris—smashed gun positions, trucks, vehicles and a few bodies, mostly Italian, I am glad to say. As we pushed down the mountain out of the town, we encountered the civilian population, which had taken to the hills, streaming back into the village, in carts, on donkeys, on foot. They all seemed cheerful and were surprisingly cordial to their conquerors.

We had been told that there was an old Roman road, not marked on our map, which was a short cut to the first place which we wanted to go to, so we decided to take that. Old Roman was the word for it—about 3½ feet wide, tiled with blocks of stone. We wound up and down the hills for a few miles, cursing the Romans and everyone else and then lost the road in a field, which was quite a relief as cross country going, even though it meant circumnavigating or bumping across several wadies, was comparatively smooth.

As far as we knew we were in enemy territory, so we went fairly slowly. I scouted each hill and corner on foot before we ventured out of cover with a peep, and then we shot the point peep fast to the next point of concealment under the cover of the machine guns of the next peep. We had two false alarms when I spotted what I thought were enemy tanks or vehicles. The first turned out to be a noble cactus plant; the second (not so humiliating!)—a threshing machine in the middle of a grove of trees! When we couldn't decide with glasses what the objects were, the Captain and I scouted them on foot and then we pushed ahead. When we reached our first objective, we found that the enemy had been knocked further back than we thought, so we went on to our second objective at a faster pace and again met no resistance. While the Captain went on the C.P., I took the patrol on another brief, and equally fruitless, reconnaissance;

145

and we headed homeward shortly after midnight, reaching there between one and two.

*   *   *

D Day plus 5. Had a bath, believe it or not, in a trickle which goes by the name of a torrento in Sicily. It was only a few inches deep, but by filling my helmet, I could get at least wet—a great luxury.

About 10 o'clock, the whole platoon moved out on a mission, the scout section having the assignment to "contact the enemy." Unfortunately, or fortunately as the case may be, we couldn't carry out our job as we ran into a full-fledged tank battle, which we were able to watch from a grand stand seat high on a hill, and were forbidden by the C. O. of the battle to proceed further until nightfall. While we were watching the battle, on the plain just below us, an infantry Captain came up in a car and jumped out with much pomp to survey the situation. He stood right on the skyline, watching through his glasses with his car silhouetted against the hill top, too. In about two minutes, there was a loud familiar whistling sound and a shell landed about 100 feet away from our observation post. Seeing that the enemy had discovered our position, thanks to that idiot of a Captain, we decided to pull out and did so to the accompaniment of another crash.

We decided to make our night patrol a dismounted one. So I picked eight men to accompany me and we were all set to start out at about 21.00, working in conjunction with an infantry patrol, when all plans were cancelled as a night attack was slated—quite an anticlimax all round, for us, at least, though probably not for the attackers.

The next day I took my peep section on a long cross country flanking reconnaissance which aimed to work behind the enemy lines on the flank. I think we got behind the enemy lines though we never actually encountered any enemy forces—just friendly Sicilian farmers who tried to embrace us and showered us with fruit and wine. We came up close to one enemy gun position. It was on one side of the hill and we were on the other, but it conveniently withdrew before we had to make any further advance. We were in constant radio communication with platoon but, short of exchanging pleasantries in the

146

rather stilted radio lingo, there wasn't a hell of a lot to report. I started the patrol back about 8:30 P.M. as I didn't want to make it all in the dark and we pulled back to platoon along about 10:30, the return trip being much faster as we didn't have to scout each hill crest and corner.

Even scouting these points very carefully with glasses (you can imagine what a godsend the Zeiss glasses are—about three times as good as the GI variety), you can never be actually sure that there isn't a well camouflaged enemy position ahead, so the only thing to do is to be as cautious as possible while scouting, and then throw caution to the winds and go like hell till you hit your next cover. A peep's a pretty hard target to hit anyway, particularly if it's going fast. You've got to have some sixth sense, however, and judge when you should take a risk and when you shouldn't, which is solely a matter of instinct.

It's quite a feeling of responsibility to realize that one mistake on your part can cause the whole scout section to be wiped out, but at least you have the comfort of knowing that you're leading off and that they can probably get out if there is a trap ahead.

Well, I shall continue later.

*　　*　　*

I have a little spare time before going on patrol so will try and continue, though it won't be too lucid an account as there's a hell of a racket going on in the CP and I will doubtless get some assignment any moment.

D Day plus 7: My notes read as follows: Message from Company: "Send out patrol to contact enemy." (The patrols, as you must have realized by now, are always the peep section!) Am running platoon as platoon leader called back to CP . . . Move platoon north of —— so as to keep radio contact with patrol . . . Am just moving out with patrol when radio message comes in: "Return with platoon to assembly area immediately." Try to get permission to let patrol go on its way, but permission not forthcoming. Return reluctantly about two P.M. . . . Find whole company is moving into other area, where

147

we are to take part in a big offensive sweep . . . swell . . . long trip in column. Bed down about one in new site. . . .

D Day plus 8: Maintenance vehicles and weapons in A.M.—Ready to move by two. Actually move at about seven and hit new bivouac spot about ten . . . "The real thing at last," the Captain tells us. The offensive starts at five in the morning. We pull out at about two to contact the infantry forward patrols and then push on.

D Day plus 9: No sleep at all. Have to get maps organized, everything planned, in total blackout. Pull out at two. Contact last friendly patrols 4 A.M. and at five push forward. Am "especially watchful," as they say, for mines, so we move slowly, but patrols have already been on roads so we aren't overcautious. Receive a terrific reception at 7 A.M. in a small mountain town. Entire population out clapping, cheering, throwing fruit in cars—whole town bedecked with white sheets. A queer race these Italians. You'd think we were their deliverers instead of their captors. Capture first town with help of 3rd platoon about two hours later. A little desultory shooting—one short burst from my Vickers and a couple of shots from the 37 and the village gives up. My peep first vehicle to enter town . . . Round up about 75 prisoners. Italians can't wait to be captured. If you don't pick them up, they run after you begging you to take them along. Humiliating really, as they don't even put up a semblance of a fight. . . . Peeps go out on reconnaissance of byways, etc., while rest of platoon rests—a common occurrence! One shot fired at us by a sniper —everyone else in ecstasies as we approach . . . It is war à la musical comedy. That's the best you can say.

D Day plus 10: Move forward early as platoon. My peep and one other on flank reconnaissance.

Capture town of ———————— high in the mountains at 8 A.M. Mayor formally surrenders town to me and is most disappointed to discover I have no intention of staying to take over. Populace almost mobs my car—have to wave machine gun around to clear space to get out . . . Really, what *is* this? Two peeps with six men take a town that could have held out for three days against our whole company . . . Obviously, they're not holding out . . . Rejoin platoon and sweep through two more towns, encountering no resistance . . . Set off on

148

flanking mission to reconnoiter another mountain town and discover an Italian machine gun nest . . . Go back to platoon and get reinforcements—throw 3 mortar shells short of position—out comes the white flag! Capture 28 prisoners, 8 machine guns—push on up the mountain with 3 peeps and a scout car and take town of ————————, right on peak of mountain, at 6 P.M. Get 25 more prisoners and set them to work clearing TNT from a road block—enough TNT to blow up the whole mountain top. Italians very reluctant to do this work— "very dangerous," they say. All the better. Mayor presents us with a large flagon of wine and we guard road block and have supper. Get orders to stay there until relieved, so bed down. Set guard over prisoners and road block. At midnight, Mayor and Chief of Police arrive very agitated . . . Civilians are threatening to storm monastery to get shoes and I have taken the police's only pistol . . . I give it back and we go out and quiet things down . . . At two get orders to pull out, so have to leave prisoners. Won't they be disappointed when they wake up and find their guards gone?

The odd part of it is, they will be. . . .

*   *   *

I have been writing of my combat "experiences"—few and far between as they have been—in as much detail as censorship regulations permitted, because (a) I thought you would be interested to hear of them, and (b) I thought they would interest *me* to look over them later on. It has just occurred to me, however, that it might possibly be a source of worry to you to discover that we did have occasional close shaves, and I wondered if I might have done better to play down any such occurrences, few and far between as *they* have been. . . . I know you are sensible enough, however, not to worry about something that is over and done with. As to the future, well, that's in the lap of the gods, as you know as well as I do. So I shall continue what I fear is a pretty uninspired bit of reporting by describing D day Plus 12 — July 22nd — which was our last day in combat.

Our little war up to this point was almost pure musical comedy, as you can tell for yourself by reading the preceding letters. We met no

149

real resistance anywhere. In fact I only fired one burst of about ten shots from my Vickers machine gun during the whole time. Of course, being out in the front, we could never tell when we'd run into the Germans or, *mirabile dictu,* an Italian force that would be willing to fight for even three minutes. We had to assume all the time that a real enemy lay in wait ahead, though it was hard to do so when the Italian soldiers, if you can dignify them by the name, would pour out of every building and machine gun nest urging us to take them prisoner. In one instance some Italians even telephoned to us from a town ten miles ahead of where we were, imploring us to come and get them.

SICILY, AUGUST 3, 1943

Here is the last, and final, installment of the Sicilian chronicle: It is entitled: D Day plus 12. Time: 00.05: I had just got my scout section bedded down—we had been off on a scouting jaunt through a range of high hill tops overlooking the company bivouac site—and was eating a can of meat and beans when I discovered, to my fury, that my own peep, which I'd left behind to have some maintenance work done on, had been sent back to B'n to guide the gas truck to where we were. All my stuff was in the car, except for my bedding roll, and I had a hunch, which proved correct, that the peep would never get back in time to take off with us the next morning. I took out my rage on my meat and beans, which made them extremely unpalatable, and lay down in what seemed like a rock pile for a little sleep. I was so angry I couldn't sleep (you can't imagine how infuriated a little thing like that can make you), which didn't matter much as all the officers were assembled shortly and told to be ready to roll at 4 A.M. for the big drive on —————————*. Our platoon was leading the Division down one route, the 3rd was taking part of the Division down another and the 2nd was in reserve.

Well, all my maps were in my peep and worse still, the peep itself was gone. I rearranged the section, took another peep for myself and was still thoroughly annoyed when the time came to move out,

*Palermo.

after a nice cold breakfast of, could you guess, meat and beans.

I led off the column in my bastard peep and we soon got orders to keep pushing on at about 15 to 25 miles per hour, so there really wasn't time to do any reconnaissance. I sat on the hood of the peep to watch the road for mines and we charged forward. Due to not having the right maps, I led the column on a wrong road, which made for a good deal of ill-natured confusion, but we finally caught up on our time schedule and by 9:30 A.M. had entered the village of ———————. There we ran into a lot of prisoners, who begged us to take them in tow, but we didn't have time to bother with them, so I threw their guns into our peep and was about to push on when one of them told me to be careful going up the next pass—that there were mines and a gun position. I passed the word back but orders were to push ahead on schedule, so on we went. The platoon leader got into my peep and we started down the valley towards the pass. It was a perfect spot for the defenders to hold; the road rose in a series of hairpin turns to a narrow pass in the cliffs. A gun at the top could command (as, indeed, it did) the whole valley and all the corners where the road circled up to the defile.

Obviously, it was suicidal to move a whole column up the road without scouting each corner and going by "bounds" (leapfrogging your cars from one point of cover to the next.) But the orders were explicit to push on without any halts. So onward and upward we went.

As we had been warned about mines, I told the platoon leader that I would concentrate on the road from my position just athwart the bumper and let him search for the gun. We pulled a scout car in behind us to give us a little more firing power cover. And started the ascent.

Reconnaissance by fire, we decided, was about the only type we would have time to do—that was to shoot at random to the head of the road when we neared the top and see if there was any answering fire.

We ran smack into the mine field just around the next to the last corner. The road was all dug up in small round craters and the mines were all stacked along the side of the road waiting to be laid. Next to the mines were a group of some 30 Italian soldiers who were obviously there to lay the mines. Although they could easily have wiped us out had they chosen to fire as we came round the corner, they promptly threw up their hands, and threw down their weapons.

It was difficult to know what to do. We were in the direct line of fire of anything at the top of the hill, so I didn't want to stay there. Yet I didn't like to have them loose. I finally shooed them up the hill on the double and raced the car about 100 yards ahead to where there was a bank which gave it some cover. The soldiers themselves had indicated that there was something ahead, so now was the time for reconnaissance by fire, if ever.

We got out of the car and scouted the position, lying on our stomachs back of the protecting bank. I spotted two soldiers at the head of the pass running back. And we opened fire on them with our rifles. Simultaneously the two machine guns on the scout car which was covering us from the corner behind opened fire.

Everything happened very quickly now. There was a roar from the head of the defile—a flash of flame—as a heavy gun fired. We ducked behind the bank. There was another roar and a crash and I looked behind me to see the scout car a mass of flames and thick black smoke.

The platoon leader and one of the men went quickly up to the bank to our right. I had my driver pull the peep forward to where there was more cover—put him behind the machine-gun but told him not to fire, as I didn't want to draw fire on the car—and went up to the crook of the corner myself with my corporal.

Our own 75's opened fire just now, the shells bursting, so it seemed, right next to us, though, actually they were a good fifty yards away. A bullet zinged down at us from the hill to our right and we saw some of the Italians we had shooed up there taking pot shots at us. We got under partial cover and raked the hill with rifle and carbine fire and the Italians beat it for dear life.

We saw a soldier on the opposite hill across the ravine, so the corporal took one side and I took the other and we fired intermittent bursts. Our own guns were pounding the gun position now at what seemed like every few seconds, making a terrific roaring sound that

reverberated through the pass. There was nothing but a thick column of oily smoke to show where the scout car had been and the road behind us was effectively blocked until the flames from the car died down. The ammunition loaded in the car now started to go off, cracking away like fire-works and every now and then making a sudden boom.

The Italians on our right flank had meanwhile all disappeared over the hill. I don't know whether we actually winged any or not. But I didn't see any of them fall. The left flank, across the ravine, was quiet, too.

We couldn't go forward, as we would run smack into our own artillery. We couldn't go back, as the road, for one thing, was blocked. And, even if we could have, nothing would have been gained. So we sat down on the bank and had a cigarette.

There was no way for us to communicate with the column as we had no radio, so we couldn't tell when our own fire was going to be lifted. There was nothing to do but wait and hope our 75 gunners didn't get their sights a fraction of a mill in the wrong direction and crack down into our little nook.

As soon as five minutes had elapsed without hearing our own fire, I decided that we should reconnoitre round the corner. Meanwhile we investigated a little wayside shrine at the corner and then just sat down and relaxed, if you can call it relaxing under such circumstances!

I learned later that one of our car crews planned to spray the entire area we were in with mortar fire. Fortunately the mortar, when they got it set up, wouldn't function.

It's luck, pure and simple, this game. There's no other way you can look at it. . . .

It seemed like hours, before the uproar quieted down. Actually, I don't believe it was more than fifty minutes. After about four minutes silence, we were just about to start up to the gun position when two Lieutenants from our company came up the road marching a group of Italian prisoners ahead.

All the men had jumped from the scout car in time they told us, which was a great relief. The fire had died down enough for them

153

to get by. With the Italians in the lead, two of them crying hysterically like snivelling babies, we went up to the gun. Two of the Italians were killed on the gun. The rest had fled.

The dead soldiers looked so incredibly like bad stage props that it was hard to believe they were really bodies. We got their papers, a gun, some field glasses and a watch, investigated two other guns which had never even been fired and their sleeping quarters. Then we started on a slow foot reconnaissance up the defile. The prisoners warned us there was a German gun position at the other end of the defile, so we went ahead very cautiously for about an eighth of a mile.

One of the Lieutenants suggested that we were getting in a rather badly extended position as, indeed, we were, so I told them to leave me and the corporal on guard where we were and go back with the prisoners and send up about twenty foot scouts. If we fired, I told him, send reinforcements "on the double."

The corporal was a wonderful man in a crisis, just as calm as if we had been on maneuvers or on a picnic. We climbed up a cliff on one side but could not see to the end of the defile. Just then a couple of enemy planes went by, so we flattened ourselves against the rocks and remained motionless. Then we sat and waited.

In about 15 minutes the foot scouts arrived and we started up the defile. About 100 yards on we spotted an Italian soldier, waving frantically from a position on the road about 200 yards across a defile to the right. We couldn't tell whether he was signalling to us or to some other soldiers round the corner, so we dropped behind the low wall which edged the road and opened fire on him. He too disappeared and that was the last we saw of him.

One of the scouts then called out that he had spotted the German gun. "Watch my dust," he said and fired up the valley. I couldn't see any gun through my glasses but we fired several shots in that general direction and then: Bang! A shell exploded on the cliff a few yards beneath where we were lying, fragments of dust and rock particles shooting round us.

If it took two seconds for those 20 men to get out of that spot and back to the road to where a friendly cliff gave us cover, I should be amazed. It was all one simultaneous motion with the crash of the 88

154

shell—all of us running at a low crouch, which really didn't do us any good as the wall was only knee high. But you somehow felt that it did do good. However, there wasn't a man in the exposed position when the next shell cannoned over and crashed behind us.

Just as we were catching our breaths and wise cracking about how undignified our retreat was, a machine gun gave a quick burst from our rear, one of the shells zinging into the dust not six inches from my foot. This time we really did dive for a cleft in the cliffs to one side, as we thought we were surrounded. (This was the time one of my sergeants went so fast, he ran right up my back!!)

We couldn't figure where the machine gun position could be, but we found out soon enough when a sheepish American soldier peered round the declivity where we were all flattened out and said his machine gun had gone off by accident when he was trying to dismount it from his peep. He hoped no one had been hit.

No one had, by the grace of God.

A Captain came up now with a mortar in his peep and the young private who had said "watch my dust" volunteered to climb the cliff and point out the position of the 88 for the mortar crew to fire.

"We'll knock out that son of a bitch," he said enthusiastically. "I know we can."

I wish I could report that he had been successful, but the mortar fell short and the man in his enthusiasm exposed himself too prominently on the cliffs. He was blown literally to bits by the next shot from the mortar. I climbed up with a sergeant to try and find some identifying marks, but it wasn't any use.

Just after this, all personnel from the 82nd were ordered back. I made a brief report of the situation to the General and we found the rest of the company drawn off the road at the foot of the valley.

It was only about 1:00 P.M., though it seemed much later, and I realized that I was pretty tired, as I hadn't had any sleep the night before. So after reporting in to the Colonel and the Captain, I lay down in the shade of a peachtree and fell sound asleep.

The platoon leader, I discovered, when I was waked up at about two, had been hit by shrapnel exploding from the scout car and had gone back to the hospital. We were pushing on now (the gun had

155

finally been knocked out by the infantry) with our platoon in reserve and with the 2nd platoon leading.

We retraversed the pass, and all went well until we were almost down the mountain on the other side. Then, bing—we ran into more artillery. As our platoon was back of the 2nd, there was nothing for us to do but to pull the cars into cover and await events.

There were about three or four enemy guns and they hammered away in front of us and over our heads. A half track just in front of us caught fire and started to spray about 200 rounds of 37mm shells all round us—to add to the general confusion—but we sat against a protecting cliff in safety.

Oddly enough, while I didn't mind the morning fire at all, I disliked this, which was far less dangerous, intensely. It all goes to show that there is no rhyme or reason in one's reactions. I think they're purely chemical!

Well, the artillery eventually knocked out the enemy guns and we pushed on again in what turned out to be a triumphal tour through the outskirts of the city—women crying, embracing us, throwing flowers, fruit, etc.

We finally stopped at about 9:00 P.M. just on the city limits, had some more C rations, watched the big shot* push into town for the official surrender and then bedded down right on the sidewalk where we were to fall into a profound slumber.

So much—too much—for D Day plus 12.

SICILY, AUGUST 4, 1943

Had to lay off a few days, as I had to go out on some very dreary but very long patrols and haven't been able to get to a piece of paper since.

Incidentally, we had a whiz of an air raid last night, or rather at 4 A.M., the noisiest damn one I have been in. (We are now in a new locality, by the way.) I had, I am ashamed to confess, a wonderful time, as I beat it out and grabbed one of the unmanned 50 caliber machine guns on a car, and pounded away into the sky for dear life.

*General George Patton.

156

I doubt if I did the slightest good, but I shot about a thousand rounds of lead up in the direction of the Jerries and hope I, at least, singed one of their wings. A couple of men were injured slightly by falling shrapnel, but otherwise, no harm was done in our area.

I am so damn busy patrolling various areas (out every eight hours, on a four hours on and four hours off basis) that God knows when I'll ever get a chance to finish this! I'd better send this off, anyway. For heaven's sake do not worry about me. We haven't been in combat for over 10 days now and won't be again, I fear, for months!

SICILY, AUGUST 4, 1943

This is another attempt to start, or rather to continue, the Sicilian chronicle. But I think it's doomed to be abortive, as I have to go on patrol in a couple of hours. I also have to pack up all my junk—junk is no exaggeration—as we are making a short move. So I fear I won't get very far.

Had another air raid at four this morning; that seems to be the Jerries' regular hour for dropping their calling cards. Rather a wash-out this one, though one of our patrols on guard out of town had a narrow escape when a bomb destroyed all their rations and equipment. A good deal of our own shrapnel dropped around our area but that, I'm glad to say, was all. I didn't do any firing this time as, for one good reason, the gun jammed and wouldn't fire! Also there were no planes in range.

I suspect these raids are largely of the nuisance variety, simply calculated to make us lose sleep, as a lone plane returned about six and the uproar started all over again, making sleep impossible. Damn them anyway! That's carrying things a bit far, don't you think?

Speaking of bombing, part of the town of Palermo, which we passed through two weeks ago, is a shambles. The waterfront area is just a mass, or rather a mess, of rubble, and the whole downtown section is filled with craters and destroyed buildings.

If the other German and Italian cities fare in like fashion, and I have every reason to believe that they will, or already have been

157

worse hit, there won't be much of them left to salvage. Which will be all to the good! Though I hope for sentimental reasons we don't hit Venice or too much of Rome.

Today is the first time I have had a chance to relax and take things easy since we got on the boat to make the invasion. I am keeping my fingers crossed as, at any moment, I may get some assignment; but officially I have no duty until I go on patrol at 4 P.M. tomorrow, which is a glorious feeling. I was getting so wound up that I just kept going like an automaton, but this patrolling keeps you almost as busy, as far as hours are concerned, as combat and it is fifty times more boring. . . . Actually we haven't been in combat since July 23rd, so we have had our fill of policing and acting as M.P.'s, which I regret to state is just what we have been doing. At present we are quartered in an Italian garrison—"somewhere in Sicily"—and live in some barracks once used by Il Duce's heroic warriors. The plumbing is bad—that goes without saying—but at least there is running water, so we can take showers for the first time in God knows how long.

The mail started coming in three days ago and I did nobly, getting about 22 letters, the latest being yours dated July 14th.

I had to laugh, as the first letters I opened were two of yours in which you expressed your deep concern about my having left my winter overcoat and warm things in Africa!! This just after escaping unscathed from the fire of German 88's, 75's and the rest of their warlike projectiles!

Don't worry about my not being warm enough when the time comes to get back into winter things. Either my overcoat will catch up with me, or I'll be issued another. If I'm not, I'll steal one, if I have to kill a German to do so. But I won't be cold, I can assure you.

I went to bed at 7 o'clock last night and slept without stirring until seven this morning—the first uninterrupted sleep in a month and one of the pleasantest I have ever had—even though it was on the floor and the flies were so thick you could eat them if you opened your

158

mouth. I feel like a million dollars this morning and am all ready to start in all over again, though I fear we'll probably be here for months, by the look of things.

It is amazing, really, how little rest a human being needs, if he's got something really important to do. The Captain figured out that he'd only had six hours sleep in the six days that constituted our big offensive, so called, and none of the officers got more than two to four hours sleep a day, if that. Of course, you can't keep up indefinitely on such a schedule, but as long as the work's interesting and exciting enough, you can keep going. I confess I found myself nodding occasionally on some of the recent routine patrols of the countryside. But in combat I was always wide awake.

It's probably got something to do with glands! When you're under pressure, your system probably fills you up with adrenalin.

Speaking of glands, the only physical reaction I've noticed to being under gunfire and under real pressure in combat conditions is that your mouth tends to dry up after a time and your voice sounds (as *you* hear it), a little hoarse. But that may be purely a personal eccentricity! And chewing gum is the perfect antidote to that.

As to fear, as I wrote you before, you really haven't time to think about being scared for the most part. It's foolish to pretend that you're never scared, because, of course, you are; but there seems to be little rhyme or reason to account for why you are scared one moment and not the next. Air raids, for instance, don't frighten me at all. I suspect that's because they're such a marvellous show that you're too excited watching them to think about anything else. I wasn't the least bit scared, either, on the occasion, described earlier, when my car was trapped in a curve at the head of the mountain pass with an Italian-75 fifty yards round the hairpin turn firing away at the rest of our column and our own artillery blasting away at the Italian gun—though actually that was one of the tightest spots I was in and we didn't have the faintest idea how large an enemy force was round the corner. My corporal and I, as I wrote, were shooting at snipers on the hills on both sides of us and our own 75's were blasting away at the gun just a few yards from us and might at any minute hit the spot we were in. Yet, an hour or so later, after the gun position had been "silenced," and we scouted forward on foot, I found I was scared as hell to poke into that camouflaged blackout tent and see what, if anything, was within. I knew damn well there wasn't anything alive, but it was still scary lifting the flap and peering into the gloom.

It doesn't make much sense, does it?!!

SICILY, AUGUST 6, 1943

Delighted to hear Grenny* was made a 1st Lieutenant. As far as I am concerned, I told you when I came here that this was the end of promotion for me and I meant it. You don't get promoted in combat units, only in staff. If I were to be promoted now, which God forbid, it would mean I'd have to be taken out of my company and put into B'n Headquarters, which I'd *loathe!* The highest rank you can be in a combat unit and still be in actual combat is a Captain, and then you have a whole company; and a Captain in a combat unit is about the equal of a full Colonel in Washington or even, if you take the Air Corps, a Brigadier General! I am happy as a clam right where I am and I expect to be discharged from the Army a First Lieutenant and to be proud of it. I think I am going to be given the whole platoon instead of just the scout section, at least that's what the Captain tells me is in the wind. I'll like that, because I'll then be sole boss of the platoon. But aside from that step up the ladder, that's as far as I want to go, at least until the fighting is over.

Chauncey† was perfectly right when he said that the Army wanted the younger men for combat jobs and that my age was slated for staff work and staff work only. Well, I succeeded in putting back the clock by some miracle, but I can't have my cake and eat it, too. You may quarrel with the whole system and say that staff gets much too much rank, and there I'll be inclined to agreed with you. But I wouldn't exchange my present job for all the rank in the world. So pray don't be disappointed that I'm still a 1st Lieutenant when you see me next.

*Grenville T. Emmet, Jr.
†Colonel Chauncey G. Parker.

It is now pouring cats and dogs and a series of drops are falling right on my bed at a point where I, stupidly enough, stuck a safety pin through the tent to hold up my mosquito bar. The tent Frank Jordan and I rigged up for ourselves is one of the most unorthodox you have ever seen. It consists of one kitchen fly over our heads rigged up on trees, with ropes and but one pole to support it. The sides are composed of three American shelter halfs, one German shelter half and one Italian radio tent. What the Colonel will say when he sees it, I shudder to think, as he is a stickler for things to be done in the orthodox GI manner. However, we are extremely comfortable and have a very congenial time.

We took a five mile hike in the rain this A.M. and tomorrow we are going to do the same (I assume it will still be raining) with full packs. It's high time we got into condition again!

Well, it is now pitch dark and it is almost impossible to write.

SICILY, AUGUST 10, 1943

Your letter of July 24th, V mail, received last night—fairly quick time, considering everything. I was interested to hear that you knew already in the States that our Division was in the fight, although actually our combat period ended July 22nd in the Palermo sector, where we turned, alas, from soldiers into policemen. It is quite an anti-climax, this damn patrolling, but I suppose someone has to do it, so why not us! We live in some Italian barracks and a picture of the Queen of Italy stares down at me every time I eat. The plumbing, needless to state, is atrocious, and the flies are even worse. Otherwise, we are quite comfortable and life is more boring than arduous.

SICILY, AUGUST 11, 1943

Everything has been very quiet and uneventful in this vicinity the past few days, not even an air raid—at least not one that woke me up—for the past five nights. We had an alert last night while I was on the night patrol, but it fizzled out just after I had found myself a beautiful grandstand seat on a high pedestal beneath a statue symbolizing, I believe, Italian strength and solidarity. It being a so-called cultural monument (God knows why, since it is perfectly hideous), I figured it was a fairly safe spot and the stone pedestal afforded a good protection from our own shrapnel. I also had a view of the whole city. But, as I said, nothing happened, somewhat, I rather ignobly confess, to my disappointment.

We live, as I told you, in some former Italian barracks, stylishly in one respect, as we have a floor under our feet, beds with actual springs, and we have showers and running water. But I think I would rather be out in some olive grove. Certainly, the flies would be better, though we are gradually getting the windows screened in with cheesecloth.

Sicily is much better than Africa, though, oddly enough, it is a good deal hotter. Life has about returned to normal in the district we are in, except for the bomb damage, which is very great in the towns. One city is hardly more than a shell in at least half its area, but life still seems to function pretty normally. The city is plastered with blue arrows, which seem to be always pointing round the corner, labelled *Recovero*. I thought at first, they were proclaiming, à la President Hoover, that recovery was just around the corner, but discovered shortly that they were pointing to air raid shelters, of which there are literally hundreds.

SICILY, AUGUST 12, 1943

Got a telephone message yesterday when I came in from patrol to call a Captain Coffin at Cedar 222. I did so and learned that Cabot* had whizzed through town in the morning on the way to the front and was expected back here this afternoon. I can't wait to see him and to hear all the home news.

I got a call from an unknown colonel at 3:30 telling me to be at the Royal Palace at 4:20 where Cabot would see me. It was more royal than royalty—not 4:15 or 4:30, but 4:20 exactly. I got to the big shot's

*Senator H. C. Lodge, Jr.

162

quarters at 4:20 precisely and found, to my relief, that no one was there and that Cabot was expected any moment. Actually, he came in at about 5:30, having flown back from the front that afternoon. Meanwhile a captain, who was aide to one of the numerous generals here, had arrived to take Cabot out to dine with the General, and an Air Corps colonel arrived who thought he was flying him back to Tunis that evening. Cabot arrived alone, in uniform, and promptly got rid of everyone, deciding he would go out to the General's, and we had a delightful half hour's chat. Then the big shot* strolled in, much to my discomfiture. I shook hands and he went out with Cabot to see about his sleeping quarters. Then he came back and told me he had been a great friend of Father's at Chaumont and said he was really very glad to see me. He asked me particularly to remember him to you and to tell you how much he admired Father and how fond he was of him. He was much quieter in manner than I had expected from what I had heard—had none of the "blood and guts" manner the newspapers always associate with him and he couldn't have been nicer.

Cabot said he would cable you that he had seen me, as soon as he reached Cairo. He has a fascinating round the world trip ahead of him and I envy him. Will you tell Emily I saw him and that he was in fine form? He is a real friend, I must say, to have taken all the trouble that he did.

SICILY, AUGUST 12, 1943. LATER

I had an amusing, though slightly exhausting and anti-climactic experience last night, when I spent the night in the shell that once housed the Fascist Party Hq. here, in the hope of trapping a spy who was reputed to be giving light signals to enemy planes from the place. Lieut. Jordan, who is from Virginia and whom I like very much, decided to go with me and we each took two men. We sneaked into the house individually, set up our headquarters in a room, the floor of which was littered with Fascist propaganda and broken glass, set a guard on the stairs and proceeded to wait. Fortunately, we had

*General George Patton.

had the sense to bring some ice and vino, so the time passed fairly pleasantly, with the conversation centering chiefly on combat experiences. The spy, alack, never turned up. I was hoping he'd have the sense to come in when I was taking the guard shift and I was all prepared to shoot him dead without any questions being asked! We returned to our headquarters at 6 A.M., slightly rheumatic from sleeping on Fascist pamphlets, but otherwise none the worse for wear.

SICILY, AUGUST 17, 1943

I went on a fascinating two-day jaunt the other day with Frank Jordan and just got back at 1 A.M. this morning. We decided we were both getting tired of sitting around and acting as MP's and that we'd like to get at least a look-in on any fighting in the east. We fixed our guard schedules so as to give us the requisite time off and hot footed it in a peep up the coast bright and early one morning. As bad luck would have it, the fighting, except for a little intermittent shelling across the Messina Channel, ended the evening before we set out; but it was still a most interesting trip, though it made us both feel rather like quartermaster officers to wait until the day the fighting ceased, to appear on the front, particularly as we took enough arms and ammunition with us to blast out a whole Jerry platoon, if not a company.

As we neared the eastern shore the wreckage of the recent battle was strewn all around us, including a lot of bodies that filled the air with that peculiarly unpleasant and unique sweet odor. The Germans had blown every bridge along the road, so the going was not very fast, but we finally, at about 12.30, reached the summit of the mountain range overlooking the town of Messina and saw across the channel of silvery blue water the toe of the Italian boot—so close, it seemed as if you could throw a rock at it.

We had heard over the radio the night before that advance elements had entered Messina that day, so we expected to find the place full of troops. Instead, as we finally wound our way down into the suburbs, we found it a city of the dead. Not a soul was stirring anywhere; the reason why was soon obvious. There wasn't anybody there. The

164

entire city—population of about 75,000, I should imagine—had been literally wiped out. Three quarters of the buildings, at least, I should say, were totally demolished—the remainder were just hollow shells, and this went for the *whole* city including the suburbs, not just the dock area as at Palermo. It was a sight I shall never forget—tragic, if you will, but at the same time extraordinarily encouraging. For it made one see what havoc must be being wrought in Germany where much heavier explosives are being used. We wound our way down carefully through the littered streets, watching for shell holes, mines or booby traps, expecting at any minute to run into troops or some civilians. But we got all the way down to the dock area, which was an indescribable mass of debris and hollow-shelled Renaissance-type buildings, before we saw a soul—a Canadian soldier who told us that at least part of a brewery had not been destroyed and that ice cold beer could be obtained in the cellar.

This required immediate investigation! Finally we located the Birra Messina brewery and drove into a courtyard filled with wreckage. A couple of our own G. I.'s and two British soldiers were there and we crawled down a narrow staircase into the total darkness of the cellar (where Jordan almost fell into an open vat of beer) till we discovered the ice cold vat. We filled our five gallon water can and then came up and had lunch of beer and German cheese (the latter captured from the enemy and issued to us) and washed some of the dirt from our faces. There was a dead body not far off in the brewery offices, as you could tell all too easily; but we'd become accustomed to the stench by then and so we didn't move off but just parked in a shady spot in the courtyard and had our lunch. The beer wasn't good but it was beer and that was all we asked for at that time.

After lunch we went on a tour of the city; we'd already found out from the British that all fighting had ceased even to the south and that the majority of the Germans had escaped across the Straits, so there wasn't the same pressing hurry to join up with the 8th Army. We drove out onto the mole which goes three-fourths of the way around the harbor, picking our way gingerly, as you never can be too careful after the Germans have evacuated a place. We looked through a couple of barracks, hoping to find some German pistols; but without success, and then decided it might be interesting to climb the light-house and look at Italy through our own field glasses. The light-house, extraordinarily enough, was practically intact and we inched our way up the stairs, watching for booby traps, wires and the like and then got out onto the balcony on top—no loot (like telescopes, etc.) but a fine view.

When we got into the car, Jordan suddenly started to scratch and I noticed that his neck was literally black with fleas. We stripped promptly and found that our clothes were full of them, right down to our boots and we spent the next half hour picking them out. It didn't do too much good, as the sand was full of them, and they'd hop right back up, but we had to do something. Then, regardless of the 88's across the Straits or of possible mines in the water, we plunged into the sea to drown such of the verminous creatures as still re-mained on our persons. Then back through the ghost city to go down the coast and join the 8th army, coming up (so we planned) around the foot of Mount Etna and spending the night at Taormina, which I'd heard was attractive. About eight miles down the coast we ran into a small detachment of the 8th Army which had made an amphib-ious landing the day before, but the road was insuperably blocked below them. One whole side of a cliff had been blown up so we had to retrace our steps back across the mountain and then cut down towards Mount Etna on another road.

Just as we were leaving the town, which was now completely de-serted, we ran into a British RAF truck and an officer stopped us and asked us if we knew what hotel they could put up at! We told him the only place we knew that even had a cellar intact still was the brewery, upon which there was a wild shout from everyone at the mention of the word beer, so we retraced our steps to lead them to the place and then sat around and chewed the rag with the RAF officer, a very amusing fellow, until 11 when we once again went up the mountain top, in blackout, and there bedded down with a cannon company.

I read the story of the fall of Messina in a newspaper last night and never did I read so many lies and discrepancies. In fact, the more I see of newspaper and magazine articles on battles of which I personally know something at first hand, the less I think of them. Another article on Palermo was false in every detail; at least every one in which I was on hand. As for Messina, it spoke about the throngs in the streets, the welcoming populace, when I doubt if there were more than twelve people in the whole town, including Jordan and myself and a couple of other soldiers. It mentioned the blistering shellfire from across the Straits, which scattered shrapnel among the vast crowds—all a pure fabrication. The shellfire was so intense that we went swimming in the direct view of the enemy and never even drew a shot! I doubt strongly if more than one shell fell every hour, certainly not more than every half hour. The trouble is that the average newspaperman thinks he has to make a good story, full of emotional excitement. It's unfortunate, but I don't know what can be done about it, and the public seems to eat it up.

Well, I have no news and have to go to B'n shortly for a formal dinner which promises to be deadly in the extreme.

SICILY, AUGUST 23, 1943

I'm afraid I have to break the news to you that I have been awarded the Silver Star,* as the enclosed order will show you. There is a good deal of bunk about my "coolness," as I was far from cool when I dashed away from the 88 or from our own machine gun fire! However, I suppose they have to exaggerate these little tales. Actually, I don't know who put in the recommendation, as it came as a complete and startling surprise to me. It probably was the Captain, though I'm not sure.

The first I heard of it was when I got word to report in person to the Colonel with the Captain and a sergeant of our platoon. I thought over all my sins, my most recent one being the trip, without any

*See Appendix, page 238.

official permission, to Messina. But, lo and behold, the Colonel was all smiles and handed us, the sergeant and myself, the medal and the ribbon. He said we'd have to give it back later for a formal presentation in front of the whole battalion; that sounds *ghastly*, doesn't it? but he wanted us to have it now so that we could wear the ribbon. Needless to say, I haven't yet availed myself of that privilege! But I will, when as and if we ever have occasion to wear a blouse.

Although I rather deprecate the awarding of any medals, as there's so much bickering and hard feeling involved in almost every case, I won't be so hypocritical as to admit I'm not glad I got it, chiefly, really, for your sake, as citations always mean a good deal more to families than to the recipients themselves. It also helps, I feel, completely to vindicate the step I took in transferring from the Air Corps. Lt. Jordan, who is my real sidekick in the company, also received an award, the Oak Leaf Cluster to the Silver Star he'd already got for the North African landing; and I may say he richly deserved it, as his platoon saw a great deal more action than ours and he was always in the lead car.

Please, if you do show this order to anyone, tell them from me that it is a highly colored version of what actually occurred!

Well, so much for that. . . .

I went to hear a speech today by the big shot who knew Father. He is an excellent speaker, very dramatic, almost melodramatic, and he ended his peroration by saying that he loved every bone in every head of every man in the 2nd Armored Division! Quite an order, what!

SICILY, AUGUST 29, 1943

Lt. Jordan and I have taken an apartment together, so when we are not on duty we can go there, which is pleasant. I wrote Margey to tell you that you absolutely must not worry about me. For one thing I fear (though God knows I don't know a thing) that it may be months before we see any action again. Remember one thing, also, that I enjoy what I am doing, and particularly the combat element of it, so don't ever think that I am going through hell!

168

We had our first rain today—a humdinger of a downpour—which practically flooded the town. Thank goodness, if the rainy season is about to start, that we are living in barracks.

SICILY, SEPTEMBER 5, 1943

Today, being Sunday, the captain decided that perhaps we should have a church service, as we haven't had one for several months. So we borrowed a chaplain from some outfit, whom he knew, and had him come over. We corraled as many men as we could into the mess hall, lined up the piano which I, in turn, had "borrowed," to put it politely, from Fascist Party Headquarters and I took my accustomed place as organist.

The chaplain was late in arriving, so we had a preliminary sing song, which could hardly have been called religious in character. The chaplain arrived as we were all singing lustily "My Wild Irish Rose"; and when the chorus had ceased we picked the hymns—you can probably guess them—and then he asked me to play a prelude. The most appropriate thing I could think of was my own master-piece, "Please Don't Say Yes," which I interpolated into "Rock of Ages," and played with due solemnity and downcast eye. It made a very appropriate number to set the mood. We then had "My Coun-try 'Tis of Thee," "Onward Christian Soldiers" and ended up with (the chaplain's choice) "He Leadeth Me." I managed, I think, to infuse my usual organic rhythm into each hymn and the service went off very well—a nice sermon, short, in which we were exhorted to live up to the Ten Commandments—always a safe exhortation and one impossible of attainment—and a few prayers. I noticed, in the Army Edition of the creed, that they have changed "Holy Catholic Church" to read "Holy Christian Church"—a wise precaution, I imagine, since otherwise they might be accused of proselyting for the Catholic Church. And that would *never* do!

Speaking of the Catholic Church, I was quite interested to read in *Time* of the reaction to the bombing of Rome. I was glad to see that the Commonweal and several other important Catholic leaders showed some intelligent understanding of the problem. There is no

169

more reason in the world why Rome should be spared than Messina, London, Rotterdam or any of the thousand towns and villages which have been bombed.

The two pencils arrived—the first real gift I have received from the States (I don't class Ephedrine Nasal Jelly as a gift)! and they were most welcome, just what I wanted. I am now looking forward expectantly to the arrival of my camera and am only scared that it may be stolen en route, cameras are so scarce and so very much in demand.

The news of Italy's surrender reached here at about 7 o'clock last night while I was on patrol in the town. We already had an inkling that something big was afoot. In fact our patrol had been doubled in case there was any double cross or backfire. The news spread like wild fire through the town and soon people were running from door to door yelling *"Finito!"*, waving and cheering at us. The church bells began to peal. Little processions carrying candles started on the back streets and it was our unpleasant duty to curb all the enthusiasm, get all the population back into the houses and get the lights out. Poor simple souls, they couldn't seem to realize that we—and, indirectly, they—were still fighting Germany and that the danger from bombing was greater than ever.

I can't agree with you about this bombing of cities. It's an absolute essential and will save thousands of lives in the long run for every one it kills now. Besides, not many people are killed anyway.

I told you a few days ago of being called out to see the G-2 officer at Division Headquarters. Well, it appears that he had looked through all the classification cards of all the officers in the Division and had decided that I was better qualified than anyone to take over a very important job. With visions of being dropped behind the enemy lines in a parachute, or something of the sort, I beamed all over. In the next breath he told me what the job was—Public Relations Officer for the Division. I was so mad that for one of the few times in my life I didn't care what I said. The fact that he was a Colonel made no more effect on me than if he had been a first class private! I told him I had abhorred public relations work for twenty years in private life and that I despised it even more in Army life! I told him I'd go to the General if all else failed; that I'd go "over the hill" or failing that that I'd just sit at my desk and sulk if he dared to take me out of my present job to put me into public relations!! Having made my position unequivocally clear—to his distinct astonishment—I saluted smartly, turned on my heel, and departed. I then post-hasted it some 35 miles to Battalion Headquarters and saw the Colonel and told him I simply wouldn't take the job. He said he'd fight to retain me and not to worry.

As the G-2 told me I wouldn't have to worry if I didn't hear anything further in three or four days, I am now moderately sure that my vehemence saved the day.

It was a close call, however!

We hope constantly to be on the move but God knows when that great day will dawn, if ever. I'm so scared Germany may sue for peace before we have a chance to take a crack at her on her own soil that I wake up nights in a cold fury.

SICILY, SEPTEMBER 17, 1943

I was glad to hear that my three long letters describing the Sicilian campaign had apparently arrived, though with a considerable gap between letters. Apparently, too, they weren't censored, not that there was anything in them which was censorable; but you are never sure what the censor will let go by when you are discussing battle experiences, if you can call the limited amount of fighting we saw "battle."

What our experiences did teach us were a lot of lessons that will be extremely valuable if we ever get in combat again—all kinds of things that you "left undone" and that you "ought not to have done," and there's really no other way to learn those things except by actual combat experience. Maneuvers help, but there's no umpire in combat to tell you you've won or lost; you either win or lose.

Incidentally, as I wrote to the Lunts, there's more sheer bosh written about what people think and say at the zero hour than you can imagine. Bobby Sherwood's scene, when the scientist and the other soldiers discoursed on life and death just before going out to be killed, made an extremely effective scene in the theatre; but it just couldn't happen in real life, anymore than Maxwell Anderson's battlefield discussions in Bataan could take place. What all these writers overlook is the fact that everyone is either too tired or too busy to think about anything, except the immediate thing they have to do, to indulge themselves in any philosophical ruminations.

Most of your men are sound asleep until the last possible moment. That takes care of their philosophy. When they wake the first thing they think of is getting a C ration, and then they're so busy getting their equipment lined up, their vehicles or weapons tuned up, that they haven't either the time or the inclination to think about life, death, love or the pursuit of happiness. The officers are so damn busy plotting out the details of the campaign, getting their orders straight and arranging their maps, overlays, etc.—plus getting the men up and ready for action, that they certainly haven't an instant to indulge in philosophical flights of fancy as to whether it's all worth it, what they're fighting for, what it all means, etc., etc. Actually, and I really don't mean this flippantly, the only time I said a prayer during the fight was the night before, or rather the early morning of the start of the big push of the 2nd Armored Division.

We didn't get into our bivouac site until about midnight and the officers were immediately called into the Company Commander's blackout tent and told that we had to pull out at four A.M. and given elaborate routes to mark out on the maps for a whole week's operations. Well, we each had about a thousand maps and by about 2:15 A.M. I was still sitting with a shelter half draped over my head, trying to make head or tail of my maps and to find the odd two dozen I needed.

I was practically suffocated from the heat, as the darn shelter half was just draped over my head to black out my flashlight, and was practically out of my head, as I couldn't find the G-d--n maps I needed. I knew, if I didn't find them and locate the route, we were lost. Besides I had to lead off. I knew I wouldn't get any sleep at all—at the most a half hour's rest, as I had to be up at 3 to start the ball rolling. And I was, frankly, frazzled to the point of taking all the maps and just tearing them into small pieces. Finally I collected myself, found the maps, pieced them together (each map only takes you a few miles), and it was then 2:40 A.M. I lay down then on the ground on my shelter half (which had almost driven me insane as a light shield) and just made about a 10 second prayer—thoroughly sincere, I assure you—urging that the half hour's rest would relax me and that I could start out fresh in the morning without making a mess of things! I didn't sleep but I really did rest and got up just after 3, feeling just as wide awake, calm and clear headed as I ever had in my life! Incidentally, I never felt tired at all that entire day, though I didn't hit the ground again until about midnight!

Of course, if it had been the theatre or literature, I'd have sweated out the last half hour wrestling with my soul, thinking of all the possible horrors that lay ahead, wondering if it was worth the candle, deciding, by God, yes—that the fight for men's freedom, etc., etc.—whereas, actually my mind was a total, and very pleasant, blank; and when I did get up I had to curse the hell out of half the platoon to get them on the ball in time to pull out at 4 A.M.

SICILY, SEPTEMBER 17, 1943

Yesterday, Frank Jordan and I went down in the evening to see the Colonel and to put our names down as volunteers to go to the Fifth Army, when, as and if they call for replacements, which they assuredly will do before long. The Colonel gave us a polite but unequivocal "No"; said he wouldn't consider releasing us, that his first loyalty was to the Bn. and to the Division and that he wouldn't consider for a minute letting his best officers (ouch!!) go to other units. He was reassuring on one score, however, in that he didn't think this inaction would continue indefinitely, though he wouldn't give us any hint as to when or where we might get on the move.

There is no news to speak of. I saw Dick Story for a few minutes yesterday and think I am going to have dinner with him tomorrow night. Haven't seen Archie Alexander again yet as really, I've been too busy; well busy isn't exactly the word, but this six hour shift every 24 hours or so keeps you fairly occupied. . . . On the night shift we always used to have air raids or alarms to liven up the dead hours, but during the last month there hasn't been even an alarm. Fortunately my driver is an exceedingly entertaining creature, which helps the hours to pass.

I have just had "stimulating shots," for typhoid, tetanus, small pox and typhus—all in one session,—so if my arm begins to peter out before finishing this letter, you'll know the reason why.

SICILY, SEPTEMBER 25, 1943

Life continues on its safe, sane and humdrum course. I feel I know every stick, stone and bomb crater of the area we patrol. Certainly, few people have ever had occasion to traverse over and over again, daily, for months, the same identical routes in a city! There isn't a back alley, in fact, hardly a room in the bombed out areas, with which I am not familiar, for we conduct occasional raids in an effort to stamp out the migrant women who move from one bombed room to another.

Incidentally, in one of the houses we found a dead horse on the second floor and, on the third, a woman who had better have been dead! Don't ask me how the horse got upstairs. That's as great a mystery as the "where is the Luftwaffe" one.

Ah me! These Sicilians!

I dislike them more every day. But I mustn't shock you with such sentiments. The world knows that the Italians are a cultured, charming and gay race, who have just been led astray by a horrid dictator. If Lieutenant Eustis knows otherwise, it is unquestionably he who is in the wrong.

No other news to speak of. Raids, black markets, riots at bread lines, sorting drunks to the stockade—these are our daily stock in trade. Sordid, but occasionally it has its lighter moments. A baby was all but born in my peep the other night. I, thank God, was not out with that patrol. The brat was born two minutes after they reached the hospital!

174

We had a company party for the enlisted men last Saturday night. Forty odd girls of questionable virtue, a good orchestra, all in all lots of fun and I think they all really enjoyed themselves. I had to help corral the girls and we swamped the town with invitations, written in Italian, addressed to *"Gentile Signorina,"* telling them a truck would pick them up at such and such a time and place. There may have been some small question as to just how *"gentile"* the girls were that accepted, but who cares in that kind of a party. Only two of them had epileptic fits, which I gather was the best record set for any company party in the vicinity!

Afterwards, we, the officers, went on to a party at our Officers' Club —not nearly so much fun, even though the entertainment, provided at the piano by one Lieutenant Eustis, was of the highest calibre.

I had dinner with Frank Jordan and Dick Story last night at the Officers' restaurant in town. Jordan is more like Bobby Bishop than Bobby himself, and so you can imagine that he is a very pleasant companion indeed. He comes from Pulaski, Virginia, just outside of Roanoke, and knows a lot of people that we know in Richmond, Warrenton, etc. Incidentally, he is about as good a soldier as there is in the Army and I have learned a great deal about soldiering, tactics, etc., from him. It makes the greatest difference to have one really close friend in an outfit, as it means you can have a good time together under almost any circumstances. It also means a lot to know that you have the enlisted men of an outfit behind you, as without their cooperation you are lost. And I really think, without in any sense blowing my own trumpet, that the men do like, and what is far more important, respect me. Quite a number of them told me so when they were a bit intoxicated at the company party, but it's more something you can sense and feel.

Actually, in one humble opinion, there's a good deal of plain unadulterated nonsense in the theory, so widely expounded in the

175

officer's guide, that an officer must be so remote from his men and live on another plane from them altogether; otherwise that familiarity will breed contempt. That's all very well in garrison, maybe, but in combat where you live, eat and sleep with the men and are on terms of the most complete intimacy, it all breaks down. And they respect you then, if they do, not because you wear bars but because you can lead them—if you can.

We are still patrolling, patrolling, patrolling! God knows if we will ever fight again.

SICILY, OCTOBER 19, 1943

There is no news that I can think of. We had a party at the Officers' Club last night, given by a former Battalion Commander, which was pretty good fun once the generals had departed! Red Cross girls and nurses, the former much the nicer, I find.

I really wish that you would have a chance to see a really good air raid (provided, of course, you weren't hit!), as it's a sight to remember all your life—one of the most beautiful and exciting shows you can imagine.

The N.C.O.s, not to be outdone by the officers, have formed a club of their own—in a house just near the barracks. They asked Jordan and me to be honorary members and we assented cheerfully. In many ways it is really nicer than our own club, though, of course, we don't hang round there very much.

SICILY, OCTOBER 23, 1943

You may set your mind at rest about the possibility of your son going without Xmas presents this year. For today, exactly one year and three days after it was mailed in Washington, your 1942 Xmas package arrived, containing cigarette cases, poker dice, cigarettes and that invaluable address book. If the next one takes as long to reach its destination, it may have to follow me back home, which would be all right by me. Many thanks to you all for the extremely useful

176

presents and for the Xmas messages you sent. I shall keep the latter
and read them over Xmas day!

SICILY, OCTOBER 25, 1943 TO R. G.

I occupied my spare time in that hell-hole of "C———," in arranging an acting version of *Macbeth* for Lynn and Alfred Lunt. I had a
lot of fun and the play that emerged was unquestionably far better
than the original. Ha, Ha! I cut, transposed and rearranged in ruth-
less fashion—the most daring alteration being a new ending to the
sleepwalking scene when I have Lynn return (awake), pluck a
dagger from the wall and say the lines "Naught's had, all's spent when
our desire is had without content. 'Tis better to be that which we
destroy than by destruction dwell in doubtful joy," before she exits
to kill herself. (The lines are Shakespeare's, as I imagine you know!!
But I swiped them from an earlier scene). I have all kinds of wonderful scenic effects—the whole thing melodramatic and lots of fun.

SICILY, OCTOBER 29, 1943 TO R. G.

Your letters with proofs of the article (*) on Josephine Baker
arrived. You did a swell job of editing the letter. But I was somewhat
horrified to see a mention of the Silver Star in the caption of the
picture. Please let the episode die a speedy death. I didn't do a damn
thing except let nature take its course and anyone else in my position
would have done the same thing and probably something a good
deal more constructive. The greatest danger I faced, with the possible
exception of the 88, was from our own machine gun which spattered
us accidently from the rear. Incidentally, if you can get through the
war without being shot by your own guns or bombed by your own
planes, you've got a better than even chance of not being hit at all.

I am waiting hopefully for the October issue. "Theatre with
Father" was a grand success. But Theatre in New York seems to be
appallingly bad. Maybe Mr. Coward will bring his new plays over

*Letter from Lt. Eustis—"Double Feature in North Africa," printed in *Theater Arts,*
October 1943.

from England to brighten up the outlook, or possibly O'Neill might be persuaded to release six or seven of his nine plays.

I am hoping that fate may be so kind as to fix it so that I can see the Lunts again before the war is over.

Don't you agree with me that Lynn and Alfred should do *Macbeth*? Of course, you haven't seen the Eustis acting version (which may be just as well!), but I know they could do a swell job and I think the time has come in their careers when they should do a real classic and match their wits with those of the great actors of the past. Lynn is just made for Lady M.

I do think, all joking aside, that the Bard got lazy at the end of the play, after the banquet scene, and just threw together a lot of scenes to end his play. The construction is almost perfect up to that point, but there it goes all to pieces. There are still *great* passages, but much extraneous matter. And the way he treats Lady Macbeth is just shameful for an actor-playwright—just leaves her hanging in mid air with no last scene. Prof. Eustis has fixed that up a little by transposition, but even then Mr. S. should have thrown his battle scenes out of the window and let us see more of the Lord and Lady— which is all we're interested in anyway.

ENGLAND

••

NOVEMBER 13, 1943 TO JUNE 2, 1944

The sands are numbered that make up my life.

SHAKESPEARE

Once again I am writing in the dead hours between midnight and dawn. 4.10 A.M. to be exact,—while I am on guard in a company compartment of a troopship. This time the quarters are on A. Deck instead of below the water level, in the room that used to be the smoking lounge in pre-war days. But the setting is much the same— four tiered bunks crammed together with aisles just wide enough to walk through, men sleeping, mostly with their clothes on; down at one end a quiet high stake crap game going on on the floor—men on guard coming in, others going out. And your correspondent whiling away the hours from two to six by reading *Years of Grace* and writing letters that cannot convey any news. . . .

It is a nice boat that I am on, and we are not too crowded—nothing like the nightmare of the trip to Bombay—we only have nine in my cabin in three-tiered bunks and have a bathroom and shower to ourselves. Although we only get two meals a day, the food is excellent and we eat candy and crackers from the PX the rest of the time. The pangs of hunger do grow acute about three in the afternoon, but I think its probably healthier to eat lightly and certainly no one seems the worse for it.

As I can't tell you anything about this voyage, I might tell you a little something about the trip from Africa to Sicily, which I don't think I ever mentioned in any of my old letters. There isn't much to tell but you might be interested just to round out the record.

About a week or ten days after I joined the 82nd (before I had even been actually assigned to the outfit), we got wind of the fact that an invasion was going to take place somewhere, sometime and that our company was almost certainly going to be in the first invasion wave. We had an amphibious "Dry-run" that week, embarking from the beach with our vehicles in LCT's one evening just at sundown, spending the night offshore and attacking the same beach, which had since been mined, during the next morning. That went off very smoothly on the whole. Then we moved into a new bivouac area and got word that we would probably pull out within a few days. Actually we moved to another area and stayed there darn near a month, as you may remember, but finally the long expected order came and we loaded up on trucks under cover of darkness and drove to the port where we boarded a transport. We stayed in port all the next day—I remember that it was July 4th, as we all thought we might have a gala of fireworks, if we were bombed. The next night, a lot of the other transports were loaded up and we actually set sail about 11 o'clock the following morning.

We sailed right past the prison camp where I had fretted and fumed for so many weeks and I gave it a delighted glance through my glasses. And then we settled down to shipboard routine.

We still, believe it or not, had no idea what our destination was. I had originally been positive that it would be Sicily but was at this point betting, (largely wishful thinking) it would be the south coast of France.

The next morning the commander of troops called all the officers together, told us the mission, outlined the plans and alternative plans and gave out maps and landing orders, etc. We were pretty busy right up to D day studying the problems, plotting our maps, etc., plus pulling guard duty.

The convoy kept growing larger all the way along the African coast. And by the time we passed Malta, about sunset, D. day minus One, there were ships as far as the eye could see. We pulled into, or rather, near to Gela just before midnight on the 9th and from then on you know the rest of the tale, probably better than I do myself! . . .

It looks now as if I will spend the second successive Thanksgiving day aboard a troopship.

AT SEA, NOVEMBER 22, 1943

As you must have gathered in my previous letters, I do not agree *at all* with your theory and that of Aunt Helen* about the bombing of enemy towns. God knows, I don't advocate the wholesale slaughter of enemy civilians in cold blood, though, in the case of Germany, some of that medicine won't do them any harm. But if civilians must

*Mrs. H. Morton.

be killed to attain your objective, why then there's nothing to do but to kill them.

You might as well say that you wouldn't attack a defended road block because it was located in a village and there was a good chance that a shell would hit a few civilians, as to say that you won't bomb a big industrial city because, in doing so, you are bound to kill some women and children and hit a few churches, hospitals and schools.

Quite cold bloodedly, too, the few thousand or hundred thousand killed now may save millions of lives—the enemy's as well as our own—later on. *Anything* one can do is justifiable in my estimation if it helps to win the war and bring it to a speedier end.

You may deplore "total war," at least in theory. But, as long as you are in the midst of one, you won't ever win it except by using total war facilities to the utmost.

One reason that I may seem to stress, unnecessarily, you may think, my bloodthirsty opposition to any campaign of mercy originating on the home front, is that there are seeds of great danger to the forthcoming peace, as I see it, in just such a point of view. It is only a small step, from thinking that this mass bombardment is "frightful" (as, indeed, it is, in one sense) and deploring it as such, to thinking, once Germany is brought to her knees: "Oh the poor Germans. Think how terribly they have suffered and after all, it wasn't the German people who were to blame—just the Nazi leaders." And the next thing you know we'll be giving them money to rebuild their homes and factories and the whole damn thing will start all over again in another twenty years.

I think the Germans—the German *people* should suffer, and suffer for many years. God knows their suffering can never atone for the crimes they've committed, but it may prevent their committing any more for some time to come.

The simple solution of the problem—complete extermination of the German people—is, I realize, a consummation that can never be realized, however devoutly it may be wished (by M. C. Eustis)! But, for heaven's sake, let's not start getting sentimental about the enemy for some time to come.

I realize, of course, that your views are prompted by the highest and most Christian and most sincere motives. But I honestly think that they are wrong.

If America had had any bombing of its own, it would feel quite differently, I feel sure. That's the major trouble of our home front. It's too far away to feel any effects of the war, except by small and no doubt irritating privations.

ENGLAND, NOVEMBER 29, 1943

To the Staff of Theatre Arts:

I really can't tell you what it meant to open the package that looked like a bound edition of Theatre Arts and find such a marvellous assortment of presents. (This looks like an insult to the bound edition, but it is not intended as such!)

The book, the games, the candy—were each works of art of their kind. The Altman caramels, incidentally, were the best I have ever eaten. (You will note, I hope, the past tense, in the reference to the caramels and that isn't a hint either—at least not too obvious a one, I hope).

The package arrived at a peculiarly opportune moment and made a gala day out of what had threatened to be an unusually boring one. Each item in the assortment was, as I have indicated, perfect of its kind. But more than anything else, the gift brought with it a real feeling of Theatre Arts, and all its associations, into an otherwise bleak and depressing atmosphere. It was cold and raining all day and I went to bed brimful of warmth and Xmas cheer. You really were too good to take so much trouble and I can only tell you in a stilted way how much it meant to me, because I should grow horribly sentimental if I let myself go. And that would never do.

Each issue of Theatre Arts which I receive depresses me by its excellence, because I see that you have absolutely no need of any assistance from me. Keep up the good work and don't do anything I wouldn't do (which gives you practically a clear field of action).

This is a joint letter to you and any and all other members of the family who sent me such a wonderful collection of Xmas presents. I can't tell you how gratefully they were received, how much they meant to me and what a real and heartwarming pleasure they brought.

There were so many of them and such a multitude of items included that I am a little hazy as to just who sent what. I opened them in such a frenzy of excitement and, of course, lost all the cards, as I moved into a new room ten minutes after opening them. Many of the boxes had no cards either; and I received one extraordinary present of a pair of pinks from a total stranger.

The food is just what I wanted. The books were what I would have ordered myself. The cards, dice, games, pencils and knick-knacks were just made to order for a soldier overseas. The camera also arrived and I was thrilled beyond measure to receive it. I shall make up for lost time now by taking a host of pictures. Please send all the film you can.

I am now rooming with Frank Jordan and Ely and, since we all three get on beautifully and see eye to eye about everything, it couldn't be a better set up. It couldn't be a more untidy one either, which doesn't bother us one whit! The presents arrived at just the right time, after a long hiatus with no mail, and I think it will take at least until Xmas to consume all the food that the three of us have received.

I think I'll save the pâté (which Betty wrote me was Margey's gift) and the fruit cake with the hard sauce for Xmas day itself (at least that's what I think at this moment!) The gloves, scarf and sweater and foot jackets (!) were *most* welcome too, particularly at this time.

The best of all, though, was the feeling of home it brought into a foreign land and the knowledge that each gift brought with it so much love and affection. They may say what they like about families but there's nothing quite like them. And you appreciate them to their utmost at times like these!

At 3 P.M. yesterday, an order came out saying that soldiers at this camp could now disclose the fact that they were in England. At 3.20 P.M. I cabled you the news, as I was most anxious for you to know it after the long hiatus in receiving mail.

Well, I can't tell you much but I can at least write in a slightly less stereotyped and self conscious manner than formerly. You try writing a letter from London pretending all the while that you are still in Washington and you'll see how hard it is to say anything at all that makes sense!

I am in a nice brick barracks with no central heating but coal grates in every room. The weather is chilly and damp but we have plenty of warm clothes.

They say they are going to be liberal with passes and leaves, so things may be very pleasant—eight-day leaves every two months, week-end passes quite often and you can go out almost every night you want to—not that there's much in the vicinity to go to. So far, I haven't strayed farther from camp than the local pub in the village— a kind of club run by elderly dart-shooters which took us in on the strength of a little liberal tipping. Not very exciting, but it did have beer which is quite a treat. Everyone has been most cordial. They act as if they were really glad to see Americans, which, indeed, they should be!

The blackout here, oddly enough, is much stricter than it was in Sicily, which was much nearer the combat zone. You just don't see any lights anywhere and you have a devil of a time getting around at night. However, there is no curfew, except that all the local pubs close at ten, which is just about the same as a curfew!

It was nice to wake up and see green grass again and civilized, cultivated looking country out of the windows.

Well, that's about the long and short of it. I am in England and glad of it, which is quite an admission from an old Anglophobe!

I haven't written Cousin Poppy* yet, but will do so tonight. Also the Lunts, who, I understand, are in London, and Avy and several other

*Mrs. James Annesley.

friends. I won't be able to tell them where I am but I can at least find out where they are, so I will know where to look if and when I get any leave.

ENGLAND, DECEMBER 5, 1943 TO T. H.[*]

Mother writes me that you are no longer at the Embassy but are now commanding officer of, I think, a Group. That is most impressive. I hope like hell I run into you some time when I get leave. In the meantime I have a favor to ask of you. Another lieutenant and I are *most* anxious to go in a bombing raid some time. I know it is not the custom to take passengers and, as far as that is concerned, I wouldn't want to go as "dead weight." But both of us have had plenty of experience with a machine gun and I am sure we could carry our weight at some unimportant gun position.

I am told we would have more chance to get in on a medium bombing raid than in a heavy bomber but I won't, I assure you, be particular! As far as getting permission at this end is concerned, we can manage that. If you could fix it at the other end, I should be eternally grateful.

Seriously, I realize it is probably impossible, but my army experience has taught me that anything is possible if you're only sufficiently persistent, even transferring from the Air Corps to the Cavalry (which I succeeded in doing after six months of trying!).

I am located only 64 miles from London and not very far from Winchester. If there were any bombing squadron in this vicinity, we could easily arrange to get over to the field in a peep—just taking a two-day pass.

ENGLAND, DECEMBER 9, 1943

I am writing in bed after a hot bath, wearing my long woolen underwear which, as David well knows, is an essential item of clothing in this climate. We are on the whole, very comfortably settled, three to a room as Jordan, Ely[†] and I managed to secure one to our-

[*]Colonel Thomas Hitchcock.
[†]Lieutenant Ely.

selves. There is hot water, coal for the fireplaces, and the food, which we eat at an officers' mess about a mile from the barracks, is good.

Re the affair about the "Big Shot" which you have commented on in your letters, I am simply disgusted both with the American press, America and American womanhood, which last I am sure is largely to blame for the whole idiotic performance. I heard the story—or rumors of same—many weeks before it broke (and why may I ask did the War Department allow Drew Pearson to publish it?). I still don't know the exact facts of the case, but I strongly suspect, if the tale, as published, is true, that the recipient of the slap richly deserved it.

Whether it was deserved or not, it strikes me that it is nobody's business but the Army's and that the public should have nothing to say about the matter. He is the best general we have, I think, in the field and it would be a national tragedy to have him thrown out because of a lot of sentimental women.

I saw Noel Coward's movie *In Which We Serve* before leaving Sicily and was woefully disappointed. It seemed to me synthetic from start to finish and curiously unaffecting. In a word—ham. I can't understand all the hosannas from London and New York—except that maybe people who have never seen any war at first hand think that it is realistic in its approach.

ENGLAND, DECEMBER 14, 1943

I got a letter from Cousin Poppy, asking me to visit her whenever possible. Dodo* wired me, too, giving me a London telephone number, and Lynn Fontanne wired from Manchester, telling me they were opening in the new version of *There Shall Be No Night* on Wednesday (tomorrow) and will be staying at the Savoy. I'll try and stay there, too, when I go up. Jordan and I hope to go there the 18th of January, at least, that's when we've applied to go. It is cold as the devil now, regular New England weather, and I am swathed in heavy woolen underwear, for which I am most thankful! I have been once to town, the nearest village; otherwise, life has been fairly uneventful. Your packages were swell. I am still eating the food. Tell Anne the

*Miss Annesley.

188

chocolate bars she sent were the best I have ever had. Can she send some more? Margey's pâté from Altman's was excellent, too. More would also be welcome! I can always use books, too, any of the latest.

ENGLAND, DECEMBER 15, 1943

Today, God help us, we had the formal presentation of the decorations to the B'n., on a green football field at the outskirts of camp, cold as sin, too. All the men getting Silver Stars—four officers and ten enlisted men—had to line up and march across the field, with the band playing, from the B'n., which was massed in formation, to where the Division Commander was standing.

From then on we stood at attention in the frigid breezes for what seemed like hours, first when the National Anthem was played, then for the reading of the citations and while the General pinned them on us. He shook hands with each person and said "congratulations," upon which we automatons said: "Thank you, sir" and saluted. Then we marched and lined up next to the General and the B'n. "passed in review" before us. Then there was a formal retreat formation, another National Anthem, another passing in review and then we hied us to the nearest coal stove.

Thank God *that's* over with!

I have read more about the P. affair in English papers and think it's too ridiculous for words. And the silly part of it all is that P. cares more really for the soldier and for his welfare than nine-tenths of the officers in the army. Well, it looks as if the army is being sensible and is just going to ignore the whole affair. I hope so.

How could you describe the multitude of Xmas presents as mere trifles? Six more came yesterday, and I am overcome with joy and gratitude. The sewing case, comb and mirror set are just what I want and the cold pills, etc., though not needed at the moment, are sure to come in handy, if not for me then for some less hardy compatriots. . . .

I wish I could describe our location, but that as you know is *verboten*. It is pretty country, however, whenever the sun shines brightly enough to enable you to see it, and there are several interesting spots nearby to see,—one particularly beautiful cathedral—the most satisfy-

189

ing English cathedral I think I have seen—one of the few that has not got a screen between the choir and the nave that cuts the church in half. This country reminds one constantly of Thomas Hardy and, save for the vast numbers of temporary barracks all over the place and the airfields, I don't imagine it is much different than it was at the time he was writing.

ENGLAND, CHRISTMAS DAY, 1943

It seems hard to believe that today is Christmas—the 2nd Xmas since I left the States. I had an even more un-Xmasy day, if possible, than I did in "Kilo 13," the dust-swept camp in the Middle East where I was stationed a year ago. I did not, I am ashamed to say, go to church, as we were restricted to the post and the service in the mess hall had no great appeal to me. My daily routine was prosaic in the extreme: a late breakfast at 10, Xmas dinner at 2, an excellent meal, I might add, with some good beer—a lazy afternoon reading and sleeping. A light supper at 7, a bath, and now, in bed at 9 P.M., a letter home.

The way things are going now it really looks to me as if we may all be together again next Christmas. I don't think the Jap war will be over by then, but I do think Germany will be on her knees.

Well, thank you again, all of you, for the wonderful Xmas presents you showered upon me and still more, for the love they represented.

LONDON, DECEMBER 31, 1943

I am in London for a course and will return to my post in a couple of days. The course has only occupied the daylight hours, so I have managed to have quite a lot of fun on the side.

The first day I got here I lunched with the Lunts at the Savoy, where they are staying. They were charming, as usual, and were thrilled at the reception they had received. Then, after signing in for my course, I looked up Avy* at the Red Cross and went back to his

*J. Averill Clark.

apartment where Young Tommy* was. Helen Potter—Chi's friend—who is driving a clubmobile came in, also Jack Potter, who is in the Canadian Army and somebody who had been a teacher at the Aiken School. I dined with Tommy, who is awaiting assignment to an RAF Squadron, and then met Avy at his apartment. As it was a long way back to my hotel and I had no flashlight, they persuaded me to spend the night there. It was like old home week seeing so many familiar faces.

The next night I dined with Dodo and Cousin Poppy at Dodo's flat. Had a very nice time, and an excellent meal, cooked by Dodo, who was very entertaining. I finally picked up a taxi—a monumentally difficult task at night—and got back to my hotel.

The blackout is intense and it's hell to get around at night in consequence. There are a few bootleg cabs but they're very difficult to get. Food is plentiful in the restaurants, drink is scarce, especially spirits. Picadilly Circus is a mad house after dark and a man can't walk without being attacked by dozens of women. But then it always used to be bad.

ENGLAND, JANUARY 8, 1944

I appreciate your feelings about the invasion but I can't say that I agree with you! I don't want Germany to collapse until we have had a chance to strike her good and hard from the West, and I hope that my platoon is the first to set foot in Berlin.

I am crazy about the platoon I am now in charge of—a hell of a nice bunch of men and, even more important, a splendid bunch of fighters—men all of them who really are eager to get into a scrap and men you know you can rely on in a crisis. I also like being the boss instead of second in command.

ENGLAND, JANUARY 22, 1944

Cousin Ethel† wrote several London friends I was here. I am accordingly going in half an hour or so to have "a glass of sherry"

*Thomas Hitchcock Clark.
†Miss Sands.

with Sir Archibald and Lady Sinclair at the Air Ministry and on Tuesday I go to cocktails at Margey and David's friend, Lady Colfax's.

We had a very nice theatrical evening with Adrienne Allen and two friends the night we got here, went to Ciro's and ate, drank and danced until about 1:00 A.M., which is *very* late for wartime London.

We had two air raids last night, one right after the theatre and one at 4:00 A.M.—neither one amounting to much, though there was a lot of noise. I was surprised at how generally apprehensive the populace seemed—much more tense than you would expect after all these years.

Tonight I am supping with Lynn and Alfred at their apartment after the show. Tomorrow we are going to Westminster Abbey for church, if we wake up; then I may play bridge with Dodo.

It seems incredibly silly to be doing all this at this time and I wish they'd hurry up and get their invasion started.

I have just made a date for lunch with an alluring young actress for Monday. She was on our party with Adrienne Allen!

ENGLAND, JANUARY 29, 1944

Well, it's back to duty again after a nine-day holiday and just as well, too, or we wouldn't have a cent left in the world. London is *fabulously* expensive. One modest dinner and dance at Quagalino's for six cost us some 18 pounds, if not more. I'll admit we did have champagne, a wartime luxury, but that was only 10 pounds for a magnum. The rest just goes up in smoke or down the gullet. Either way, you're licked.

Although leave was swell, nine days was long enough where we were. You began to get bored, so I'm not sorry to be back. I only wish they'd get going in a hurry now on this invasion and get it over with.

By the way, the Annesleys saved our lives, and they couldn't have been nicer. And believe me, it's quite an effort in London to go out at all, when you work nine hours a day as all the women do. You can't get taxis except by a miracle. You have to walk home. So it's not just a question of saying "Who wouldn't be nice to three young men?"

Not many people, I can assure you, would have been as nice as they were. Patricia* even cooked an egg apiece for Frank and me on our farewell night or rather morning—and that's the equivalent of selling yourself, I can assure you, as eggs are just unheard of and the greatest present you can give anybody is an egg and some oranges or rather one orange.

ENGLAND, FEBRUARY 4, 1944

I have just finished reading an article on "Anglo-American relations" in *Time*. If I quoted passages from same, I would probably be subject to court martial for saying things which the Americans should never hear re what the British feel about the Americans here and vice versa. The gist of what the article has to say is true in its essence. It sums up what you hear in most conversations on the subject—the Americans have too much money, they are too loud and boisterous, they are stealing the British girls, etc., etc. At the same time, it boils down, as an argument, to a lot of poppycock.

The only thing wrong with Anglo-American relations in Britain at the moment is that there are too many Americans in England; or, as the Limeys might put it, "too bloody many Yanks around."

It would drive Americans crazy if our towns and villages were swamped—and I mean swamped—with British, Russian or Chinese soldiers—no matter how much we loved them as individuals, no matter how vitally we needed their help. Once the novelty and the first fine flush of enthusiasm had died down we would be bound to resent the foreigner in our midst—in much the same manner as small towns near big army camps almost always come to resent the military. That's only human nature.

After about five days in London, sweating out lines at every restaurant, bus stop, taxi stand, ticket counter, laundry, tailor and men's room, I began myself to wish I'd never see another American soldier. In Cairo, where the British outnumbered us in about the same ratio as we do them here, it was all: "these————Limeys, they think they own the place"—the same thing in reverse.

*Lady Norman.

Which is another way of saying that the major deterrent to friendly Anglo-American relations at present is merely too much of a damn good thing.

Once let normal conditions reestablish themselves—as they do, paradoxically enough, in abnormal situations like combat or life in the field—then we'll go right back to calling each other arrogant bastards and get on, on the whole, about as well as can be expected of any two peoples who are as much alike as they are unlike and who respect fundamentally each other's characteristics, no matter how irritating the superficial manifestations of these characteristics may be.

Un point c'est tout.

Which, being interpreted for the censor—foreign languages being frowned upon—means: "That settles that"—I hope.

We are so rushed now that we literally hardly have time to sit down; certainly the time for letter writing is almost non-existent. Today is the first time I've had time to catch my breath of an evening since returning from London. Yesterday I had to lecture to a class, or at least keep their attention, for eight solid hours. Since they'd been up, including the lecturer, most of the night before on a problem, it was something of a strain! I've gotten so now, however, that I can at least get on my feet in front of a group and speak, which I never could before, as you well know. But eight hours to one group of men is too much of a good thing!

ENGLAND, FEBRUARY 15, 1944

The news just broke today of the bombing of Cassino monastery —tragic, but just a prelude, I fear, to wholesale destruction of Italy's *monuments historiques.* I was pleased to see that almost all the English Catholic hierarchy approved of the bombing. I hope they did in America, too; approved is, perhaps, the wrong word, but you know what I mean. It had to be done and that was all there was to it. The Pope's summer home will be next. I only hope that they can spare St. Peter's and the Vatican; but even that may not be possible if the Germans make a concerted stand at Rome.

ENGLAND, FEBRUARY 28, 1944

A week ago we had a visit from Gen. Eisenhower, Gen. Montgomery and Air Marshall Tedder, which, curiously enough, the censor said we could mention. My platoon was picked to give a "demonstration" problem for the dignitaries and, needless to say, there was a hectic two days of cleaning equipment and vehicles, etc., not to mention of dry running of the position itself. Actually, I never saw the generals myself, as I was glued to a pair of field glasses looking at an "enemy" position back of a haystack. The TNT I was supposed to set off (to simulate gunfire) at the start of the problem failed to ignite, but I'm sure the generals didn't care as they only stayed a few minutes and were gone by the time I arrived panting at the haystack, to observe the next position, thank God. General Montgomery told our chief of staff he was very impressed by us, which means all of nothing as he didn't see enough to impress him one way or t'other.

ENGLAND, MARCH 16, 1944

I finally got over to Cousin Ethel's last Sunday afternoon and had a delightful visit. She lives in a sweet little brick house practically in a country churchyard, just two miles outside of Marlborough. She hadn't changed at all, and was fascinating, describing her last weeks in France and her escape.

I enjoyed myself thoroughly and was sorry to leave at 9:30 when my peep came to pick me up. She has a French couple, refugees, who live with her and cook, most excellently, I might add! It was the most civilized evening I have had since leaving Washington and was really delightful. She has such an interesting mind and is so quick and so alive.

ENGLAND, MARCH 24, 1944

We had another "very distinguished visitor" yesterday, higher still than the last, who also trailed along; and we put on a big show for him. My platoon was picked to put on a combat problem and we blew up enough TNT (simulating gunfire) to blow up a battleship. I had to make a hair-raising dash cross country, with half the platoon, round the flank of the enemy and we finally, in rehearsal, got it down so that we did three miles in about four minutes. Why anyone was alive, at the end of the trip, I don't know! It all went off very well for the big shot and he watched the whole show and, so the Colonel said, seemed to like it a lot. . . .I'm afraid that the platoon I inherited from Frank is unquestionably the best combat platoon in the B'n (which is no credit to me unless I make it better), and this next week we are taking special tests to go through another exercise for the Commanding General of the Combat Command. It works out very well, as it means I can take the platoon off by myself and really teach them—and more important still—learn something myself, instead af wasting time on routine garrison training of the same type we had at Devens.

Patricia has reserved rooms for what she calls the three musketeers —and the enlisted men call "the Piccadilly Commandos"—at the Berkeley from the 14th to the 17th. We decided we really should do it up brown and the Berkeley is my favorite hotel in London.

I am in the best of health and spirits and only hope this invasion comes off before we all get grey hairs. Don't worry about me. It's all luck and I have a hunch my luck is going to be good. If it isn't— well there are worse ways of saying adieu. But we won't cross that bridge just yet.

ENGLAND, MARCH 25, 1944

The weather, these past three days has been unbelievable—actually hot in the daytime and not a cloud in the sky. The English, the poor idiots, are lamenting the fact that it isn't raining. I'm planning, if I ever get round to it, to send home all my summer things—practically a footlocker full of things. . . . I'll also send back some extra junk I don't need. It's fantastic how much junk you can accumulate in a few months, even though you never seem to buy anything.

Next week I'm slated to give a lecture to a Reconnaissance outfit on the Sicilian campaign. Can you picture anything more awful? It's just to the officers, thank God.

I had to give a repeat performance for another company today of my orientation lecture. You would have blushed to hear me asserting myself as an authority on French habits and customs. But at that, I probably knew more of what I was talking about than anyone in the audience. I gave the French as much of a build up as I could to counteract the running down they get from the British. Next week, God help me, the subject is "The Soldier's Bonus," or what the hell we can expect to receive out of the Government on our return to civilian life. For myself, the best present they can give me is a nice Certificate of Discharge—honorable, I trust!

Now for a brief lecture. There should be more glamour on the *Theatre Arts* cover. The "Men listening to the Radio" was terrible, I thought. We get enough war everywhere else. Incidentally, I sent down a lot of magazines to my platoon the other day and, by a horrid accident, included a copy of *Theatre Arts* that had my Baker article and my picture in it. The next day I walked in and found my picture on the bulletin board in the platoon squad room. And ever since then they have been hiding it and bringing it out when they thought I couldn't get around and steal it.

Did I tell you that Lynn and Alfred saw the gentleman whom Cabot stayed with in Palermo? They told him they had just seen me (imagine *his* excitement, can't you?!!) and that I'd told them I would rather have General Patton lead us in this invasion than anyone else. He seemed pleased, they said, and told them that he'd known Father very well in the last war and admired him immensely. A coincidence, wasn't it? I was glad to hear, too, from them, that our mutual friend seemed very well. And more than happy that he's on this side of the channel rather than back home. . . . Now something really may get done.

It seems hard to believe that two Xmas's and two Easters have passed since I saw you. Although there have been long moments of infuriating inactivity in that time, I have had so many varied experiences and have covered so much ground that the time has passed very quickly. I'm betting now that by next Easter, I don't dare suggest Xmas,—we'll be back in the States. And I made a bet of £10, the other day, that we'd be in Paris by July 14th. Rather rash, that last one, I realize, but I am still hopeful, though a little less so, than I was a month ago.

So please try, and I know this is easier said than done, not to worry too much. For all I know we may sit in England some time after the Invasion starts and may be miles away from any danger. There probably won't be any way to let you know we are not on a beachhead, as I imagine they will stop all mail and telegrams for a period of time just before and after the invasion. But I want to beg you to try and be philosophical about it all, to leave it all in God's hands (which is all anyone can do) and to say to yourself that you will not let your imagination picture me in every tight spot you read about, in the papers. Discount 90% too, of what you read in the papers, as their battle reports are woefully inaccurate.

ENGLAND, APRIL 11, 1944. LATER

I called up Cousin Poppy Saturday night in the country and she sounded very well and cheerful. Dolly,* it appears, had quite a harrowing experience in one of the recent bombings. A bomb first shattered all her windows and blasted in all her doors. Then, just when she had gone back to bed, having nothing else to do, a warden arrived, telling her to be out of her house in 30 seconds, as there was a time bomb under it. So in her night gown and fur coat, out poor Dolly traipsed into the streets, and was put up at a shelter, sitting up until

*Miss Dorothy Dawkins.

six on a wooden bench. At six she took off in her night gown to Dodo's and stayed there for four days until they got out the bomb and let her go home. In another raid a bomb blew in the wall of adjoining flats and a man and woman, who had been dying to meet each other, found themselves hurtled into the same bed together. Dodo, herself, was hurled out of her chair on to the floor by the blast of an explosion. But everyone takes it all very much as a matter of course.

ENGLAND, APRIL 14, 1944

I am now established at a British anti-aircraft range for a week's firing. It ought to be pretty good fun. I say "ought" because today it is raining so hard that no planes can get up and we are getting organized in camp instead of firing. But I know that, fun or not, it will be a welcome change from the routine of garrison life, with all the endless paper work, policing and emphasis on "spit and polish."

Although it is a British Camp, the only thing British about it, save for the training aids, etc., is the rations. And British rations leave much to be desired! After eating them I can see where the word subsistence got its derivation. You subsist on the British ration. But that's about the whole story.

This is as bleak a spot as you could imagine—not a tree for miles and, if the weather remains as is, the only firing we'll get is in the indoor dome where you fire with lights instead of bullets—something like a world's fair contrivance.

British hours being what they are, I will probably have more time for writing than I thought. They are much more leisurely, to put it mildly, than our own, for, as you know, the Englishman must have his cup of tea at 10:30 in the morning and again at 4:30 in the afternoon. And "tea" means about an hour's break in the day's routine! Still I don't doubt they get as much done in the long run as we do. Their ways seem rather strange to us but, as long as they get results, we shouldn't let it worry us.

The honeymoon is over, or almost over. We return tomorrow to camp and start in once again with the "training schedule" that won't come to an end until we finally take off for foreign shores, if we ever do anything so rash! I don't credit the Army with being sufficiently far sighted to make their training so boring that men are really anxious to go into combat just to get away from it, but that is actually what happens. I don't believe there's a man in our company who wouldn't rather be under enemy fire than in garrison over here. And I know that they're itching to get going and get this over with, rather than to sit around for months and even years. All this applies only to the combat troops.

I have had a very good time at this anti-aircraft school and fired off a good many rounds myself at these sleeve targets they tow behind planes, which is not nearly so much fun, I might add, as shooting at enemy planes. But it's all good practice and I think I learned a good deal. The work wasn't too hard either and I got off almost every night in my peep.

At another town—this one overrun by the American Navy—I found a delightful bar presided over by a woman who was the split image of Mrs. Pat Campbell and almost as funny. And there, I am glad to relate, there was an apparently unlimited supply of what they call "spirits" over here. I had to indulge wisely instead of too well, you will be pleased to hear, because I was in charge of the recreation trip and had to assemble my charges at 10:45 and lead the little dears home to bed. Oddly enough they all turned up and none of them seem to have got into any fights with the Navy—an extraordinary occurrence, even though I had lectured them severely on the subject in advance and told them to be sure not to get in any fights but, if they did, to be equally sure it was the Navy rather than themselves who were knocked out. They did cause me a little trouble by bringing four girls back to camp in the truck with them and I had to cart them home wailing in the middle of the night. But that wasn't too serious, though I had to pretend to be outraged at such behaviour.

We start off at the crack of dawn tomorrow and probably in the midst of a howling gale, judging by the way it is blowing at this minute. Incidentally I am curled up in my sleeping bag in a Nissen hut, after having taken a hot bath in the "ablution hut," as the British call it. (Honestly, there *are* times————!!) I am writing on my map board and plan to retire soon, preparatory to getting up at 04.30.

Incidentally, after *much* endeavor and scouring the English countryside, I was able to obtain, from the Navy, this time, some much needed spare parts for our British machine guns which I got in Africa. It took a telephone call to the First or Third Lord of the Admiralty to get permission to transfer them to the American Army from the British Navy, and I signed my soul, and probably my pocketbook, away on endless requisition sheets, but the important thing is that I *have* what I needed. I also secured some 30,000 rounds of ammunition from the Navy. I must say the British are wonderfully cooperative about this sort of thing, much more so, I think, than we would ever be. Imagine what would happen if a British officer tried to secure guns and ammunition from our QM with nothing to show that he had any right to them save his own guileless expression!

A very nice British Naval officer was the one responsible for my getting what I did get and I am more than grateful to him, particularly as I have to make another trip to his town to pick up what the Admiralty is sending down!

Just read about the British torpedo propelled by two human divers. That's *one* job I would not like to have. I'll take my chances with anyone on dry land, I hope, but under water I think I should be a pure coward. It is extraordinary, isn't it, what people will do under pressure? Also how fundamentally nice the average person is—the average American GI anyway. I have the greatest respect for the American soldier from what I've seen of him in all kinds of circumstances. I don't think there's anyone in the world who can touch him —not necessarily as a soldier, though he's no slouch there, but as an individual. I don't think we have much to worry about our future when we can produce a race of men as good as our GI's.

Wasn't it too bad about Willkie? Those stupid Republicans! They deserve to lose and what's more they will lose, and I, for one, will vote against them just to register my emphatic protest against their shelving the only good candidate they had. . . . I wish really the whole damned election could be postponed, as it will only serve to prolong the war and stir up all kinds of bitternesses back home, when everyone ought to be thinking of and working for just one thing—winning the war. Oh well, I obviously can't do anything about it, so I shall not worry unduly, particularly as I have great faith in Roosevelt's ability not only to win the war but, even more important, to win the peace.

ENGLAND, APRIL 28, 1944

Wasn't it tragic about Tommy?* I happened to be at his base after it happened and made what inquiries I could. I talked to several officers and they all were broken hearted about the accident. They said that Tommy was idolized by his Group—that he would always insist on carrying out any dangerous tests that the rest of them did, even though he didn't have to. He was in the midst of a test, diving his plane in order to let photographs be taken of the bomb burst, when the plane cracked up. No one seemed to know exactly what happened as everyone was watching the ground, but they seemed to think that a wing had snapped. Anyway, it was a mercifully quick thing when it happened and he was killed instantly. I asked where he was buried, as I wanted to go to his grave, but it wasn't near enough for me to go to in the limited time at my disposal. Well, he died the way he would have liked to, I know—in action, even if it wasn't, as it happened, in actual combat. Tommy was never one to sit around and let others do the dirty work, which is one reason, I suppose, why he was so admired by all his officers. There was no reason for him to be doing what he was doing, but he wouldn't have been happy letting anyone else do it while he watched from the sidelines. It was that quality, after all, that made Tommy what he was. If he'd been an armchair leader, he wouldn't have been Tommy.

Well, there's nothing more to say about it. But I like to feel that Tommy himself would not have had it otherwise, if it had to happen to someone.

*Colonel Thomas Hitchcock.

That delicious chocolate arrived yesterday and the package from Pierce's today. Incidentally, I should like some more of the same chocolate as often as you can get it! Also books would be appreciated.

I suddenly remembered that I owed you some more money to give to St. Anthony for making my request come true—which I had promised to do. $50 will fulfill that obligation, with much gratitude; the other $100 is for another request with a promise of $100 more if my request is granted. I have great faith in him, as you can see.

ENGLAND, MAY 2, 1944

The English climate, believe it or not, has been delightful this past two weeks, and I actually have discarded my woolen underwear and taken to sitting in the sun in my shirt sleeves. The Gulf Stream must be working overtime.

It is hard to write about anything without touching on the one subject which is paramount in everyone's mind at this time. But since I know less—a great deal less—than what I read in the newspapers about it, it won't be very difficult for me to desist! I suppose America is in a frenzy of excitement, suppressed or otherwise. I can just hear the radio commentators!

I am writing in the usual supine position, stretched out on my cot, and find it very hard to stay awake, to tell the truth, even though it is only noon. The sun is actually beating down on me and it wouldn't take much prodding to make me fall asleep.

9:30 P.M.

Morpheus won out. I fell sound asleep, with my map board on top of me and woke up 45 minutes later, just in time to stagger down to the mess hall. Spring fever is certainly in the air.

I have just come back from a short peep ride through the countryside with Frank, partly business and partly pleasure. You have no idea how much the country looks like Virginia at this time of year. We both remarked on it. The flowering fruit is out and a lot of those pale carpets of yellow and purple flowers in the fields and on the road banks. I have always somewhat decried the beauties of the English countryside, as you know!, but I must admit I was wrong. Parts of England are as pretty as any country I have ever seen—for beauty of landscape, that is. Everything is so green and fertile—though the English claim the countryside is burned up now, as they haven't had more than an inch of rain in the last month.

Tomorrow I have to give one of my weekly information talks to the company—the subject this time being France again. God knows what I will say that will keep them still for an hour. But I'll try and give them a little geopolitical picture of the country that is not too unfavourable towards it. At least it will be more interesting for me than some of the other subjects I have had to cover, such as "British law and government," "the good General," "Post war jobs."

Well, it is getting dark outside, so I will now say goodnight, before I plunge into the nethermost recesses of my sleeping bag.

ENGLAND, MAY 3, 1944 TO M. E. F.

Your letter of the 23rd, needless to say, did not reach me in France! So your fears were groundless.

I know you won't worry too much and I feel confident that Mother won't either. I do know, however, that this whole show will be a much greater strain on you at home than it will be on those of us who will—or think and hope we will—take part in it. The only emotion we experience here is one of boredom—the "My God, will it *never* start" type of feeling—and I haven't seen the faintest sign of apprehension, or even excitement. We are all intrigued, of course, to know how the plan is going to be worked out and I confess that we wouldn't mind being told when it was going to be carried out. But that's about as far as our emotional reaction goes. Whereas, at home, you must, I know (and, God knows, I don't blame you) be on pins and needles, hanging on the radio.

I am delighted with the platoon I am now in charge of. It is the best platoon in the B'n, thanks entirely to Frank Jordon, who commanded it before he became Executive Officer of the company. And

I would rather go into combat with these men than with any group of men I know.

My peep driver, funnily enough, is from Virginia. He lives about forty miles from Roanoke, and a better driver I couldn't ask for, nor a better fighter. Our peep is a veritable arsenal now. I have mounted two machine guns on it—one for him, one for me, and we have, besides a rifle, a Tommy gun, a Browning automatic and my pistol, not to mention a rifle grenade and a flare pistol that I talked the Air Corps out of. We ought to be able to do *some* damage with that amount of fire power!!

Let's hope it won't be too long before we'll all be sitting round the pool at Oatlands again. Next Spring, what ho!

ENGLAND, MAY 14, 1944

Frank and I had another break two days ago, as we were sent to London on official business to buy some things the battalion needed. We went down in a peep which was great luxury, finished our purchases by noon and had the whole rest of the day and evening in town. I had lunch with Lynn and Alfred at the Savoy. She told me she had written you a letter. Did you ever receive it? I had a very amusing time with them and then met Frank at the Berkeley. . . . I am glad that you are coming around to my way of thinking about the bombing (of Germany). I thought you would. They are certainly getting their full measure of it now and, whatever happens, they won't be able to say this time that their homeland was not touched by the war. Personally, it's O.K. by me if every stick and stone in Germany is razed to the ground. That goes for every German, too, though we will probably start that idiotic sentimentality about the poor, nice Germans the minute the war is over. If so, we ought to have our collective heads examined.

ENGLAND, MAY 21, 1944

Lieut. Jordan and I took our twenty-four hour leave on Wednesday and had a day so similar to the last we had that it is hardly necessary for you to know what we did. Dodo got us reservations at the Ritz, the Berkeley being full up, and we settled down there in the early afternoon, very plush and ornate and not nearly so nice as the other—also one of the coldest spots I have ever been in. We had to sit with overcoats on while we sipped beer in our sitting room.

After the theatre we went back to see the Lunts and I took Alfred a present that ordinarily you would have been ashamed to give to a rummage sale—two old pairs of silk pajamas that I have not worn or washed since Cairo, a battered pair of pinks covered with grease stains, a couple of old books and a half-gallon can of grapefruit juice. Well, you would have thought I had brought diamonds, he was so pleased. (I forgot, I also brought along a pair of old bedroom slippers that you wouldn't have given to Basil!) He called in individual members of the company to see the "wonderful" present he had received and packed it all lovingly to take back to the hotel. They can't buy anything, you see, except through coupons, and that allows them about one suit of clothes a year. We stayed back stage until they were dressed and then, as it was raining, they took us back in their taxi several miles out of the way to a restaurant. They were in especially good form. Dodo was completely captivated by them. We dined and danced and when the place was closed up about one A.M., called for the bill. It was just over seventeen pounds! A mere bagatelle for a three course dinner with cocktails and wine.

We had to catch a ten o'clock train home the next morning and Dodo and Gillian insisted on taking us to the station, so we had a tearful "cavalcade" farewell scene at Waterloo and headed back to the grim contours of our present home. As we reported for duty we received the pleasant news that there was an all night problem ahead of us, and what a problem! It was, or rather seemed like, the coldest night of the year, especially as we had turned in most of our heavy clothing and we did not get in until seven in the morning, and never closed an eye during the whole time.

I seem to be fated not to have a camera at the time I want one most, as my Eastman was obligingly stolen out of my room while I was on the night problem. I am enraged beyond description but there seems no way in which it can be traced, so there is nothing to do but lump it.

ENGLAND, MAY 25, 1944

This evening, during an "officers' school," the Adjutant presented me with a bulky package, or rather letter, and there, lo and behold, was the wallet I lost three months ago, battered and mud stained, minus all cash (some 60 pounds), but with everything else intact in the way of credentials, letter of credit, identification card, AGO card, etc., etc. It had been sent from ETO Hq. to which point it had been forwarded by another Army unit which found it in a vehicle. As far as I can make out, some civilian must have picked it up in the fields (I lost it on a night problem), helped himself to the cash and then tossed it out of kindness into the first Army car he saw. Well, it was like meeting an old friend who has been through the wars. I was very pleased and promptly transferred all the vital elements to the new twin which you had sent me.

ENGLAND, MAY 30, 1944 TO M. E. F.

It seems almost impossible to believe that it was a year ago today that I attended a Memorial Day Service on a dust swept hill in Africa. Today we had an assembly on a green English parade ground and shot off a few salutes for good measure. It was so hot that you broke into a sweat even in your shirt sleeves—quite a change from a week or so ago when it was so cold that it seemed worse than mid-winter. . . . I have now shed all my English wool—for the duration, I hope! But one can never tell these days. . . . I think of you and David basking in the sun at the Oatlands pool and grow quite jealous, but I have hopes now that by this time next year we might all be reunited again. . . .

ENGLAND, JUNE 2, 1944 TO R. G.

You may be amused to hear that I have just christened a new vehicle in my platoon after Katharine Cornell. All my cars are named, or supposedly named, after people or characters in the amusement world. Some, I frankly confess, I have never heard of, such as the great Indian witch doctor (I presume), CHIUAHUA, not to mention CRUSADER, who, they tell me, was an actual person. I ride, myself, in a comic-strip peep (and *that's* no lie!) entitled CRICKET, the other peeps are called CANTOR, CORKY and CRAZY CAT. The armored section goes by such redoubtable and blood curdling names as COHAN, CROSBY, COLBERT and the mysterious CRUSADER. The assault gun, more appropriately, is named CAGNEY, and COLUMBO (whoever he is) brings up the rear as an ammunition tender with CORNELL just ahead, bristling with mortars and machine guns. You note the names all begin with C. They have to, as that designates Co. "C." . . . Also I didn't have the idea; I merely inherited the platoon. Unfortunately, I couldn't fit in Lynn and Alfred, however hard I tried!

FRANCE

And now, those waiting dreams are satisfied,
From twilight to the halls of dawn he went,
His lance is broken, but he has content
With that high hour, in which he lived and died.

HERBERT ASQUITH

We were told last night that we could start writing letters. We can disclose no information or tell of 'battle experiences,' as they call them, until fourteen days after the event. So don't expect a very scintillating account of the invasion. I can't tell you where I am but I can tell you that I have never felt better and that it is a great relief to be out of that confounded British climate and in this lovely country.

Today is fairly cool, almost like British weather, but yesterday was lovely and warm and I lay in the sun for two hours by my peep reading *An Eye for a Tooth*—one of the detective stories you sent me in the last batch.

Quite a tough war, isn't it!

The worst feature of it is that all of you back home probably envisage us lying in pools of blood and sweat all the time, when actually the picture is very different. So don't worry, please—which may be easier for me to say than for you to do.

A nice old French woman brought out four jugs of cider for me yesterday when I was out on one of the roads and it certainly was nice to see how friendly the populace is—French flags everywhere, people throwing flowers. I got quite a scratch from a rose a woman threw at me. Ought to get the Purple Heart for it!

A peep is about the most comfortable base to live from that I know. We've got all the equipment in the world and I haven't yet been in a foxhole and don't actually expect to be. As you can probably see, reading through the lines, I am enjoying myself thoroughly and just can't wait for the day when we march triumphantly into Paris with, I fondly trust, my platoon leading the parade.

P.S. I enclose a couple of R.A.F. leaflets which I picked up in our bivouac site and which might interest you.

MESSAGE URGENT .
DU COMMANDEMENT SUPREME DES FORCES
EXPEDITIONNAIRES ALLIEES
AUX HABITANTS DE CETTE VILLE

Afin que l'ennemi commun soit vaincu, les Armées de l'Air Alliées vont attaquer tous les centres de transports ainsi que toutes les voies et moyens de communications vitaux pour l'ennemi.

Des ordres à cet effet ont été donnés.

Vous qui lisez ce tract, vous vous trouvez dans où près d'un centre essentiel à l'ennemi pour le mouvement de ses troupes et de son matériel. L'objectif vital près duquel vous vous trouvez va être attaqué incessamment.

Il faut sans délai vous éloigner, avec votre famille, *pendant quelques jours,* de la zone de danger où vous vous trouvez.

N'encombrez pas les routes. Dispersez-vous dans la campagne autant que possible.

PARTEZ SUR LE CHAMP!
VOUS N'AVEZ PAS UNE MINUTE A PERDRE!

The morale of the men is excellent. They are all so glad to be in action again that they are like a bunch of kids on vacation.

FRANCE, JUNE 14, 1944

First a word of warning. The bad thing about being able to write letters in a combat zone is the fact that they will arrive in such an irregular fashion that the recipient of the letter is apt to read all kinds of conclusions into long periods of silence. So remember, please, that the fact that I haven't written, or that *you haven't received,* any letters for a long spell, must not be construed as meaning anything other than the obvious fact that letters coming out of a combat zone are bound to be erratic.

I am sitting in the sun now on a shelter half leaning against the camouflage net which is draped—with great artistry!—round my peep. My car crew is preparing lunch, judging by the sounds emanating from the other side of the peep, and I shall shortly join them.

It is peculiar weather—not quite settled yet—hot in the sun but quite cold at night. Fortunately, I have my sleeping bag which I wouldn't get rid of for $1,000, and so I am extremely warm and comfortable in any kind of temperature. A peep also is a wonderful vehicle to have as your C. P., as you can carry a great deal of equipment which wouldn't fit in the armored cars. I have had my peep equipped with every known type of box, racks, etc.—not to mention weapons and so am extremely comfortable and efficiently set up. Speaking of weapons, we counted up yesterday and discovered that we had, for a car crew of three, eight weapons, not to speak of an assortment of knives, grenades, a rocket launcher and a flare pistol, which isn't bad, all things considered! especially since two of the guns are machine guns (the ones I got from the R.A.F. in Africa) and one is a Browning automatic. Maybe we will be able to corner Herr Hitler behind the lines sometime and riddle him with a few of the thousands of bullets we have available.

Another leaflet picked up in a field! Ironic, isn't it, to pick up a message from Bobby Sherwood in a field in France? Ironic, too, to be visiting France to the accompaniment of a constant artillery barrage and the roar of hundreds of planes in the air.

I must say, I feel sorry for the French, as, in order to get back their freedom, they have to see their country ravaged all over again from another direction. But I have come to the conclusion that bricks and mortar, however beautiful, are not nearly as important as we used to think. It is the spirit of a country that really counts; and if France had been a little less worried in 1940 about saving Paris, they might not have lost France. Now they are going to lose out both ways.

FRANCE, JUNE 17, 1944

Another note before the sun goes down. It is now 9:15 and the sun should set in about 45 minutes. Funny, you know, I don't recall these

213

late summer nights before; but then, of course, we are on double summer time.

In about three days the ban on descriptions of the landing will be lifted and I can perhaps give you a few more details of the operation.* Until then nothing but idle chatter is allowed.

I do hope, in one way, that the Germans give in before the whole of France is virtually in ruins, as is pretty much bound to be the case if they fight a delaying action to the German border. The French are taking it wonderfully, however. In all the ruined towns French and American flags are flying and the inhabitants hurl flowers at the soldiers. I saw one house that had been totally destroyed. Nothing but rubble was left, but stuck in the rubble was a flagpole and an old man and woman sat with beaming faces on the ruins with the French flag flying above their white hair. A gallant people, I must say. In the countryside, the farmers tell me, the people did not fare so badly even though they had to send most of their cattle to Germany, but they at least got enough milk, butter and eggs. But in the towns food was very scarce. They hate the Germans with a towering passion, and a woman in a farmhouse told me there was just one thing to do to each and every Boche—and she pulled her finger quickly across her throat. . . . Slit the throat of every German, she said. Then this won't happen again. I must say, I agree with her and I think I'll be happier after I've attended to a few of them in person!

FRANCE, JUNE 24, 1944

I haven't written for the last few days, not because I was too busy but because I was too lazy. Actually I had plenty of time but I seem to have wasted most of it, in such trivial—but important!—items, as scouring the countryside for eggs, butter, potatoes and onions to supplement our rations. Today we had a gala lunch of fresh beefsteak, fried onions, fried potatoes and for breakfast I had four fresh eggs.

Two day ago I had a bloody encounter—with a deer! We finally brought him down, after shooting up a veritable storm and had venison for the whole platoon the next day. It sounded louder—the

*That letter was lost in the mails.

chase—than the front lines and was certainly as bloody, as the poor thing had all its insides shot out. However, he tasted very good. The next day Frank went deer hunting and came home with the hind quarters of a cow. The whole company had meat the next day. No more need be said about that!

You see that total war is not as bad as it is cracked up to be!

Soon I'll be able to tell you in more detail my daily experiences, prosaic as they have been. But I can tell you that on D. day, D-day plus one and D-day plus two, I was still in Merrie England, champing at the bit.

I am very comfortably settled now. I have put up an Italian tent I stole in Sicily which is much roomier than our pup tent and I have our platoon C.P. therein.

I have just heard a report that the town of Bayeux fortunately bears hardly a mark of war. The Cathedral is intact, they tell me, and the shops, cafés, etc., are all open. That is lucky, isn't it? I only hope they can spare other towns like Chartres, but I fear that Rouen is doomed—such a beautiful town, too.

Well, Mother dear, keep your chin up, as the saying goes. I know you will and I am confident that your prayers will bring me through with flags flying.

Tell Cousin Tina* that France is still one of the most delightful spots in the world, even sitting on the ground at the edge of a field and looking at a contented cow. I wonder if that cow would feel so contented if she knew I had designs on her life.

FRANCE, JUNE 28, 1944

We are living in style here. We have had venison every day for three days and we had brook trout for lunch today. Trust a GI, particularly from the 82nd, to look after himself!

There is no news until the bar is let down and I can begin to give you back news. Then there's not too much.

We are receiving all types of mail now. It is almost like England, so maybe my camera will come along soon.

*Mrs. Charles Bohlen.

215

I can tell you that up to D plus 12—that's the date, I think, that I can go back to — I underwent no great hardships! In fact I got far more rest and relaxation than I did in England when that damnable training schedule kept us busy night and day. The nights were noisy as the devil, due almost entirely to our own artillery batteries, which would bang away merrily from dusk till dawn. But after the first fifteen minutes of that you would go right back to sleep. The first few shots would usually wake you, as the ground shakes, if you are close enough to them, but then you turn over and that's that.

The enemy used very little counter battery fire. One of the mysteries of this campaign, in fact, is where the devil the German artillery is. All the authorities said that they would have artillery zeroed in on almost every square inch of the beachhead. But they certainly didn't. An occasional 88 or 150 would shell the rear areas without any apparent objective, but none of them ever came any closer to us than four or five hundred yards—not enough to make one bother to turn over in bed, much less get into a slit trench. Actually this slit trench business is vastly exaggerated in one not so humble opinion! There are times, I concede, when they may be necessary, if you are in a dug-in position and under steady fire. But, by and large, they're a complete waste of effort. If the same energy was used to advance from one hedgerow to another as is thrown away in digging, I have a feeling we'd be in Berlin a good deal sooner than we will be! The Luftwaffe has been conspicuous largely by its absence. The first night a few stray bombers were over our area. One bomb landed, as a matter of fact, a few feet away from one of our cars. An occasional flight (three to five planes) of Focke-Wulfs has been over strafing, with very little result, but that's about all. The most fun I had the first week or so was in taking small patrols—just two peeps—up to reconnoitre the front lines and contact the infantry units there. The sniper menace has been much exaggerated, I may say. I've been shot at about four times by snipers, I guess, and they've never hit yet.

One of the most interesting features of going up to the front is to try and find it before you are behind the enemy lines. It's such a fluid front that you can go right down the road and be in enemy territory without even knowing it—(in some spots, at least, in others you'll know it right away!) The information you get at headquarters as to the location of the front is invariably incorrect, so you have to rely on a sort of sixth sense to let you know when you'd better slow down and take it easy round corners. This, mind you, is when both sides are dug in and there's not much shooting going on. Usually, you get a little warning tingle in the back of your neck which says, "Better take it easy." But that's about the only warning you do get and several times that tingle has come just in time, when I thought the front was actually a good deal farther away than it was! You feel like a Quartermaster just going up to the front lines to visit and get information, but it's better than not going up at all.

One day Frank and I were out on an informal reconnaissance trip in our peep. We were sailing along merrily, chatting about Virginia for all I know, when we noticed that there was none of our wire strung along the roads (one infallible way of telling where the front lines are) but only German wire and no signs saying the road was clear of mines. We knew the line was uncertain at this spot—that is, if we were reading our maps correctly—but it seemed as if we should be able to get through this road, as, indeed, we had. We checked our maps. I put the machine gun at full load and we went on, but a trifle more cautiously. We saw two Frenchmen in denims ahead, trudging along the road and we pulled up to ask if we were on the right road. I noticed that they walked in step and looked rather military, so I kept an eye on them when I asked them if such and such a village was ahead (in French). One of them answered in good French, but he pronounced the name of the village very queerly, so I hopped out and covered them with my paratroop carbine (one that has a folding stock) and got my driver and another enlisted man to search them. Sure enough, they were Germans, though they had no soldiers pay-cards or military identification or arms or uniforms. They admitted, at the point of a gun, to being Germans—said they were trying to find our lines. I wanted to shoot them on the spot! but it is pretty difficult to do so in cold blood and they were only nineteen and twenty and scared stiff, I may add. So we put them on the front of the peep and told them *'Achtung minen'*—to watch for mines—and proceeded onward to see if we could locate a PW station. The younger turned bright green when we told him he was going to watch for mines and be the first to be blown up if we hit one, but that was all right and, God knows, it was the truth. Well, we went on a piece and passed several deserted German gun emplacements, and then at a corner where I had gone on foot ahead to scout around it, I saw a man in uniform pull back quickly behind a hedgerow. I was pretty sure it was our own uniform (we were headed then down a road which should have led to our own lines, assuming, that is, that we were behind the enemy lines). But the chances of his shooting were good, whether he was enemy or friendly. So I figured the best thing was to walk forward as if you owned the road and make no attempt at concealment. That would give them a chance to get a good look at the uniform, in case the peep with the two Germans in overalls on the front had mystified them. I went up further around the bend, saw they had an elaborate road-block one hundred yards ahead, took out my field glasses, and scanned the road back of it. I saw we had a machine gun position in one ditch and a soldier scurried across the road and joined the two men who were on it. He was American, too. I don't think they would have shot if we had moved the peep forward, but there was a chance that they were the trigger-happy type who would shoot first and ask questions afterwards (and in this case they would have had some justification, as they were a good four hundred yards away). So I turned, walked slowly back to the peep, turned it around and went back the way we came. When we did hit our own lines, we were told we were in an area which was 'strongly held' by the Germans in a pocket between two of our forward prongs and that the Americans were just about to lay a barrage of artillery on the area. Incidentally, the road block was our own, as I had thought. We merely approached it from the wrong side! We notified them that the enemy had already withdrawn, went on and dumped our 'prisoners' at a PW station and headed homeward.

I am sitting now in my Italian tent, propped up against a tent pole, which may account for my handwriting. It is pouring rain and has been raining intermittently for days. I've never known France to be like this before. In England the sun shone for a month before we left. Here, where it should shine, it's hardly ever stopped raining. Damnable, if you ask me.

FRANCE, JULY 3, 1944. LATER

The sun has at last come out, thank God, and I am seated in the middle of an apple orchard propped up against a tree. The darned artillery has just opened up a field or two away from us and it is loud enough to split your ear-drums, then, the whirr and you can't even hear the explosion except as a faint clap like someone beating on a pan in the distance. It's a far more pleasant sound, however, than the whine that draws closer and closer over your head.

I can give you now a little description of a combat patrol I took out sometime ago to penetrate behind the enemy lines and knock out a strong point. The main point of the mission actually was to capture some prisoners dead or alive, for unit identification purposes. It is perhaps incorrect, too, to say 'enemy strong point,' as we didn't know it was a strong point until after we had gone in.

Frank came and woke me up one night to tell me that we had been ordered to send one platoon on a dismounted patrol the next evening—that we would draw straws the next morning to see which platoon went. I won the toss, thank goodness, and Frank and I went down and reconnoitered the territory that morning. I took thirty-six men and a lieutenant and four sergeants from another outfit. Frank was in charge of the unit and took one squad; I took another, and my scout section leader another.

When we got down to the spot at about 7:30 p.m. (we trucked down instead of using our vehicles), we found that the Germans had moved into the village since we were there in the morning and were now just in spitting distance across the road from an infantry platoon that had an outpost there. That made us change our mission and we decided to attack and drive them out of the village where originally we had planned to penetrate deeper and find out where they were.

Frank took the most important and most dangerous assignment, that of a direct attack on the barn where they were situated and attacking the left flank; my mission was to hit them just to the right of the village, advancing through an orchard up to a hedgerow where we knew they had two machine guns. The object was to draw their fire and keep them occupied while Frank smacked them frontally and from the left. The third squad we sent way round the right flank to secure the flank and to trap any Germans that escaped from the village toward their main lines to the south.

Our plan was to attack about 8:30, so that we could make the attack in daylight and be able to withdraw under cover of darkness in case we got trapped or pinned down. We figured the fight should be over by 11:30 P.M.

We briefed our squads and then took off—No. 3 starting first, as it had farthest to go, then my squad, last of all Frank's.

I got to the road fairly easily, without drawing fire, and deployed along the hedgerow. I observed movement where infantry had told us there was a machine gun and, as soon as I thought Frank had had time to get his men into position, I opened fire.

That was the signal for every thing to open fire at once, so it seemed. The machine gun sprayed the hedgerow; enemy rifle fire and machine pistols opened up all along the hedgerow at the head of the orchard. And I heard Frank's squad opening up on our left.

I realized we could never advance up through the orchard, as we had planned on paper. The terrain favored the Germans, as there was a slight incline all the way up, and there was practically no cover. The only way we could hope to get up was along the west side of the hedgerow where we had excellent cover from anything along the main strong line. There was no cover at all from anything in the hedgerow just ahead, but it was unlikely that there was anything more than an outpost stationed there, if that. And there was only one way to find out. Leaving half the squad along the road to cover us, I accordingly scrambled through the hedgerow, scratching myself to shreds, it seemed, and started up the hedgerow. I got halfway up to where there was a break in the hedgerow, leading into the orchard, and was observing the line with my glasses when a machine gun opened up from the right corner of the hedgerow just ahead. I hit the ground, as did everyone else who was following, and crawled forward a few feet, so that, if he sprayed the ground, he wouldn't find M. C. Eustis lying there. I passed back word for the men deployed along the road to try and knock out the position with rifle grenades and took another man with me to crawl up along the hedgerow. There was no cover except high grass, but we didn't gain anything staying where we were and we might be able to get through the hedgerow and knock him out at close range. As luck (and excellent firing) would have it, we knocked out the gun or the gunner on the third round of rifle grenade fire and we were able to reach our point without drawing any further fire from the flank.

From there we could observe activity at the next point, in fact all along the hedgerow, so I pulled up the bulk of the squad and deployed them along the hedgerow, leaving two men back to protect our left and right flank.

I tried to radio to Frank and the Lieutenant on the right flank to see how they were getting on, but the walky-talky would do nothing but play dance music, thanks to Jerry jamming, so we had to do the best we could on our own and trust to luck and sense that we wouldn't fire on our own men.

We each knew where the other was, or was supposed to be, and we could hear each other plainly even if we couldn't see each other. The Jerries complicated our lives a bit by having two of our own B.A.R.'s, which they had captured, but we had been warned of that in advance and the sound of their other weapons is quite different from our own.

We were throwing fire steadily at every flash and moving thing we saw behind the Jerry's dug-in position and then hell let loose as they opened up with everything they had. They threw mortars and grenades into the field just back of us, but never did seem to get our range; and there was a constant spray of fire along the top of the hedgerow. I told my men to open up with everything we had and to keep changing their positions so that we would seem to be a much larger force than we actually were. Frank had evidently done the same and from the racket we made we sounded more like a Battalion than a platoon! Which was what got us through so well, I feel convinced.

The Germans were there in much stronger force than they had been G-2'd to be and, if they had had any idea of how small our force was, they could probably have overrun us at any time. They'd have lost a good deal in the process but they could have done it, I feel sure.

Our tactics throughout were completely unorthodox from an infantry point of view. We went about it as if we were hunting rabbits rather than Germans and pushed ahead about four times faster than any infantry patrol would ever have done, as the infantry told us the next day! The net result was, however, to surprise the Jerries completely, to make them think that a real attack in force was being made. They accordingly opened up with everything they had, including some heavy artillery, which our artillery was able to spot and knock out. And we learnt twice as much about their strength and positions as if we had not had a knock-down, drag-out scrap.

Well, to go back, we held our position for about an hour, I should guess, peppering them constantly but not able to advance, as they had all the ground ahead of us covered. I wanted to try and flank them through the orchard to our right but didn't dare, as I knew that, if I were successful, I'd be firing directly at Frank and he at me. I got no word from our 3rd squad on the extreme right flank, but they seemed to be having a considerable fight, too, judging from the sound over there.

Then the Jerries opened up with 150 mm. howitzers. They ranged in first on the village, disregarding completely, it seems, the fact that their own troops were still in there. Then they started hitting the road just behind us, and it looked as if they might be about to range in on our hedgerow. I ordered the squad to move down to a point along the hedgerow to the right, so that we could withdraw through the orchard if we had to, and stayed up at the higher point with another man to cover them. The Germans started coming down the hedgerow towards us, so I figured we'd better withdraw in a hurry to prevent their getting to our rear and cutting us off. We were also getting very low on ammunition, as we frankly hadn't anticipated such a spit and fire session. Withdraw we did along the line, as we found that the hedgerow was too thick to penetrate and we couldn't get into the orchard.

Everything was quiet now for a change, except for an occasional

222

sputter. I'd ordered my men to cease firing unless they saw a definite target and our artillery had evidently got the 150 howitzers. We got back to the cover of the road just in time, as the Jerries opened up from the back of the hedgerow just behind where we had originally been, and we deployed again along the road to hold the flank.

It was about 11:30 by then and just dark, so I sent a man back with a wounded man I wanted to evacuate, to get the dope from Frank's section and find out what he wanted me to do. He returned shortly and said that the attack was over and to return to the assembly point, which we accordingly did.

We then checked our squads over and found, all things considered, that we had fared darned well. We know we accounted for at least ten or a dozen Jerries killed and I don't know how many wounded. Our own casualties were negligible in comparison, though we did lose one man that I hated to lose. By the time we had collected everyone and walked back to the trucks, it was about 1:00 A.M. and we got to bed about 2:00, exhausted but, on the whole, well satisfied.

It was the best possible experience we could get, particularly to have to fight dismounted, as you have to, for the most part, in this terrain, and to be under as heavy and as concentrated fire as we were for about two solid hours. The platoon is a seasoned one, but we hadn't fought for over half a year and we had several new men. So the knowledge we gained was invaluable and everyone who went seemed to agree about this.

It's always a help to be under fire and to realize how great the odds are against your being hit. And how much less of a strain the whole thing is than you might be wont to imagine.

We went back, Frank and I, the next day and found that the infantry was full of our attack! They'd never heard anything like it, and it stirred up a hornet's nest! But best of all, they were definitely pleased and most appreciative of what we had done. They got more information as a result of our patrol than from dozens of their own they had sent out, they said, and we had penetrated farther into the enemy lines than they believed was possible. We had, however, actually failed to accomplish our mission. We didn't take the town and we didn't bring back any prisoners, dead or alive. But it would have taken a force three times as strong as we had to do that, and we gave ten for every one we took. I think frankly the infantry was a little leery of us coming into their territory at the beginning. Any outfit is apt to distrust another. But the next day they were all smiles. The Colonel said that any time we'd like to come back, he'd be delighted to have us, mounted or dismounted. Which is all to the good.

I am frankly exhausted now. This is July 4th, as I couldn't finish last night, and I think back to Oatlands invariably when I think of the 4th. Well, next year, perhaps, we'll have the fire-works there.

FRANCE, JULY 9, 1944

We are required to get up at 5 A.M. each morning, regardless of whether we have anything to do or not; and as you rarely go to bed until it is dark at 11.30 P.M., you are apt to take cat naps during the day. In fact you do take them! And so your time for letter writing is spent blissfully in the arms of Morpheus. . . . The last letters I have from home were dated the 27th of June and I got them three days ago, which isn't bad at all. In fact the mail seems to be coming through just about as well as it did in England. And life is just about as normal as it was there, save that it is far less nerve wracking, owing to the absence of any regular training schedule.

It is amazing how really comfortable you can be in the field, even in weather like we have been having, in which it rains every day without fail. I have had only two complete baths since June 5th and one of those was out of a bucket and the other out of a saucepan. I have slept every night in my clothes, minus shoes only, except for a couple of nights when shells were dropping moderately close and I kept my shoes on. And yet I have never felt better or more relaxed, and actually my tent is luxurious. I can black it out and read at night by flashlight. I am sitting now in the parlor, on a ration box outside my tent, under an apple tree and in about two minutes it is going to start raining with a vengeance.

The only thing that irks me really in this whole set-up is the inaction and the caution we are displaying. I wish we'd blitz right in and get the thing over with in a hurry.

224

It is now 10:15 P.M. and I am seated on a box of rifle grenades leaning against a tree, next to my Italian tent. Most of the platoon are lying in a circle in front of me playing poker under an apple tree, while the radio from the radio car is playing a jazz program.

Not such a tough life, is it?!!

Actually it has all been a perfect cinch as far as we were concerned ever since we have been here; and the papers have vastly exaggerated the fierceness of the fighting everywhere.

Frank and I went up to Cherbourg the Friday before it fell, when the papers and the radio were full of bloody hand to hand combat. That was the day, incidentally, that we spent three hours behind the enemy lines without knowing it and ran into one of our own road blocks from the wrong side!

Actually, there was very little fighting and hardly any hand to hand combat. We got up to the fort overlooking the town from the right flank—the infantry had just taken it—and there was scattered machine gun fire whizzing round but nothing even to make you duck your head. Largely, I would say it has been an artillery and Air Corps war so far.

And again I urge you to believe *nothing* you read in the papers.

Because, it just ain't so!

I went up to Caen the day before it fell and got up to the last outpost where a tank battle was just starting. It was interesting but not as exciting as you might imagine. A certain amount of artillery fire was dropping round, but most of that was directed at the airport hangars, which were already in shreds, and not much was falling round the tanks. The outskirts of Caen were just about five hundred yards away across a slight defile and the British were laying a heavy barrage of mortar and artillery fire on the German positions. A Canadian officer in one of the tanks told me that there already was a patrol in the town that had come in from the North (we were at the Western approach on the road from Tilly); that the Germans had evacuated the town and were just holding at suicide strong points round the outskirts.

We came back down the streets of a little town that was almost completely a shell. Here they *had* had hand to hand fighting for three days. We went through several ruins in search of booty—particularly liquid booty—but the Canadians had already combed the area and had collected 1,500 bottles of cognac in a dugout the day before.

*   *   *

Some Canadian soldiers beckoned to us from a bombed out house and gave us some wine. I collected a nice aluminum pot for cooking and we went back to the peeps and headed homeward through a mass of knocked out tanks (British and German) and heavy artillery firing with almost machine gun precision toward the Jerries!

Caen fell about three hours after we were there, so I took a patrol up the next day to see the town before the M.P.'s took over and put everything "off limits." The town itself is a mess. All the outskirts are a shambles; then there is a ring of about five hundred yards that is hardly touched, but the center of the town is the most completely obliterated town that I have seen. Rubble is piled two to three stories high in all the streets. We picked our way through the debris, keeping an eye out for snipers. A few French people were wandering back to see what was left of their possessions, but the town had the same rather ghost-like atmosphere that Messina had. It was all so quiet—just a shell of something that had once been a thriving metropolis.

In a second story café that was all open to the sky we saw some Canadians seated at a table, eating and drinking. We picked our way upstairs and they invited us to have some wine with them in their palace restaurant—*"le meilleur du monde,"* the sign said. We drank a few toasts to each other, and then we pushed on through the ruins back to our peeps and back home. The Germans were still putting up a stiff defense to the south about five hundred yards from the road we had to take, and we watched the British peppering the area from the rear with artillery. The Germans were shelling the road sporadically but not enough to cause us any concern, and we got through easily.

That evening, in a search for eggs, I ran into the nicest French family I have seen so far. They were refugees from Boulogne and

226

they had many interesting tales of the four years under the German heel. The soldiers, by and large, they said were *"très correct."* But this good behaviour went hand in hand with the most savage atrocities and then they (the Boches) wondered why everyone didn't love them. In one village, they told me, where a railroad tressle had been dynamited several times by the Maquis, a German officer ordered everyone in the station shot (no matter what they were doing there), then rounded up the Mayor, the Curé and the village's leading citizens, had them shot in front of all the rest of the inhabitants, and then marched all the remaining men, women and children into the church—locked them up there, saturated the building with gasoline and set fire to it. Something very similar to that happened in another village not too far from where we are.

A newspaper man told me he saw a captured German officer who was raving about the American "terror bombings" of innocent women and children. He reminded the officer of Rotterdam, Warsaw, Coventry, London, etc., etc., but made absolutely no impression. Anything these people do is all right as long as *they* do it. But give them their own medicine and they whine like babies.

If I don't kill at least ten of them personally, I shall be most unhappy!! I'm pretty sure I accounted for some on our combat patrol, but they were seventy-five yards away and I never could get up to see the damage.

Well, enough of such bloodthirsty talk!

*   *   *

We've just been issued some new camouflage uniforms—"Zoot suits" as we call them—two piece uniforms in varying shades and splotches of greens, browns and yellows. Twenty yards away you can hardly see a man and I'm sure we'll look, to the Jerries, as if our vehicles were approaching without any personnel in them. I'm going to have a picture taken and will send it to you, only you probably won't see anything at all but a bush!

Had a fascinating experience in the platoon the other evening during an air raid. A couple of F.W.190's tried to get through to the beach but were driven back by the ack ack. We were standing watching them coming closer in a veritable blaze of fireworks when suddenly there was an explosion just behind us. I looked back and saw one of our pup tents going up in smoke and a few men nearby racing for the ditch. All the rest of us dispersed in a hurry and hit the ditches or slit trenches as our own ack ack began pinging round in the area. As soon as the planes passed overhead I dashed over to the tent and saw that it was a complete shambles; blankets, clothes and everything torn to shreds. Just then a pale face stuck its head out of the ditch and one of my men followed it. He was in the tent writing a letter when the shell hit it. It was a 40 mm dud—one of our own—that failed to explode in the air and by some miracle he wasn't even scratched. He'd just moved his head when the barrage started and was reaching for his helmet, and the shell hit just where his head had been. He showed me the letter he was writing and the last line was "At the moment I'm still feeling fine." (I'm not exaggerating!) I told him to finish the letter and repeat the phrase again! And carted the debris down to HQ. to be salvaged.

It all goes to show—I don't care what anyone says—it's luck, pure and simple. If your number's not on the shell, you're O.K.

I'm delighted you're enjoying yourself in Quebec. Take care of yourself. May be the way things are going it won't be so long now before we'll all be back. And don't, I repeat again, don't worry about me. I am sure, between you and all your saints and my own bull luck, that I'll be OK.

And remember, too, it's nowhere near as bad at any time, even the worst, as you can picture in your imagination.

I've got the best platoon in the B'n, they really know how to fight, and they like to fight. And that kind of platoon makes its own breaks.

The weather finally has cleared.

Pray God we don't have any more rain for a time.

FRANCE, JULY 22, 1944

I am sitting for the first time since England at a table. I'll grant you it is only a collapsible company mess table under a spreading

228

apple tree. But it is at least a solid foundation for this miserable scratch pad.

It stopped raining this afternoon, for the first time in three days, and I celebrated by taking a hot bath in a small tin bucket and then boiling my dirty clothes in the same bucket. That is the way I do my washing when I don't get some accommodating French woman to do it for me. I let it boil for two hours, then rinse it out in cold water and hang it out. It doesn't look white but I figure that it must be clean. And please don't disillusion me about the results!

You should see one of the road intersections not very far from where we are bivouacked àt present. It happened to have been a thoroughly bombed out spot but the engineers rapidly made it passable. Well, I didn't see it for about two weeks and the last time I crossed it, I almost fell out of my peep. They have made a huge circle, bounded by felled trees. It looks like nothing much that I can think of except one of those super-intersections in the Saw Mill River Parkway—beautiful road signs at each of the eight roads that meet at this point—M.P.'s with white helmets waving you to the right. All it needs is a Good Humor sign in the center to take you right back to America. And all this not six miles from the front lines.

I can't help feeling—not to be disparaging to our Engineers—that more of this type of effort expended *at* the front and less behind the lines would end the war sooner. But still you have to take your hat off to some American quality—I don't know just what it is. If we don't like something the way it is, to hell with it. We'll build it our way. And we *will* and have, all over the world.

Actually I am enjoying myself here, though I'd be happier if we were seeing more action.

I saw one fascinating sight at the British front lines not far from Caen. We went up in our peeps through quite an artillery barrage, got to a point which was practically on the front lines and asked a soldier in a ditch if we could leave the peeps anywhere. He said "The parking lot's just this way, Sir." And, sure enough, there was a sign in the woods: "Visitors, please park your vehicles here." About two hundred yards further up a hedgerow was a sign: "Visitors will please crawl from this point." That was two hundred yards from the German front lines.

A wonderful people, the British!

FRANCE, AUGUST 1, 1944

Your letter of July 20th received this A.M. Quick, isn't it? I had to smile, I confess, at the statement, "I am so glad that you are not in London with all those robot bombs!" when I thought back a few days! But I, too, am sincerely glad that I am not in London—though, frankly, I should like to see one of the flying bombs.

The German morale is certainly getting low. The prisoners we capture now are not at all the arrogant crew they once were. They have reached the whimpering stage instead. They can't understand why America is fighting Germany anyway. Their only real enemy, they say, is Russia. If only America and England would join them in polishing off Russia—but no, we kill defenseless women and children instead and make their own life, incidentally, a living hell, what with the incessant air bombing and strafing and the artillery barrages we hammer them with! Most of them look nervous wrecks and poor physical specimens to boot. Not at all the master race. They are a terrible people, aren't they? They bully when they're on top and whimper when they're down.

FRANCE, AUGUST 3, 1944

Just a short line to let you know that all is going splendidly as usual. I have just had an early supper and am sitting in my peep sunning myself. I regret to tell you that you have a shock in store for you—another one of those damn decorations—the Bronze Star this time, awarded (*if* it is actually awarded) for the part I played in one of the recent actions. I say "if" as it has not been awarded as yet. The Captain merely told me he had put in the recommendation and by mistake the papers on the case were just given to me to sign, instead of to the Captain. So don't say a word about it to anyone until,

or *unless!*, it is made official. Actually, this time I was in a far more dangerous position than in the Sicilian affair. Also I had much more fun, as I led the column riding in the turret of a medium tank, and nothing I know gives you quite the sense of power as that. You feel that nothing can stop you—and nothing much can, except, of course, an anti-tank gun or a Mark VI.

It shouldn't be too long now before the war will be over and then we'll have a grand and glorious reunion.

Give my love to everyone, and take care of yourself.

FRANCE, AUGUST 10, 1944. TO E. P.*

I have had a fairly exciting and, at times, nerve racking time during the last three weeks but so far am well and in the best of health. I have had many, many close shaves, and at times you get a little bit fed up with being under fire, usually when you are just sitting under artillery fire and can't fire back, but, by and large, we have made out as well as could be expected, considering the type of missions we have. We are almost always deep in enemy territory, subject to attack from all sides, and you can see that that type of operation can be pretty damned exciting.

I ran smack into the enemy lines the other day in a peep. I had been told the road was clear and the enemy was so startled they never even fired. I was somewhat startled, myself! Another time, some dismounted men let us sneak forward, dismounted up the road on to a machine gun position and then had the nerve to open up on us from the rear. They never hit one of us, but for a few moments I thought we'd never get out.

And so it goes. It gets to be all part of the day's run and the rest periods seem rather tame by comparison.

I shouldn't mind, however, if the whole affair wound up before many more weeks are passed, as your luck can hold out just so long in this type of game, and sooner or later someone's aim is going to be good, especially when you are sitting out most of the time in the point vehicle.

*Mrs. John Parkinson.

The following excerpt is taken from "The Stars and Stripes" which was published on Monday, August 7th, three days before his last letter.

"On the third day of the battle that cut the Normandy peninsula, while radios blared success and victory to the four corners of the world, a small force of American armor was catching merry hell at Notre Dame de Cenilly crossroads. The veteran reconnaissance battalion* which spearheaded the Second Armored Division in one of the most spectacular cross country drives had experiences, good and bad, which were probably duplicated by every advance guard unit in the fight.

"Immediately after the break through above St. Lo, the battle for this battalion—which had units and patrols always ranging behind the German lines—started with a defeat. At Canisy one of the assault guns was knocked out and the light reconnaissance force was stopped by heavy German armor.

"Heavy American armor came up and with crushing P47's flying close support, the Germans were crushed.   ·

"From there on the Battalion's keen young commander, Lt. Col. Wheeler G. Merriam, who was in the middle of practically every fight, insisted on drive and more drive—and that is what his men gave him.

"When a patrol under Lts. Frank Jordan and Morton Eustis took a cross road far in advance of everything else American, three truck loads of German infantry followed them down the road. It was a situation where the Germans, if given the split seconds they needed, could wipe out the Yanks, so Jordan, who was a lawyer in Virginia and Eustis, who wrote drama criticisms in New York, parked their jeep behind a hedgerow and as the German trucks approached, the Americans obliterated them with machine gun fire. . . .

"From dawn of the first day of battle until sundown after reaching the objective, it was that way—heavy fighting, relaxation, then more and heavier fighting."†

*The 82nd Reconnaissance Battalion.
†See Appendix, page 241.

I wrote you a line about five days ago but was never able to get it off and it is sitting right next to me now. I hope both these letters can get off in the near future, as I want you to know that I have survived the Blitz-krieg in good shape and am in the best possible health—a little sleepy, perhaps, but that is all.

At the moment I am sitting in my peep stripped to the waist, taking a sun bath. And save for the fact that artillery is banging away around us (our *own* artillery, I am glad to state), the whole setting is very peaceful.

A mortifying article appeared in yesterday's continental edition of The Stars and Stripes, in which it described the drive our company made to the S.——— River in the latter part of July and credited Frank and me with knocking out *single handed* (which was a complete lie) two truckloads of German infantry with machine guns! And it said that Frank and I were the prize "pilferers" of the B'n in that we "appropriated" two medium tanks and kept them with us for the drive! Well, we did get the two tanks, but we asked permission for them, so why shouldn't we! I rode in the turret of the point tank during the two-day drive, mowing down Jerries with a 50 cal. machine gun.

We had several interesting fights at one time or another and came out on the whole pretty well. This campaign is a good deal nearer the real thing than Sicily was, but Sicily was invaluable experience none the less and probably saved us many lives in this foray.

I can't write much in detail now, as I haven't too much time and we can't write details until two weeks after the event in any case. I have had about every type of lead the Germans have to offer hurled at me at one time or another, but so far (touch wood) haven't been scratched, which is more than I can say for many, many Germans who have come up against my platoon.

Well, Mother dear, take care of yourself. Your letters are wonderful, we get mail almost every night. And don't worry. And give my love to everyone.

On August 13th our Battalion was ordered to start an attack on Domfront, France. We had run into some German Infantry along the main road leading into the town from the west. Morton was riding in the turret of a tank and was leading the column. He was sitting in the turret manning the 50 cal. machine gun and was exposed from his waist up. I was walking beside the tank and we were shouting to each other, speculating on where the Germans had gone. We were moving about as fast as I could walk. Suddenly we were fired on by rifle and machine gun fire. Morton was returning the fire with his machine gun, when the tank was hit by a type of anti-tank rocket carried by the Infantry. The tank behind us was firing by this time and the Germans were falling back. I managed to climb up on the tank and into the turret in a matter of seconds and soon had Morton out of the tank. However, it was useless, because a fragment had hit him in the head and I am sure that he died instantly.

*Wounded October 8th, died of wounds in Germany, October 15th, 1944. Also see Appendix, page 246. *The Stars & Stripes,* December 28, 1944.

APPENDIX

EXCERPTS OF LETTER FROM
LT. COL. WHEELER G. MERRIAM,
BATTALION COMMANDER
82nd. ARMORED RECON. BATTALION

Germany, May 17, 1945

Morton was one of those persons that will not be forgotten. Together with Frank Jordan he made his platoon as complete an entity as any regiment or division in the army; just as fiery in its loyalties, just as quick and loud in shouting for its due. Frank and Morton represented what is best expressed as the "loyal opposition"; never content to passively accept what they thought was wrong or unfair. The men literally worshipped them both. I mention Frank Jordan with Morton because they were inseparable—in spirit too.

Morton had apparently composed a song for every occasion. I dare say some of the choicer ones never reached my ears. Everyone of our officers' parties had the interlude of gathering about the piano while Morton tunefully put colonels, majors, in fact the whole army in its proper place—we loved it. His men sang too. He had one of those things, so rare among American troops, a singing platoon.

His idea of leadership was superb. Never aloof from his men he stood above them on his character. When the going was difficult he was at the spot where it was roughest. It was thus that he was killed as he led his platoon which was spearheading our attack on Domfront.

Much of the glorious part of the war he saw. The days of the St. Lo breakthrough; of tearing apart the confused German army in Northern France. I say glorious, only as a comparative term as opposed to the ghastly weeks of calculated death in the Siegfried line and the long frigid nights in the snow of the Ardennes.

Wheeler G. Merriam
Lt. Col. U. S. Army

82nd Arm. Rec. Bn.
A.P.O. 252, Postmaster, New York

CONFIDENTIAL
HEADQUARTERS 2ND ARMORED DIVISION
OFFICE OF THE DIVISION COMMANDER
A.P.O. 252
20 August 1943.

General Order No. 46.

Award of Oak Leaf Cluster Silver Medal Star I
Award of Silver Star Medal II

* * *

II Award of Silver Star Medal

Under the provisions of A.R. 600-45, as amended, a Silver Star Medal is awarded each of the following named officers and the following named enlisted men:

1st Lieutenant Morton C. Eustis, o-1575303, Company C. 82nd Armored Reconnaissance Battalion, United States Army. For gallantry in action. On 22 July, 1943, near S. Ciperello, Sicily, Lieutenant Eustis was given the mission as the point for the advance guard for the advance on Palermo. Because of the rate of speed at which the column was travelling and the mountainous terrain, the only possible way to determine the location of the enemy was by drawing enemy fire. When enemy fire was encountered and the column was held up, Lieutenant Eustis dismounted and advanced on foot through heavy small arms and artillery fire to locate the enemy gun positions. Lieutenant Eustis's coolness and courage under fire coupled with his aggressiveness and disregard of his own safety in fulfilling the mission given to him reflect great credit upon himself and the Armed Forces. Medal No. 23488. Residence of appointment: Washington, D. C.

* * *

By command of Major General Gaffey:

R. F. Ferry
Colonel, G.S.C.
Chief of Staff.

238

Official:
R. H. Shell
Lt. Col. A.G.D.
Adjutant General

WAR DEPARTMENT
THE ADJUTANT GENERAL'S OFFICE
WASHINGTON, D. C.

4 January 1945

My dear Mrs. Eustis:

I have the honor to inform you that, by direction of the President, The Silver Star, one Oak-Leaf Cluster, representing one additional award of the same decoration, and the Bronze Star Medal have been posthumously awarded to your son, First Lieutenant Morton C. Eustis, Armored Cavalry. The citations are as follows:

ONE OAK LEAF CLUSTER TO THE SILVER STAR

"For gallantry in Action on 13 August 1944 in France. First Lieutenant Eustis, in command of the Third Platoon, Company "C" . . . Armored Reconnaissance Battalion, with a Platoon of medium tanks and fifteen dismounted men attached, was given the mission of crossing the ———— River and attacking ————, ... France. Lieutenant Eustis, with utter disregard for his own personal safety and under heavy small arms fire, rode on the turret of the leading medium tank in order to best direct the advance. He was always present at the point when contact with the enemy was made. Lieutenant Eustis was killed by an enemy rocket projectile while firing a fifty caliber machine gun, from an exposed position, at a dismounted enemy patrol, which had forced his own dismounted men to take cover. Lieutenant Eustis's courage and habitual contempt for the enemy was largely responsible for the success of his Platoon."

BRONZE STAR MEDAL

"For meritorious service in France during the period 29 July 1944 to 30 July 1944, in connection with military operations against the enemy. First Lieutenant Eustis, Company "C" . . . Armored Reconnaissance Battalion, while riding in the point vehicle of his Platoon which was acting as advance guard for the company that was reconnoitering the right flank of the main Axis of Combat Command B. 2nd Armored Division, did, without regard for his own personal safety, come under enemy fire at least ten times and by his quick action in locating and destroying enemy tanks and ground positions made it possible for the company to move forward on its mission."

These decorations will be forwarded to the Commanding General, Military District of Washington, D. C., who will select an officer to make the presentation. The officer selected will communicate with you concerning your wishes in the matter.

May I again express my deepest sympathy, etc.,

Sincerely yours,

Robert H. Dunlop
Brigadier General
Acting the Adjutant General.

From *The Stars and Stripes,* Monday, August 7, 1944

MERRY HELL AT CROSSROADS AS RADIO BLARED VICTORY

By Earl Mazo, *Stars and Stripes* Staff Writer

On the third day of the battle that cut the Normandy peninsula, while Allied radios blared success and victory to the four corners of the world, a small force of American armor was catching merry hell at the Notre Dame de Cenilly crossroads.

The day before a light German counter-attack had cut off most of the salient which pointed into Notre Dame, but heavier American armor, infantry and strafing aircraft had come to the rescue and on this third day the Germans, with Panther and Tiger tanks, attacked with a viciousness which proved that prisoners who said the Germans would move forward at any cost were correct.

For hours it was a nip-and-tuck fight, then the Americans fell back until more and more armor came to stem the tide.

NO PUSHOVER

American numerical superiority had won against trapped Panzers of elite SS divisions, but it was no pushover victory—not for the twisted and cremated bodies left behind in the burned-out M10s, Shermans and M5s.

This engagement was typical of the four-day fight from St. Lo to the Normandy west coast. In the big picture of war the week of armored break-throughs and advances represented great victories, but to the Joes in the tanks and jeeps up front it wasn't so simple as the official reports indicated.

The veteran reconnaissance battalion which spearheaded the Second Armored Division in one of the most spectacular cross peninsula drives had experiences, good and bad, which were probably duplicated by every advance guard unit in the fight.

Immediately after the break-through above St. Lo the battle for this battalion—which had units and patrols always ranging behind the German lines—started with a defeat. At Canisy one of the assault

241

guns was knocked out and the light recon. force was stopped by heavy German armor.

CLOSE SUPPORT

Heavy American armor came up and, with bombing P47s flying close support, the Germans were crushed.

From there on the battalion's keen young commander, Lt. Col. Wheeler G. Merriam, who was in the middle of practically every fight, insisted on drive and more drive—and that is what his men gave him.

When a patrol under Lts. Frank Jordan and Morton Eustis took a cross-road town far in advance of everything else American, three truck-loads of German infantry followed them down the road. It was a situation where the Germans, if given the split seconds they needed, could wipe out the Yanks, so Jordan, who was a lawyer in Virginia, and Eustis, who wrote drama criticisms in New York, parked their jeep behind a hedgerow and as the German trucks approached, the Americans obliterated them with machine gun fire. Later a German staff car passed, and Eustis, back at work behind his machine gun, cut off the driver's head and legs.

ALWAYS UP "FRONT"

The battalion's whole operation went like that. It was scientific. Every one in the outfit was always up "front" because wherever the battalion worked it created fronts. Even the unit's rear echelon troops under Lt. J. Frank Coneybear of Philadelphia, came up at least once a day to bring supplies, mail, papers and sometimes doughnuts.

On the second day of the drive the battalion had one of its most serious "cut off" periods. Col. Merriam, who proved himself as good a leader and tactician as has been produced in Massachusetts, drew part of his force into a field well lined by hedgerows, gave orders to use grenades sparingly because they were scarce, and prepared for a last-ditch fight.

The battle raged. Within half an hour infantry and heavier tanks came up to relieve the battalion, and within three hours the recon. boys were sitting back eating doughnuts, and planning the next day's operations.

242

From dawn of the first day of battle until sundown after reaching the objective, it was that way—heavy fighting, relaxation, then more and heavier fighting.

HEROES ALL

To list the heroes of this battalion would require a listing of the whole roster. Pvt. Everett Christensen, of Kenosha, Wis., for instance, is a typical medic. In the turmoil of one German counter-attack his unit was scattered and he was lost, but refused to go back to headquarters. "I have to find my men," he said as the Germans advanced. "I believe they need me worse than ammunition."

When an armored car needed a tire changed in the middle of a fight Sgt. Paul Cooper of Kansas City, Mo., and Pvt. Mack Gorny, of Chicago, maintenance men, went forward with the tires even though they weren't positive of the armored car's location.

Early in the battle the vital radio equipment in the colonel's armored car went out. T/Sgt. Dan Hamilton, the battalion's chief expert on radios, from Cape Cod, Mass., willingly hopped on the back of that car and went around with the colonel—to keep communication open.

In Sicily this battalion, which led Lt. Gen. George S. Patton's famous end run to Palermo, adopted the battle yell, "Hitler Count Your Children."

And they used it time and again in Normandy.

During the third night the battalion's components were well scattered. The Tuscon, Ariz., captain, Clark McGee, had his company at one point near some mobile artillery; Capt. Pete Johnson's company was at a high point overlooking the Seine River; Lt. George Karl's light tank company was with battalion headquarters and Capt. Ted Large, the Illinois State graduate from Taylorville, had his company positioned at the most important road junction before the Seine.

That evening some of Large's men contacted another American force which had driven down from Carentan and had taken Coutances. The Americans had the Germans pocketed, but the pocket had plenty of holes.

At about 03.00 hours Sunday, a German armored column broke through at Denis-le Gast and headed madly for the Seine. Only Capt. Large's company plus some infantry and some 105mm howitzers protected the approaches. The Germans raced on but the Americans held their fire until they neared an ideal trap position, the crossroad before the river bridge.

Then the fighting began at point-blank range.

When the smoke and fires cleared at dawn the hulks of 20 German vehicles, including tanks and self-propelled 88s, lay smouldering where they had been stopped, and pieces of German bodies were strewn all over the roads and hedges for a half mile. The engagment had cost the Americans an armored car, a halftrack, some jeeps and guns, a light tank—and some lives.

From the first day of the fight groups of Germans were taken prisoner. Few of them were "foreigners"; almost always they were Panzer men and paratroopers and some of them gave the arrogant Nazi sneer and said "the Fuhrer knows all . . . we will win," despite their defeat. By the fourth day they were surrendering in droves. Americans like Sgt. William Price, a battalion clerk from Waukesha, Wis., when there is no fighting in progress, had a field day with snipers. Pvt. Raymond (Junior) Gray of Indianapolis, went on lone hunting patrols because he insisted that he wanted to spend his birthday in Paris. He will be 19 next week.

The recon. patrols which had pushed to the river doubled back to flush out the Germans they had bypassed. By noon of the fourth day the adjutant, Lt. Ernie Evans of Anderson, S. C., figured the battalion total was over 2,000 prisoners and they were coming in so fast he stopped counting.

SMALL ARMS VS. ARMOR

But despite all the success, there was fighting to do, plenty of it. Some of the fanatical Nazis continued to pit small arms against American armor.

Pvt. Charles Rogers, one of the motorcycle dispatch riders who did a lot of running around under fire, passed and repassed a particularly troublesome spot in one town. When he had time he went back to that place and waited. Soon a German appeared—and Rogers "got" him plus six others.

Sgt. Jim Maser's armored car accidently ran up on two parked Mark IV tanks. The American drew back, killed about 15 German infantrymen with his machine gun, then covered the tanks from a distance while heavier American armor came up to finish them off. Meanwhile more Germans appeared. Before the fight was finished ten Mark IVs and Panthers were strewn about the area and Lt. Quin Morton, Maser's Charleston, W. Va., platoon leader, went in to destroy four others.

Throughout the days of battle Cubs overhead were like eyes to the armor below. The Cubs worked with everybody. Once when artillery was requested on a point of dug-in German tanks, the officer making the request waited a while then shouted (via radio) to the Cub, "Can't we get that damn artillery?" There was another pause, then the Cub observer answered, "You don't need it . . . the planes have already gotten those tanks."

PLENTY CLOSE

The air support of P47s, P51s and Typhoons was as close as could be desired. Lt. Sam Hodgon, of Flushing, N. Y., at one time had a recon. unit within 25 feet of German tanks under air attack and he called it "plenty close."

Besides killing a horde of Germans, smashing a countless number of their vehicles and capturing prisoners by the thousands, Col. Merriam's battalion netted items like a $30,000 German payroll in francs, a German van filled with loot from American prisoners, including parachutes, major's leaves, letters and guns, an American GI truck filled with German armor, a large German oil dump, numbers of ammo dumps, and Italian and British guns, and other odds and ends.

One of the lucky men in the outfit was Capt. Sydney Norwick, Indianapolis, battalion surgeon, who was about to call for help when a patrol captured three German ambulances.

And the unit's prize pilferers were Lts. Jordan and Eustis, who, in course of the battle, managed to "appropriate" two American medium tanks plus crews for their company.

245

From *The Stars and Stripes,* December 28, 1944

BATTLE BUDDIES—PALS ON PASS,
THEY'RE TOGETHER IN DEATH

By ED LAWRENCE

With Second Armored Division. Germany, December 27

They were buddies for a long time, by war standards—a year and a half, through the North African campaign, Sicilian and Normandy campaigns. And one fixed it so that even after his death he could do one more favor for his pal.

They met in a spearhead "killer" outfit, the 82nd Armored Reconnaissance Battalion, in the Mediterranean Theatre, and found they had something in common. . . .

Captain Frank B. Jordan, Jr., of Pulaski, Va., was then a lieutenant and already had won his battle spurs. He and a sergeant swam ashore in the African Invasion, talked two Arabs out of their burnooses, roamed through enemy territory, armed only with two grenades and smeared a machine gun nest. Before they rejoined their unit, they found a leaderless infantry company which the lieutenant commanded in combat, for two days.

He and Lt. Morton C. Eustis, magazine writer from Washington, D. C., became an inseparable team. If one were given a mission, the other accompanied him. When they went on pass, it was together.

"They were good reconnaissance men, because they always wanted to know what was going on and would go anywhere to find out," their former commander said. The infantrymen who captured Messina in Sicily found them drinking beer in a cellar where they had taken cover from American shelling.

A few months ago, the Germans broke up the combination by hitting Eustis, when he was riding with a force attacking Domfront. He was pulled out of the tank by his buddy and died on the way to the hospital.

Some weeks later, Jordan heard from the executor of his comrade's estate. Eustis had willed him $5000 toward the purchase of a law library for which Jordan, a recent law graduate, had been saving. An additional bequest specified "4 cases of high-class Scotch whiskey."

The Germans spoiled that too. Shortly afterwards the Captain and his men stormed a German Army emplacement and smashed it up. He was killed in the fray.

CPSIA information can be obtained
at www.ICGtesting.com
Printed in the USA
LVHW052131300423
745716LV00034B/672